CliffsNotes®

Praxis® English Subject Assessments (5038, 5039, 5047, 5146-ELA)

3RD EDITION

by
Diane E. Kern, Ph.D.

Best exam taking wishes!
Diane E Kern

* Please re-donate to a URI student ☺

Houghton Mifflin Harcourt
Boston • New York

About the Author

Diane E. Kern, Ph.D., is Associate Professor of Education at the University of Rhode Island (URI). She supervises student teachers and teaches courses in education psychology, teaching methods, literacy education, and classroom management. Dr. Kern was a public school teacher for 14 years and currently coordinates the Secondary English Language Arts teacher education program in the School of Education at URI.

Acknowledgments

Thanks to the editorial team—Greg, Chris, Lynn, Erika, and Barbara—for their expertise, professionalism, and technical support. This 3rd edition is dedicated to URI Cohort 2015.

Editorial

Executive Editor: Greg Tubach

Senior Editor: Christina Stambaugh

Production Editor: Erika West

Copy Editor: Lynn Northrup

Technical Editor: Barbara Swovelin

Proofreader: Pamela Weber-Leaf

CliffsNotes® Praxis® English Subject Assessments, 3rd Edition
(5038, 5039, 5047, 5146-ELA)

Copyright © 2016 by Houghton Mifflin Harcourt Publishing Company

All rights reserved.

Cover image © Shutterstock / Mavrick

Library of Congress Control Number: 2016932397
ISBN: 978-0-544-62827-4 (pbk)

Printed in the United States of America
DOO 10 9 8 7 6 5 4 3 2 1   4500593928

For information about permission to reproduce selections from this book, write to trade.permissions@hmhco.com or to Permissions, Houghton Mifflin Harcourt Publishing Company, 3 Park Avenue, 19th Floor, New York, New York 10016.

www.hmhco.com

Table of Contents

Introduction

As you know, teaching English to middle school or secondary school students is a rewarding and challenging profession. One way you will demonstrate that you are ready for your teaching license is to pass your state's required Praxis English Subject Assessment test. To show that you definitely are ready for your teaching career, use this book to thoroughly prepare for your teaching licensure test. Successful teachers like you do their homework, so let's get started.

Format of the Tests

This book contains information about the four tests that make up the Praxis English Subject Assessment series. Each of these tests has a different test registration code, testing time, and format, as detailed in the following table.

Test	Registration Code	Time	Format
English Language Arts: Content Knowledge	5038	150 minutes; about 1 minute per item, with additional time needed for audio and video stimulus questions	130 selected-response (SR) questions
English Language Arts: Content and Analysis	5039	3 hours total; 150 minutes for the selected-response section and 30 minutes for the constructed-response section; about 1 minute per SR question, with additional time needed for audio and video items and about 15 minutes per CR question	130 selected-response (SR) questions and 2 constructed-response (CR) questions
Middle School English Language Arts	5047	160 minutes total; 130 minutes for the selected-response section and 30 minutes for the constructed-response section; about 1 minute per SR question, with additional time needed for audio and video items and about 15 minutes per CR question	110 selected-response (SR) questions and 2 constructed-response (CR) questions
Middle School: Content Knowledge—Literature and Language Studies subtest	5146	30 minutes for the Literature and Language Studies subtest (total testing time 2 hours for 4 subtests); about 1 minute per question	30 selected-response (SR) questions in the Literature and Language Studies subtest (total of 120 items in all 4 subtests)

Two of the four tests in this book include **constructed-response questions,** which require you to read a passage—about a literary work or a teaching situation, for example—and respond to a short-answer question. Chapter 1 of this book offers sample constructed-response questions and responses, as well as specific strategies to help you prepare for this type of test question.

Selected-response questions appear on all four of the Praxis English Subject Assessment tests. These questions require you to quickly read a portion of a literary work or a synopsis of a teaching situation, listen to an audio prompt, view a video, or a respond to a question about teaching English. Then you must choose the "credited response." The credited response is the answer that gets you points. In this new question type, the selected response comes in several formats: single-selection multiple choice, multiple-selection multiple choice, order/match, audio stimulus, complete a table/grid, select in passage, and video stimulus. Chapter 2 provides suggested strategies for approaching the selected-response questions.

When you take your Praxis English Subject Assessment test, the proctor will set you up at the computer testing station, and you will determine how much time you spend on each item during each section of the test. Suggested pacing per question is provided. You will want to plan your pacing for the specific format of your test. This opportunity is provided in chapters 7–10 of this book, which contain full-length practice tests for each of the Praxis English Subject Assessment tests.

Content of the Tests

Now that you've got a general idea of the format and pacing of the tests, let's take a closer look at each test's content. Each of the Praxis English Subject Assessment tests is designed to measure your knowledge of a broad range of topics related to teaching English. Your knowledge of these topics is usually developed in high school English classes and undergraduate or teacher-certification teaching methods courses, as well as in English courses. Each test covers specific content categories with which you'll want to become familiar.

First, let's take a look at the four broad content categories: Reading and Literature; Language Use, Vocabulary, and Linguistics; Writing, Speaking, and Listening; and English Language Arts Instruction. The following table shows you the frequency of each content category on the Praxis English Subject Assessment tests. As you can see, three of the four broad content categories—Reading and Literature; Language Use, Vocabulary, and Linguistics; and Writing, Speaking, and Listening—are assessed on every Praxis English Subject Assessment test. Clearly, you will want to study these three content categories carefully to assess your areas of strength and weakness; they are covered in chapters 3, 4, and 5, respectively.

Test Number	Reading and Literature	Language Use, Vocabulary, and Linguistics	Writing, Speaking, and Listening	English Language Arts Instruction
5038	✓	✓	✓	
5039	✓	✓	✓	
5047	✓	✓	✓	✓
5146	✓	✓	✓	

In the next section, I'll take a closer look at the specific content categories covered on each of the Praxis English Subject Assessment tests to help you better understand what will be assessed on the specific test you must take.

Specific Praxis English Subject Assessment Test Descriptions

This section provides an overview of the content covered on each Praxis English Subject Assessment test to help you acquaint yourself with the specific content categories. This will be helpful to know as you assess what content you need to study. In addition, I'll share the number of questions usually asked in each content category, as well as the approximate percentage of the test each content category comprises. This information will help you anticipate the question types and the length of the exam, while also helping you feel more prepared for your test.

English Language Arts: Content Knowledge (5038)

This teaching licensure test is designed for beginning teachers of English in a secondary school. It measures three areas required of English teachers: reading texts, which includes the study of literature and informational texts; use of the English language and vocabulary; and writing, speaking, and listening. Test 5038 is only available in computer-delivered format and contains 130 selected-response questions that you must answer in 150 minutes. The following table provides an overview of this test's specific content categories, the related broad content categories, the chapters in this book that can help you study this content, the approximate number of questions in each category, and the overall percentage of questions usually presented in each category.

Specific Content Category	Broad Content Category	Chapter to Help You Study This Content	Typical Number of Questions in This Category	Approximate Percentage of the Test
Reading	Reading and Literature	Chapter 3	49 selected response	38%
Language Use and Vocabulary	Language Use, Vocabulary, and Linguistics	Chapter 4	33 selected response	25%
Writing, Speaking, and Listening	Writing, Speaking, and Listening	Chapter 5	48 selected response	37%

English Language Arts: Content and Analysis (5039)

This teaching licensure test measures whether entry-level secondary English teachers have the standards-based, relevant knowledge, skills, and abilities believed necessary for competent teaching practice. Test 5039 is only available in computer-delivered format and contains 130 selected-response questions and 2 constructed-response questions for a total of 3 hours of testing time. The following table provides an overview of this test's specific content categories, the related broad content categories, the chapters in this book that can help you study the content, the approximate number of questions in each category, and the overall percentage of questions usually presented in each category.

Specific Content Category	Broad Content Category	Chapter to Help You Study This Content	Typical Number of Questions in This Category	Approximate Percentage of the Test
Reading	Reading and Literature	Chapter 3	48 selected response and 1 constructed response	40%
Language Use and Vocabulary	Language Use, Vocabulary, and Linguistics	Chapter 4	33 selected response	19%
Writing, Speaking, and Listening	Writing, Speaking, and Listening	Chapter 5	49 selected response and 1 constructed response	41%

Middle School English Language Arts (5047)

This teaching licensure test measures the knowledge and competencies required of a beginning teacher of English at the middle school level. Test 5047 is only available in computer-delivered format and contains 110 selected-response questions and 2 constructed-response questions, which must be answered in 160 minutes. The following table provides an overview of this test's specific content categories, the related broad content categories, chapters in this book that can help you study this content, the approximate number of questions in each category, and the overall percentage of questions usually presented in each category.

Specific Content Category	Broad Content Category	Chapter to Help You Study This Content	Typical Number of Questions in This Category	Approximate Percentage of the Test
Reading	Reading and Literature	Chapter 3	50 selected response and 1 constructed response	46%
Language Use and Vocabulary	Language Use, Vocabulary, and Linguistics	Chapter 4	16 selected response	11%

continued

Specific Content Category	Broad Content Category	Chapter to Help You Study This Content	Typical Number of Questions in This Category	Approximate Percentage of the Test
Writing, Speaking, and Listening	Writing, Speaking, and Listening	Chapter 5	26 selected response	18%
English Language Arts Instruction	English Language Arts Instruction	Chapter 6	18 selected response and 1 constructed response	25%

Middle School: Content Knowledge—Literature and Language Studies Subtest (5146)

The Middle School: Content Knowledge—Literature and Language Studies subtest is designed to assess subject matter knowledge required for teachers beginning professional careers as middle school teachers. This test is part of a middle school series of subtests (mathematics, social studies, science, and English) for those who seek licensure to teach in multiple subject areas. Test-takers have typically completed a bachelor's degree program for middle-level teaching licensure. This subtest has 30 selected-response questions designed to assess whether entry-level middle school teachers have the content knowledge necessary to teach English Language Arts. The following table provides an overview of this test's specific content categories, the related broad content categories, chapters in this book that can help you study this content, the approximate number of questions in each category, and the overall percentage of questions usually presented in each category.

Specific Content Category	Broad Content Category	Chapter to Help You Study This Content	Typical Number of Questions in This Category	Approximate Percentage of the Test
Literature	Reading and Literature	Chapter 3	10 or 11 selected response	35%
Language and Linguistics	Language Use, Vocabulary, and Linguistics	Chapter 4	9 selected response	30%
Oral and Written Communication	Writing, Speaking, and Listening	Chapter 5	10 or 11 selected response	35%

Frequently Asked Questions

You've already started on the path to success by orienting yourself with the format of the questions, planning to pace yourself, and becoming familiar with the content covered on the Praxis English Subject Assessment tests, but you probably still have several questions about the test(s) you'll be taking. Here are answers to some frequently asked questions about the Praxis English Subject Assessment tests.

Q. How do I register for a Praxis English Subject Assessment test?

A. Visit the Educational Testing Service (ETS) website at http://www.ets.org/praxis and select Register for a Test. You will need to set up an online account to register. You should note that all tests covered in this book are only offered at ETS-authorized testing centers. Some are offered continuously and others only at certain times called "testing windows." In other words, your test may only be offered a few times a year, so be sure to plan in advance and to allow plenty of time to study and receive your scores.

Q. How do I know which Praxis English Subject Assessment test to take?

A. Contact the department of education for the state in which you seek licensure. If you are enrolled in a school of education, the education department or office of teacher certification also may be able to help, so check its website or contact your advisor. I recommend that you use your favorite Internet search engine to locate your state department of education's teaching certification office. For example, for Rhode Island's teacher licensure information, I would search by the key words "Rhode Island Department of Education Teacher Licensure." When you know which test you need to take, go to the ETS website at http://www.ets.org/praxis/states and select the state in which you plan to be licensed. All Praxis English Subject Assessment tests are only available in computer-delivered format. You'll note that the number "5" is used to signify the computer-delivered format; it is the first digit of the four-digit test code.

Q. **How much does it cost to take a Praxis English Subject Assessment test?**

A. There is no registration fee, but there is a testing fee. For the current cost of your test, visit the ETS website (http://www.ets.org/praxis/about/fees). Each test has its own fee based on the format of the test, the complexity of the scoring process (for example, selected-response questions are less expensive to score than constructed-response questions), and the testing time. Below, you'll find the testing fees (at the time of this book's publication), by test code.

Test Number	Test Title	Testing Fee
5038	English Language Arts: Content Knowledge	$120
5039	English Language Arts: Content and Analysis	$146
5047	Middle School English Language Arts	$146
5146	Middle School: Content Knowledge	$120

Q. **What score do I need to earn my teaching license?**

A. Each state department of education sets its own passing score. First, you can visit your state department of education website for this answer and then check the ETS website at http://www.ets.org/praxis/states to see the qualifying score for your state.

Q. **Why do I need to take a teaching licensure test?**

A. The No Child Left Behind Act (NCLB) is a federal education policy that calls for teachers to be "highly qualified" to teach in their area(s) of teacher certification. One way teachers can demonstrate that they are highly qualified to teach English is to earn a passing score on one or more of the Praxis English Subject Assessment tests. While the federal government sets the requirements for federal funding for education programs, each state government is responsible for the education of its schoolchildren. Your state has determined which teaching licensure tests and/or other requirements are required to obtain a teaching license in that state.

Q. **Do all states require Praxis Subject Assessment tests for teacher licensure?**

A. No, but several states do. Some states have created their own teaching licensure tests. Some states use other Praxis tests. Again, contact your state department of education for specifics. States that require Praxis Subject Assessment tests will accept your Praxis scores no matter where you take the test, provided that you meet that state's qualifying score requirement and that you did not take the test too long ago (usually within the past 5 years).

Q. **How long does it take to get my scores back?**

A. Your scores will come into your online ETS account. For tests that are offered continuously, scores are available approximately 10 to 16 business days after your test date. For tests offered in testing windows, your scores will be available in your online account 10 to 16 business days after the testing window closes. You will receive an email that your scores are ready.

Q. **Are any accommodations available to test-takers?**

A. Yes. Test-takers with disabilities and those whose primary language is not English may apply for test-taking accommodations. More information is available at http://www.ets.org/praxis/register/ in the section on Registration, Test Centers and Dates. Click on "Disability Accommodations" or "Other Accommodations" for more information. The general procedure is to complete a form documenting your learning difference or status as a person whose primary language is not English and to include a document from an individual (there are specific rules as to whom you can request this documentation from) who can attest to your learning difference or status as a person whose primary language is not English. A variety of appropriate accommodations are available to test-takers with learning disabilities or differences. The one accommodation available to test-takers whose primary language is not English is 50 percent more testing time. A word of advice: Look into this information at least 3 months before you plan to take your Praxis English Subject Assessment test to allow yourself time to complete the appropriate documentation and ensure that you can register at a test center that allows for these accommodations.

Q. **What do I need on the day of the test?**

A. You need:

- Photo identification with your name, photograph, and signature. See the list of accepted forms of identification on the ETS Praxis website (http://www.ets.org/praxis/test_day/id). These must not be expired documents.
- A second form of identification with your name, photograph, and signature—just to be safe!
- Your admission ticket
- A watch without calculator functions (optional, but advised)

Important note: You do not need to bring pencils/pens. These will be provided. DO NOT BRING cell phones, smart phones, smartwatches, and/or any other electronic, photo, scanning, recording, or listening device into the test center. Test center personnel are not allowed to collect and/or store your cell phone, etc. The consequence for bringing any of these devices into the test center is dismissal from the test and forfeit of that day's test scores/fees.

Q. **What's the best way to prepare for the Praxis English Subject Assessment tests?**

A. Do just what you're doing. Become familiar with the format, types of questions, and content of the test. After you're familiar with what will be on the test, complete several practice tests, correct them yourself, and study the content related to the questions you answered incorrectly.

A Few Tips

Registration

Registration is available online, by mail, and by telephone. See http://www.ets.org/praxis/register/ for details. Most test-takers use the online registration, but those who request accommodations will need to use the mail format.

If your state requires more than one Praxis English Subject Assessment test for certification, consider taking only one test per day. Taking a Praxis English Subject Assessment test is a fast-paced, intense, and exhausting experience. Your test will be 2 to 3 hours long. If you are required to take more than one test, you may want to exercise your option of spreading out your testing time to improve your performance.

Plan ahead. Currently, all Praxis English Subject Assessment tests are only available in a computer-delivered format and, as noted previously, some are only offered in "testing windows" a few times each year.

If you're eligible for testing accommodations, complete the required documentation before registering for the test and mail it to ETS early. Be sure to double-check that the date on which you are planning to take the Praxis English Subject Assessment test allows for testing accommodations. Also, be sure that accommodations are available at the testing location you request.

Some colleges or universities will provide a waiver for the fee for your Praxis English Subject Assessment test. You can get the waiver form on the ETS website, https://www.ets.org/praxis/about/fees/fee_waivers/. Talk to a financial aid officer to see if getting a waiver is a possibility for you.

Studying

Don't wait until the last minute to study. Schedule study sessions the way you schedule other obligations, such as medical appointments and classes. Stick to your study plan.

Assess your strengths and weaknesses as a test-taker and student, based on your past performance. If you are generally a strong test-taker, review this book's content and take the practice tests. If you are generally an anxious or not-so-strong test-taker, use this book to familiarize yourself with the format and content of the Praxis English Subject Assessment tests and plan to use additional resources, such as English and education course textbooks, to thoroughly prepare for the test. If you experience test anxiety, you may want to seek the support of your university's or college's counseling services. ETS also offers a free guide about test anxiety that is available at https://www.ets.org/s/praxis/pdf/reducing_test_anxiety.pdf.

This book will help you experience the format of your test and determine the content you need to review. If you're not a great selected-response person, for example, study more of those questions. If you're struggling with reading comprehension, writing, or the fundamental English or language arts content, study and practice those sections to better prepare for your teaching licensure test.

Exam Day

- Be sure to get a good night's sleep the night before your test.
- Eat a healthy, adequate breakfast.
- Remember your two forms of identification and your admission ticket.
- Arrive at least 15 minutes early.
- Pass your Praxis English Subject Assessment test!

Study Planning Guide If You Have a Longer Timeline

When	What You Need to Do
3 months (or more) before the test	❑ Create your My Praxis Account online at http://www.ets.org/praxis/register/ and then register for the Praxis English Subject Assessment test that your state requires. ❑ Complete the paperwork for accommodations, if applicable. ❑ Complete the paperwork or speak with a financial aid officer about the possibility of a fee waiver, if applicable. ❑ Read the Introduction and chapters 1–2 of this book. ❑ Dust off your English language arts methods textbooks or borrow one from the library. More recent copies even include references to the Praxis English Subject Assessment tests! Use your favorite web browser to search for websites using key words such as "Praxis Subject Assessment" and "English." Look for sites that contain PowerPoint presentations or the names of colleges or universities. Many of these sites are created by professors and offer a wealth of information to strengthen your weaknesses and help you prepare for the content of the test. Bookmark these websites for future use.
2 months (or more) before the test	❑ Make sure you've registered for your test. Also, be sure to set aside your admission ticket and your log-in username and password for your My Praxis Account and place them in a safe place—one that you'll remember! ❑ Read chapters 3–6 of this book to help you understand the format and content of the test. ❑ Use your favorite Praxis English Subject Assessment websites—the ones you bookmarked last month—to help you prepare for the test. ❑ Take a look at the table of contents, glossary, and index of your education psychology textbook for even more information about the areas in which you are still learning.
1 month (or more) before the test	❑ Take a test drive to the building in which you'll be taking your test. Time how long it takes and note the traffic conditions. ❑ Take the appropriate full-length practice tests in chapters 7–10 of this book to simulate test-taking conditions and assess which areas you still need to study. ❑ Use suggested online resources and your English methods textbook to fill in any missing content.

continued

When	What You Need to Do
1 week before the test	❑ Set aside your admission ticket, and make a note to bring two valid forms of identification. These must not be expired documents. ❑ Retake any or all of the full-length practice tests in this book. ❑ Review chapters 3–6 of this book to refresh your memory on the test content.
The night before the test	❑ Talk only to people who make you feel good and confident! ❑ Pack a water bottle and a small snack bag. Although you can't bring these things into the test session, you'll enjoy the brain refueling after the test. ❑ Go to bed early. Don't cram all night.
The day of the test	❑ Relax. Take a deep breath. You've already put in lots of effort preparing for your Praxis English Subject Assessment test. ❑ Eat a good breakfast and dress comfortably in layers. Remember to bring your admission ticket and two valid forms of identifications. Leave your cell phone locked in the glove box of your car or at home. Bring a snack and water for the ride home. ❑ Arrive at the test center at least 15 minutes early.

Study Planning Guide If You Have a Shorter Timeline

When	What You Need to Do
1 month before the test	❑ Register for the Praxis English Subject Assessment test that your state requires. There is a late registration fee option. ❑ Complete the paperwork and submit it to ETS if you are eligible for accommodations. ❑ Talk to your financial aid officer to learn whether your school has a test fee waiver option. ❑ Read the Introduction and chapters 1–2 of this book.
3 weeks before the test	❑ Read chapters 3–6 of this book. ❑ Take a test drive to the building in which you'll be taking your test. Time how long it takes and note the traffic conditions.
2 weeks before the test	❑ Take the appropriate full-length practice test in chapters 7–10 of this book to simulate test-taking conditions and assess which areas you still need to study. ❑ Review the content outlines in chapters 3–6 of this book to help shore up any areas whose content you are still learning.
1 week before the test	❑ Set aside your admission ticket, and be certain your two valid forms of identification are not expired. ❑ Retake any or all the full-length practice tests in this book. ❑ Review chapters 3–6 of this book to refresh your memory on the test content.
The night before the test	❑ Talk only to people who make you feel good and confident! ❑ Pack a water bottle and a small snack bag. Although you can't bring these things into the test session, you'll enjoy the brain refueling after the test. ❑ Go to bed early. Don't cram all night.
The day of the test	❑ Relax. Take a deep breath. You've already put in lots of effort preparing for your Praxis English Subject Assessment test. ❑ Eat a good breakfast and dress comfortably in layers. Remember to bring your admission ticket and two valid forms of identifications. Leave your cell phone locked in the glove box of your car or at home. Bring a snack and water for the ride home. ❑ Arrive at the test center at least 15 minutes early.

Suggestions for Using This Study Guide

This book offers various levels of support to make your test preparation efforts more successful.

Chapters 1–2: Preparing for the Format of the Praxis English Subject Assessment Tests

Chapters 1 and 2 provide step-by-step instructions and specific strategies for each of the two question types—constructed response and selected response—on the Praxis English Subject Assessment tests. Please note that the single-selection multiple-choice format is now a subsection of the selected-response question type.

Chapters 3–6: Preparing for the Content of the Praxis English Subject Assessment Tests

As you know, the Praxis English Subject Assessment tests have four broad categories of content: Reading and Literature; Language Use, Vocabulary, and Linguistics; Writing, Speaking, and Listening; and English Language Arts Instruction. Chapters 3–6 contain detailed outlines to save you time (no need to go through all those methods and English textbooks!) and offer a concise overview of the key content knowledge and research-based educational practices used in teaching English today. Each practice test question in chapters 7–10 is linked to the appropriate content chapter to provide the information you need to learn so you can be more successful on the actual test.

Chapters 7–10: Full-Length Practice Tests

Chapters 7–10 offer you the opportunity to apply all that you've learned—in this book and in your English teacher education coursework. Complete the practice test for your specific Praxis English Subject Assessment test, check your answers, and then study the detailed explanations. You can even practice your pacing for the Praxis English Subject Assessment test—be sure to know the time length of your test, which will be between 2 and 3 hours.

Appendix: Resources

In the appendix, you will find lists of suggested references, major authors, and literary works, as well as online resources that will give you ideas for more ways to prepare for your test and where to get more information if you need it.

Chapter 1

Constructed-Response Questions

This chapter provides specific examples and helpful strategies you can use to approach the constructed-response questions on the Praxis English Subject Assessment tests. Constructed-response questions appear on the following tests:

- Test 5039: English Language Arts: Content and Analysis
- Test 5047: Middle School English Language Arts

If you are required to take one of these tests, you will benefit from a careful review of this chapter. If not, you will want to skip this chapter and turn to chapter 2 to learn more about the types of questions you'll find on your specific test.

How to Approach Constructed-Response Questions

The constructed-response format requires you to carefully and quickly read a short passage and then write a short-answer response to one or more questions about the passage. Let's take a look at a generic constructed-response question.

Directions: For this question, you will read an excerpt from a novel and then write a brief response.

Read carefully the following excerpt from chapter 8 of *The Adventures of Huckleberry Finn,* a novel by Mark Twain. Explain how the author uses personification and word choice to help us better understand Huck, the narrator of the novel.

> I didn't sleep much. I couldn't, somehow, for thinking. And every time I waked up I thought somebody had me by the neck. So the sleep didn't do me no good. By and by I says to myself, I can't live this way; I'm a-going to find out who it is that's here on the island with me; I'll find it out or bust. Well, I felt better right off.
>
> So I took my paddle and slid out from shore just a step or two, and then let the canoe drop along down amongst the shadows. The moon was shining, and outside of the shadows it made it most as light as day. I poked along well on to an hour, everything still as rocks and sound asleep. Well, by this time I was most down to the foot of the island. A little ripply, cool breeze begun to blow, and that was as good as saying the night was about done. I give her a turn with the paddle and brung her nose to shore; then I got my gun and slipped out and into the edge of the woods. I sat down there on a log, and looked out through the leaves. I see the moon go off watch, and the darkness begin to blanket the river. But in a little while I see a pale streak over the treetops, and knowed the day was coming. So I took my gun and slipped off towards where I had run across that camp fire, stopping every minute or two to listen. But I hadn't no luck somehow; I couldn't seem to find the place. But by and by, sure enough, I catched a glimpse of fire away through the trees. I went for it, cautious and slow. By and by I was close enough to have a look, and there laid a man on the ground. It most give me the fan-tods. He had a blanket around his head, and his head was nearly in the fire. I set there behind a clump of bushes, in about six foot of him, and kept my eyes on him steady. It was getting gray daylight now. Pretty soon he gapped and stretched himself and hove off the blanket, and it was Miss Watson's Jim! I bet I was glad to see him. I says:
>
> "Hello, Jim!" and skipped out.
>
> He bounced up and stared at me wild. Then he drops down on his knees, and puts his hands together and says:
>
> "Doan' hurt me—don't! I hain't ever done no harm to a ghos'. I alwuz liked dead people, en done all I could for 'em. You go en git in de river agin, whah you b'longs, en doan' do nuffn to Ole Jim, 'at 'uz awluz yo' fren'."

As you can see, a constructed-response question is made up of three parts: directions, one or more questions about the passage, and the passage.

Strategies for the Constructed-Response Questions

Here are some suggested strategies to use as you approach the constructed-response questions.

- **Read the question(s) first.** Most test-takers would naturally read the passage first and then move to the question(s). But remember, you are reading the passage in order to get the answers to the questions right. Before you spend time reading the passage, read the question(s) you'll be required to answer so that you can think about why you are reading it. Reading specialists call this "setting purpose for reading."

- **Actively read each passage.** As you read the passage, take notes, keep your mind on the question(s) you'll have to answer, and think about your response as you read. It's fine to make notes on the scratch paper provided to you.

- **Reread each question and then make a brief plan or sketch of the points of your response.** For example, a brief plan for the sample question above might look like this:

  - Personification: "everything still as rocks and sound asleep"; "I see the moon go off watch, and the darkness begin to blanket the river."

  - Analysis: Paints a picture in the reader's mind; sets a mood of quiet and calm on the Mississippi River; sense of oneness with nature as Huck's only companion and chance for freedom.

  - Word choice: Twain uses dialect such as "By and by I says to myself, I can't live this way; I'm a-going to find out who it is that's here on the island with me; I'll find it out or bust." and "Doan' hurt me—don't! I hain't ever done no harm to a ghos'."

  - Analysis: Word choice demonstrates the way people actually spoke in this time period, indicates characters' status in society, makes one feel right there beside the character.

- **Review the passage and question(s).** Make sure you have referred specifically to the passage and have addressed all the question requirements with examples and details.

- **Review your response.** Were you clear, concise, specific, and accurate? Did you base your response on principles of learning and teaching English? Did you answer all parts of the question?

- **Beware of multiple-part constructed-response questions.** These questions have two or more parts rather than just one, and you need to make sure your response addresses all parts of the question.

- **Remember that this is not a formal essay test.** In general, you will write a one- to two-paragraph response for each part of the question, although the length of your response will vary depending on the question as well as on the amount of testing time you have allotted to each question. This is not an essay-test format, so it is okay to use bulleted lists or brief examples. You do not have to have "perfect paragraphs" or use an essay format to earn a high score. The most important aspect of your response is the content you write and the accuracy of the examples you provide.

- **Be mindful of your testing time.** Depending on which Praxis English Subject Assessment test you take, you will have between 2 and 3 hours to complete your test. Each test-taker will need a different amount of time to respond to a constructed-response question accurately and thoroughly, so there is not a specific time to spend on each constructed-response question. However, as a guideline, a constructed-response question like the one above should take about 15 minutes of testing time. See page 1 in the Introduction for the test publisher's suggested pacing.

  You'll want to practice your timing before the actual test. Many of my students report that timing was more of a problem than content knowledge was, especially on the constructed-response questions. Several of my students simply ran out of time to fully answer one or more questions. Constructed-response questions are likely to take more of your testing time, so practice the full-length tests at the back of this guide with your watch in hand. Be sure to check your watch at the start of the test and then every 30 minutes into the testing session. Remember, you are in charge of your pacing on the entire test. While subparts of your test may be timed by the proctor, you want to monitor your time as well to ensure that you are on pace to complete the test on time.

Here is a satisfactory sample response to the generic question on this passage from *The Adventures of Huckleberry Finn:*

> Mark Twain uses personification and word choice to give the reader of *The Adventures of Huckleberry Finn* the sense that s/he is right there beside Huck on his escape from society. In the passage, Twain uses personification in narrator Huck's description of the change from night to daybreak.
> Example 1: everything still as rocks and sound asleep
> Example 2: I see the moon go off watch, and the darkness begin to blanket the river
> This use of personification paints a vivid picture of the scene in the reader's mind, setting a lonely mood of quiet and calm on the Mississippi River, evoking a sense that the river is alive and is Huck's only companion on his quest for freedom.
> Twain's word choice, specifically the use of dialect, allows the reader to feel as though s/he is right in the scene during this time period in the mid-1800s. Huck's dialect indicates that he is a boyish youth from a low level of Southern American white society. For example, Huck says, "By and by I says to myself, I can't live this way; I'm a-going to find out who it is that's here on the island with me; I'll find it out or bust." Huck is feeling lonely and impulsively decides he has to learn who has made a fire on the island. Jim, Miss Watson's escaped slave, speaks in the dialect of African-American slaves of the U.S. South. The last line of the passage shows that Jim is superstitious, afraid that he is seeing Huck Finn's ghost, and pleads with the ghost to not harm him, to return to the river, and also reminds the ghost that he was always a good friend to Huck. In addition to giving the reader a sense of the real way people spoke in this time, the dialect has a foolish charm that evokes a smile at Twain's use of humor in this scene.

How to Read the Passage

Now that you better understand the format of constructed-response questions, take a closer look at the passage itself and develop a strategy for reading the passage actively and efficiently.

Read carefully the following excerpt from chapter 8 of *The Adventures of Huckleberry Finn*, a novel by Mark Twain. Explain how the author uses personification and word choice to help us better understand Huck, the narrator of the novel.

I didn't sleep much. I couldn't, somehow, for thinking. And every time I waked up I thought somebody had me by the neck. So the sleep didn't do me no good. By and by I says to myself, I can't live this way; I'm a-going to find out who it is that's here on the island with me; I'll find it out or bust. Well, I felt better right off.

So I took my paddle and slid out from shore just a step or two, and then let the canoe drop along down amongst the shadows. The moon was shining, and outside of the shadows it made it most as light as day. I poked along well on to an hour, everything still as rocks and sound asleep. Well, by this time I was most down to the foot of the island. A little ripply, cool breeze begun to blow, and that was as good as saying the night was about done. I give her a turn with the paddle and brung her nose to shore; then I got my gun and slipped out and into the edge of the woods. I sat down there on a log, and looked out through the leaves. I see the moon go off watch, and the darkness begin to blanket the river. But in a little while I see a pale streak over the treetops, and knowed the day was coming. So I took my gun and slipped off towards where I had run across that camp fire, stopping every minute or two to listen. But I hadn't no luck somehow; I couldn't seem to find the place. But by and by, sure enough, I catched a glimpse of fire away through the trees. I went for it, cautious and slow. By and by I was close enough to have a look, and there laid a man on the ground. It most give me the fan-tods. He had a blanket around his head, and his head was nearly in the fire. I set there behind a clump of bushes, in about six foot of him, and kept my eyes on him steady. It was getting gray daylight now. Pretty soon he gapped and stretched himself and hove off the blanket, and it was Miss Watson's Jim! I bet I was glad to see him. I says:

"Hello, Jim!" and skipped out.

He bounced up and stared at me wild. Then he drops down on his knees, and puts his hands together and says:

"Doan' hurt me—don't! I hain't ever done no harm to a ghos'. I alwuz liked dead people, en done all I could for 'em. You go en git in de river agin, whah you b'longs, en doan' do nuffn to Ole Jim, 'at 'uz awluz yo' fren'."

- Remember to read the question(s) first.
- Read the passage carefully, closely, and actively. Read carefully—read slowly enough to comprehend what you've read. Read closely—consider the literary elements the author uses. Read actively—make notes on your scratch paper and think about why this information is included. As you can see in the passage from *The Adventures of Huckleberry Finn* above, some recollection of this literary work is expected if you are to earn a higher score on this question, such as the time period in which it takes place and the fact that Jim is Miss Watson's escaped slave—information not included in the passage. I have underlined some of the key points and phrases that helped me decide how to respond to the question.
- Ask questions as you read. What literary elements does this passage feature? What is the main idea? Keep in mind that all information in the passage is included on the test for a reason. Reading and knowing the questions before you read the passage really pay off here. You can read the passage actively and efficiently to get ideas for your constructed response. This should save you time as well.

As you know, two of the Praxis English Subject Assessment tests include constructed-response questions, but each of the tests uses slightly different types of questions for the passage and constructed-response section. In the next section, we'll look at sample constructed-response questions test by test. When you're finished reviewing the format of your test's constructed-response question, practice completing your answer to the question. I have included sample responses at the end of this chapter for you to review after you complete your responses.

Constructed-Response Scoring Guides

This section helps you focus on how to earn the highest score. It also helps you better understand what makes a less effective response. You'll see that your answers need to be *complete, relevant, appropriate, thorough,* and *specific to the literary work or other works in the passage*. While an appropriate response must be accurate, note that you are not required to have perfect spelling or grammar. Let's look at the specific scoring guides for the constructed-response items on your Praxis English Subject Assessment test.

How to Use the Scoring Criteria to Assess Your Own Practice Test Responses

As you'll see in this section, the two Praxis English Subject Assessment tests that include constructed-response questions have different scoring criteria. This section presents the scoring criteria for English Language Arts: Content and Analysis (5039) and Middle School English Language Arts (5047). After you review this section, you may want to share your constructed-response questions from the sample test items earlier in this chapter with an experienced teacher or educator and ask him or her to use the scoring guide to provide you with feedback. You also may want to compare your own constructed responses to the answers and explanations provided. This way, you can make sure you are addressing all the important aspects of each question.

English Language Arts: Content and Analysis (5039)

There are two constructed-response questions on Test 5039: One tests literary analysis of poetry or prose, and the other evaluates rhetorical devices used to construct an argument. The scoring range for each constructed-response question on this test is 0 to 3. Points are distributed as follows.

Score of 3

The response demonstrates a thorough understanding of the content.

- Analyzes the specified literary elements in the text accurately and with some depth
- Shows sound understanding of the selected text
- Supports points with appropriate examples from the text and explains how the examples support points

- Offers a coherent response that demonstrates control of language, including diction and syntax
- Demonstrates facility with conventions of standard written English

Score of 2

The response demonstrates a basic or general understanding of the content.

- Analyzes the specified literary elements in the text with accuracy but may overlook or misinterpret some elements
- Demonstrates understanding of the selected text but may contain some misreading
- Supports points with appropriate examples from the text but may fail to explain how the examples support points
- Offers a coherent response that demonstrates control of language, including diction and syntax
- Displays control of conventions of standard written English but may have some flaws

Score of 1

The response demonstrates a weak understanding of the content and is flawed in one or more of the following ways.

- Incorrectly identifies literary elements in the text or provides a superficial analysis of elements
- Demonstrates insufficient or inaccurate understanding of the text
- Fails to support points with appropriate text citations
- Lacks coherence or has serious issues with control of language, including diction and syntax
- Contains serious and persistent writing errors

Score of 0

The response demonstrates no understanding of the text and is seriously flawed in one or more of the following ways.

- Does not identify literary elements in the selection or does not provide analysis of elements
- Demonstrates a completely inaccurate understanding of the text
- Is incoherent, or contains writing errors so intrusive that comprehension is impeded

Also, any response that is blank, completely off-topic, or not written in English would receive a score of 0.

Middle School English Language Arts (5047)

There are two constructed-response questions on Test 5047: One tests literary analysis, and the other assesses teaching of English language arts. The scoring range for each constructed-response question on this test is 0 to 3. Points are distributed as follows.

Score of 3

The response is strong in the following ways.

- Analyzes the prompt material accurately and in depth
- Shows sound understanding of the subject matter
- Follows the conventions of standard written English

Score of 2

The response demonstrates some understanding of the content but is limited in one or more of the following ways.

- Analyzes the prompt material with some misinterpretation or provides a superficial analysis
- Demonstrates superficial understanding of the subject matter
- Fails to respond adequately or not at all to one or more of the tasks
- Contains significant writing errors

Score of 1

The response is seriously flawed in one or more of the following ways.

- Demonstrates weak understanding of the subject matter or the reading/writing task
- Fails to respond adequately to most of the tasks
- Lacks coherence or is severely underdeveloped
- Contains serious and persistent writing errors

Score of 0

The response is blank, completely off-topic, totally incorrect, or is just a rephrasing of the questions.

Sample Constructed-Response Questions

English Language Arts: Content and Analysis (5039)

Interpreting Literature—Sample Question

Directions: This constructed-response question requires you to interpret a piece of literary or nonfiction text. Plan to spend approximately 15 minutes of your testing time on this constructed response.

Read the following excerpt from "The Fall of the House of Usher," a short story by Edgar Allan Poe. Then, in your own words, identify the main idea in the passage and explain how the method of development and the style (e.g., tone, word choice, or figurative language) clarify and support the main idea. Be sure to cite specific examples from the excerpt in your response.

From that chamber, and from that mansion, I fled aghast. The storm was still abroad in all its wrath as I found myself crossing the old causeway. Suddenly there shot along the path a wild light, and I turned to see whence a gleam so unusual could have issued; for the vast house and its shadows were alone behind me. The radiance was that of the full, setting, and blood-red moon which now shone vividly through that once barely-discernible fissure of which I have before spoken as extending from the roof of the building, in a zig-zag direction, to the base. While I gazed, this fissure rapidly widened—there came a fierce breath of the whirlwind—the entire orb of the satellite burst at once upon my sight—my brain reeled as I saw the mighty walls rushing asunder—there was a long tumultuous shouting sound like the voice of a thousand waters—and the deep and dank tarn at my feet closed sullenly and silently over the fragments of the "HOUSE OF USHER."

Evaluating Rhetorical Features—Sample Question

Directions: This constructed-response question requires you to discuss the rhetorical elements of a piece of writing. Plan to spend approximately 15 minutes of your testing time on this constructed response.

Read the following excerpt from a speech delivered by Queen Elizabeth I. Then, using at least two examples from the passage, describe how the Queen used tone and rhetorical appeals to convince her audience to fight for her.

My loving people,

    We have been persuaded by some that are careful of our safety, to take heed how we commit ourselves to armed multitudes, for fear of treachery; but I assure you I do not desire to live to distrust my faithful and loving people. Let tyrants fear, I have always so behaved myself that, under God, I have placed my chiefest strength and safeguard in the loyal hearts and good-will of my subjects; and therefore I am come amongst you, as you see, at this time, not for my recreation and disport, but being resolved, in the midst and heat of the battle, to live and die amongst you all; to lay down for my God, and for my kingdom, and my people, my honour and my blood, even in the dust. I know I have the body but of a weak and feeble woman; but I have the heart and stomach of a king, and of a king of England too, and think foul scorn that Parma or Spain, or any prince of Europe, should dare to invade the borders of my realm; to which rather than any dishonour shall grow by me, I myself will take up arms, I myself will be your general, judge, and rewarder of every one of your virtues in the field. I know already, for your forwardness you have deserved rewards and crowns; and We do assure you in the word of a prince, they shall be duly paid you. In the mean time, my lieutenant general shall be in my stead, than whom never prince commanded a more noble or worthy subject; not doubting but by your obedience to my general, by your concord in the camp, and your valour in the field, we shall shortly have a famous victory over those enemies of my God, of my kingdom, and of my people.

Middle School English Language Arts (5047)

There are two constructed-response questions on Test 5047. One question requires you to interpret a text, and the other asks you to explain how you respond to student reading or writing.

Textual Interpretation—Sample Question

Directions: This constructed-response question requires you to interpret a piece of literary or nonfiction text. Plan to spend approximately 15 minutes of your testing time on this constructed response.

Saturday, 30 January 1943

Dearest Kitty,

    I'm seething with rage, yet I can't show it. I'd like to scream, stamp my foot, give Mother a good shaking, cry and I don't know what else because of the nasty words, mocking looks and accusations that she hurls at me day after day, piercing me like arrows from a tightly strung bow, which are nearly impossible to pull from my body. I'd like to scream at Mother, Margot, the van Daans, Dussel and Father too: 'Leave me alone, let me have at least one night when I don't cry myself to sleep with my eyes burning and my head pounding. Let me get away, away from everything, away from this world!' But I can't do that. I can't let them see my doubts, or the wound they've inflicted on me. I couldn't bear their sympathy or their good-humoured derision. It would only make me want to scream even more.

    Everyone thinks I'm showing off when I talk, ridiculous when I'm silent, insolent when I answer, cunning when I have a good idea, lazy when I'm tired, selfish when I eat one bit more than I should, stupid, cowardly, calculating, etc., etc. All day long I hear nothing but what an exasperating child I am, and although I laugh it off and pretend not to mind, I do mind. I wish I could ask God to give me another personality, one that doesn't antagonize everyone.

    But that's impossible. I'm stuck with the character I was born with, and yet I'm sure I'm not a bad person. I do my best to please everyone, more than they'd ever suspect in a million years. When I'm upstairs, I try to laugh it off because I don't want them to see my troubles.

Explain how Anne Frank effectively uses two literary devices in this excerpt from *The Diary of a Young Girl*.

Teaching Reading or Writing—Sample Question

Directions: In this exercise, you will answer questions about a student's writing sample. Some questions will ask about strengths, weaknesses, and errors in conventions of standard written English. Below are some examples of how you should understand these terms for the purpose of this test question. You may find it helpful to refer to these examples when you write your response, although you may introduce your own examples.

Examples of strengths and weaknesses in writing:

- Sense of voice
- Paragraph organization
- Essay organization
- Sentence variety and complexity
- Sense of audience

Examples of errors in conventions of standard written English:

- Misplaced semicolons or commas
- Nonparallel construction
- Run-on sentences
- Sentence fragments
- Subject-verb agreement errors
- Verb tense inconsistency
- Pronoun-antecedent agreement errors

An eighth-grade English class was assigned to write a personal narrative from another person's point of view. What follows is a student response to this assignment. It is a final draft. Read this response carefully and then complete the three tasks that follow.

Student Response

Broken Bones

I'm good friends with Jim. I live right next to him and on days school is canceled we usually hang out. On this day, school was cancelled due to too much snow on the roads. So I called Jim and we came to consensus that we would go to the mall at about 11:00 am. He came down to my house and we were ready to go at 11:15.

The snow that has fallen slowly last night had continued into the morning. The sky was filled with gray clouds. Jim said he wanted to go sledding too. We live right near Monsignor Clark School, and they have a good sledding hill. I said I wanted to go to the mall, so we made an agreement to go to the mall first and then the sledding hill second. I got my way.

Jim didn't have a sled, and he liked using his boogie board as a sled anyway, so he brought that. He took some other snow gear with him to stay warm. I had a sled, but really wasn't planning on going sledding. Jim was way into this stuff.

We walked over the hill toward the mall, saw Monsignor Clark School, and kept walking towards the Wakefield Mall. Jim jumped down a small hill near the Paul Baileys' car dealership. He was laughing the whole time. He sprung up and looked at me with the biggest smile on and his eyes were as wide the night sky. Then Jim sprinted to a hill that a snow plow had made on the side of the road. The plow had come to a little three-way intersection and just went straight, right up to the grass. All I could see was a mound of snow about 10 or 12 feet high and Jim disappear over it. I walked a bit further so I was parallel with the hill and could see that on the other side it was straight down and lead to a hill that was more like 15 or 16 feet high.

Jim did a "dropping in" motion two or three times on his stomach and said this was the coolest ever. Then he said what I figured he would eventually say, "You think I'll do it standing up?" and of course I said that I didn't think he would. I knew he would get up there but I wasn't sure if he would actually drop in. He got on top with boogie board in hand, and tried to place it under his feet and almost fell. He finally got his feet set and leaned forward. He was all good, going straight down the slope very fast. That's until he hit the bottom. At that moment the sky turned even grayer.

It looked like Jim was going to try to stand up when he slipped violently to his left side. Jim hit the ground with way too much force, and to make things worse, he didn't get up. I couldn't discern what had happened. Then Jim yelled, "I didn't know the ground was that hard!"

Jim picked up his boogie board and walked away to leave, without the smile on his face. Jim's face was hard to read, no expressions, which is how he usually is. He was quiet on the walk home, and then he said he couldn't move this left arm. When we got back to my house, my mom, who is a nurse, helped him get his coat off and looked at his arm. Jim's elbow was sticking out. "It's not supposed to look like that, huh?" Jim said. "No, Jim, ha-ha, it's not" my mom mumbled with a nervous laugh.

Jim's dad took him to the hospital. He had broken his ulna, and would have to wear a cast for awhile. I thought of how ironic it was that on a day we planned to have lots of fun sledding, Jim ended up breaking his arm. At least I will get to sign his cast! I hope he is resilient and bounces back soon. I think the lesson he learned is not to be a fool and do something zany without the proper equipment and protection. Maybe next time he'll replace the boogie board with a sled!

Tasks

1. Identify ONE significant strength (give specific examples) and explain how this strength contributes to the essay's effectiveness. Do NOT discuss the student's ability with conventions of standard written English (e.g., grammar, punctuation).

2. Identify ONE significant weakness (give specific examples) and explain how this weakness interferes with the essay's effectiveness. Do NOT discuss the student's ability with conventions of standard written English (e.g., grammar, punctuation).

3. Based on this student's writing sample, describe ONE follow-up assignment you would give to help improve this student's writing ability. Explain how you would address the strength (from item 1 of this question) and/or the weakness (from item 2 of this question). Your follow-up assignment should NOT address errors in conventions of standard written English (e.g., grammar, punctuation).

Answers and Explanations

English Language Arts: Content and Analysis (5039)

Interpreting Literature—Sample Response

The following response would earn a score of 3 on a 3-point scale.

In this concluding paragraph from Poe's short story "The Fall of the House of Usher," the narrator has just fled the horrific events inside the mansion. The literal main idea of this excerpt is, that as the narrator barely escapes from the House of Usher, a crack in the foundation of the building becomes so large that it crumbles to the ground right before his eyes. The figurative main idea of the excerpt is that the evils, the human and the otherworldly inhabitants of this mansion, are now completely gone and that the narrator has escaped his entrapment in this frightening place.

This story uses the classic elements of a Gothic tale, such as a setting in a seemingly abandoned castle or mansion, a sense of entrapment, an atmosphere of mystery and suspense, and metonymies of doom and gloom. For example, the metonymy "…there came a fierce breath of the whirlwind…" signifies danger, doom, and the subsequent destruction of the mansion and its eerie inhabitants. The narrator escapes the house only to enter a violent storm, another metonymy, only to hear "…a long tumultuous shouting sound like the voice of a thousand waters…" This effective use of a simile evokes a sense of fear and danger.

Score Explanation

This is a successful response because it addresses and analyzes the main idea in the passage thoughtfully and in depth. The response not only addresses the literal main idea, but it also addresses the figurative main idea with specific text citations of support, such as "the narrator has escaped his entrapment" and "the building becomes so large that it crumbles to the ground right before his eyes." The respondent identifies that Poe's work is a Gothic tale, then provides specific examples about the setting, "a seemingly abandoned castle or mansion" and an "an atmosphere of mystery and suspense." In addition, the respondent accurately uses the term metonymy and provides analysis of specific text citations such as "…there came a fierce breath of the whirlwind…" and "…a long tumultuous shouting sound like the voice of a thousand waters…."

Evaluating Rhetorical Features—Sample Response

The following response would earn a score of 3 on a 3-point scale.

Set in the mid-1500s in England, Queen Elizabeth I speaks to the troops about the imminent threat of invasion by the Spanish Armada in an effort to gain their support for her leadership and the fight that will likely take many of their lives. The speech begins, "My loving people: We have been persuaded by some that are careful of our safety…", using first person plural, a rhetorical device known as the "royal we," which asserts her authority as the ruling monarch who embodies the entire nation of England. Referring to herself as "we" and "our" creates a sense of common purpose between the speaker and audience. The Queen then immediately switches her diction to the singular pronouns "I" and "my," which is appropriate as she is literally and figuratively delivering the speech on the same ground as the soldiers.

"Let tyrants fear, I have always so behaved myself that, under God, I have placed my chiefest strength and safeguard in the loyal hearts and good-will of my subjects…" In this quote from the passage, Queen Elizabeth I uses an appeal to ethos. In referencing "under God," Elizabeth places herself under the higher authority of God in an effort to connect with the soldiers' belief that monarchs are ordained by God and operate under a higher power. As such, this appeal strengthens her credibility.

Score Explanation

This is an exemplary response because it addresses and analyzes how the Queen used tone and rhetorical appeals to convince her audience to fight for her. For example, the respondent accurately identifies the use of the "royal we" and the Queen's switch to singular pronouns to show she is "literally and figuratively delivering the speech on the same ground as the soldiers." The respondent accurately identifies an appeal to ethos and provides evidence that this appeal "strengthens the Queen's credibility."

Middle School English Language Arts (5047)

Textual Interpretation—Sample Response

The following response would earn a score of 3 on a 3-point scale.

Anne Frank effectively uses imagery to let the reader know how angry and trapped she feels in hiding and in close quarters with adults and family in German-occupied Amsterdam, Holland, during World War II. She evokes the image of being irreparably injured by her mother's words in this simile from the excerpt, "…accusations that she hurls at me day after day, piercing me like arrows from a tightly strung bow, which are nearly impossible to pull from my body." Many can relate to this time in an adolescent's life when parents don't understand and say the most awful things. The image of a screaming, raging, emotionally out-of-control Anne, helps the reader envision Anne as a typical teenager—wanting to run away from home, wanting to be free from parents and siblings, to be accepted—who is living in an extraordinarily atypical and dangerous time period.

Hyperbole is a figurative language technique in which exaggeration is used to create a strong effect, to overstate a point, to go a bit too far, oftentimes for comedic effect. Anne's overstatement of how often she tries to please everyone is especially amusing soon after she describes how angry and enraged she feels. "I do my best to please everyone, more than they'd ever suspect in a million years." She wishes she, "...could ask God to give me another personality," another outrageous overstatement as to how horrible she feels about the way she is perceived.

Score Explanation

This is a 3-point response because it accurately identifies and analyzes two literary devices used in the excerpt. Not only does the response provide an appropriate text citation of imagery, but it also demonstrates its effective use in the text. Hyperbole is accurately defined, and then two specific examples of this literary device are provided to show how Anne Frank is feeling at the time of this diary entry.

Teaching Reading or Writing—Sample Response

The following response would earn a score of 3 on a 3-point scale.

1. One significant strength of this student's writing is its sense of voice. The reader can imagine Jim's enthusiasm on a snow day with no school, as noted in the third paragraph, "Jim was way into this stuff," and in the fourth paragraph when the author describes Jim's eyes "as wide as the night sky." The author's voice is that of an adolescent, perhaps one who is a bit older than Jim and sees Jim as a younger brother. This older adolescent's voice is noted in the third paragraph, "I had a sled, but really wasn't planning on going sledding," and in the seventh paragraph, in which the narrator talks about Jim's expressions being hard to read "which is how he usually is." The sense of voice this young author creates draws the reader in to learn more about the broken bones incident and lets the reader know these adolescents have a caring, yet competitive, relationship. This makes the reader wonder if the older friend causes the broken bones and how the adolescents will handle an accident. Voice is a significant strength of this piece.

2. One significant weakness of the student's writing is the inclusion of unnecessary events leading up to the "broken bones" incident in the story. Furthermore, the student writer tends to overuse sequence of events as the rationale for inclusion of events. For example, the author includes details about why school was cancelled (first paragraph) and the snow gear that Jim brought (third paragraph). The result of this weakness is a loss of the reader's interest from time to time. In addition, the time order of going to the mall and then sledding seems important in the opening but is not clearly developed at the close of the piece. The narrator talks about the irony of the day's events, but misses the opportunity to revisit who got his way—Jim or the narrator (second paragraph), a more significant and subtle bit of irony in the piece.

3. One follow-up assignment I would give to this student writer is an author study of works that include sequential events that are important to the development of a narrative, as well as examples of other ways to organize a narrative, such as flashback, journal format, or carefully selecting events to return to later in the narrative. *Flowers for Algernon, The Catcher in the Rye,* and *To Kill a Mockingbird* all could provide excellent models for this study. Next, I would ask the student to re-examine this piece of writing in order to suggest one paragraph to revise. Specifically, I would help the student see the inclusion of unnecessary events and contrast this with the inclusion of necessary events that are important to the piece.

Score Explanation

This is a full-credit response because it addresses all three prompts with strong evidence of how to support a student in strengthening an essay and understanding features of writing.

The response to Prompt 1 correctly identifies one strength as the development of voice in an essay assignment that requires writing from another's perspective. Examples are presented of how an older adolescent would view younger friend Jim with text citations that demonstrate the effective establishment of voice in the piece.

The response to Prompt 2, identifying one weakness of the essay, discusses the inclusion of unnecessary details, which lead to loss of reader interest at times. Analysis of specific instances where the student loses reader interest follow, with specific text citations.

The response to Prompt 3 offers specific follow-up assignments to support the student writer's efforts to maintain reader interest through mini lessons using author study of use of flashback, sequencing events, and journal format techniques. These suggestions for revision are very strong, including what should be done and why these revisions would improve the essay. The response shows a clear understanding of how a writing teacher's actions support the development of a student's skills and development as a writer.

Chapter 2

Selected-Response Questions

This chapter offers you specific examples and helpful strategies to approach the selected-response questions included on all four of the Praxis English Subject Assessment tests. In this chapter, you will learn about the format and types of selected-response questions on the Praxis English Subject Assessment tests. This format requires you to analyze passages, synthesize information, and apply knowledge, all of which takes time. The selected-response questions are a new variation of the old multiple-choice question format. Selected-response questions utilize computer technology to allow for more interaction with test questions, rather than just choosing one answer and marking the bubble sheet as on paper-and-pencil tests of the past. Knowing the format of these questions will get your mind ready to recognize the patterns and answer each question quickly and efficiently. This chapter also includes helpful tips and resources to help you achieve your goal—a passing score on your teaching licensure test!

How to Approach the Single-Selection Questions

Single-selection questions require you to select the one correct answer of the four choices given. In single-selection questions, the answer choices are preceded by ovals. The five most common types of single-selection questions are as follows:

- Complete the statement
- Which of the following
- Roman numeral
- LEAST/NOT/EXCEPT
- Reading passages/tables

The example questions on the pages that follow illustrate each of the five most common single-selection question types.

> **IMPORTANT NOTE: All of the tests covered in this book are offered in computer-delivered format only. Answer choices in this book have lettered choices A, B, C, and D for clarity, but answer choice letters will *not* appear on the actual test. On the actual computer-delivered test, you will be required to click on ovals to select your answer for single-selection questions.**

Here's a sample of what your computer screen will look like for a single-selection question:

Praxis English

Answer the question below by clicking on the correct response.

During a persuasive writing technique lesson, the teacher shares the following examples from advertisements: "big boned," a person "with curves" or one who is "cuddly," instead of saying the person is obese. Which of the following persuasive techniques is the teacher's focus?

○ Voice
○ Euphemism
○ Bandwagon
○ Ad hominem

| ⬅ Previous | Question 1 of 130 | Next ➡ |

Complete the Statement

Complete-the-statement questions require you to read a statement that remains incomplete. You must choose one of the answer choices to complete the statement.

Example:

> The meaning of the prefix *ab-* in the word *abduction* is
>
> **A.** with
> **B.** into
> **C.** out of
> **D.** away from

Answer: D

Which of the Following

In this question type, you read a short question that includes the phrase "Which of the following …" This is the most frequent question type on the Praxis English Subject Assessment tests.

Example:

> Which of the following best describes the most significant feature common to both Orwell's *Animal Farm* and Bradbury's *Fahrenheit 451*?
>
> **A.** Oxymoron
> **B.** Parody
> **C.** Social criticism
> **D.** Apostrophe

Answer: C

Roman Numeral

Roman numeral questions require you to read a short passage that includes several options to consider. The answer choices are presented as a Roman numeraled list. You must use your critical reasoning to determine which of the answer choices contains all of the correct options. These questions take more time than most other single-selection questions and appear infrequently on the Praxis English Subject Assessment tests.

Example:

> Of the sentences below, which two contain a dangling modifier error?
>
> I. Running and shouting for help, the dog bit the mail carrier while making her routine deliveries.
> II. After successfully winning the gold medal, the Olympics was the skater's realization of her dream.
> III. Although he was not found guilty of any crime, Randy was fired from his law firm for an ethics violation.
> IV. Upon successful completion of the Praxis English Subject Assessment tests, I obtained my teaching license and started my career as an educator.
>
> **A.** III, IV
> **B.** II, III
> **C.** I, II
> **D.** I, IV

Answer: C

LEAST/NOT/EXCEPT

In LEAST/NOT/EXCEPT questions, one of the three terms—LEAST, NOT, or EXCEPT—will appear in the question stem. This type of question requires you to reverse your thinking and reason carefully, so take a bit more time on these!

LEAST Example:

Which of the following works is LEAST likely to be described as a romance?

A. *Le Morte d'Arthur*
B. *Amadís of Gaul*
C. *Sir Gawain and the Green Knight*
D. *The Iliad*

Answer: D

NOT Example:

Which of the following literary works was NOT written by William Shakespeare?

A. *A Midsummer Evening*
B. *Julius Caesar*
C. *Hamlet*
D. *All's Well That Ends Well*

Answer: A

EXCEPT Example:

Each of the following accurately describes common features of ballads and hymns, EXCEPT that they are

A. oral forms meant to be sung rather than read
B. written in iambic or dactylic pentameter
C. usually written in quatrains
D. rhyming

Answer: B

Reading Passages/Tables

Reading passage questions are more common than questions that require you to read and interpret a table. I've included samples of both the reading passage format and the table format to help you prepare for these types of questions.

Reading Passage Example:

> This question is based on the following excerpt from *Flowers for Algernon* by Daniel Keyes.
>
> There was nothing more to say, to her or the rest of them. None of them would look into my eyes. I can still feel the hostility. Before, they had laughed at me, despising me for my ignorance and dullness; now, they hated me for my knowledge and understanding. Why? What in God's name did they want of me?
>
> Which of the following themes from *Flowers for Algernon* helps to explain why the narrator, Charlie, was laughed at and despised by his bakery coworkers?
>
> A. The importance of redemption and forgiveness
> B. Miscommunication based on cultural differences
> C. Mistreatment of the mentally disabled
> D. Persistence of the past in the present

Answer: C

Table Example:

> This question is based on the following table.
>
> **Literary Period**
>
> | Movement | Formal Characteristic | Representative Author(s) | Representative Work | Time |
> |---|---|---|---|---|
> | Modern | Open form, free verse | T. S. Eliot | "The Waste Land" | 1900–1940 |
> | Realist | Objective, various voices | Twain | *The Adventures of Huckleberry Finn* | 1855–1900 |
> | Romantic | Imagination, transcendence | Wordsworth, Coleridge | *Lyrical Ballads* | 1780–1830 |
> | Renaissance | Order, humanism, imitation | Shakespeare | *Hamlet* | Late 14th–16th century |
>
> Poets from which of the following literary periods wrote about the supernatural, the exotic, and the medieval?
>
> A. Realist
> B. Renaissance
> C. Modern
> D. Romantic

Answer: B

How to Approach Other Selected-Response Question Types

The majority of the selected-response questions on your test will be in the single-selection format as you've seen above. However, the Praxis English Subject Assessment tests also have new, innovative selected-response question types described in the examples that follow.

1. Multiple-Selection

Multiple-selection questions ask that you select all answer choices that apply. Instead of ovals next to the answer choices, you will see boxes. When you click on an answer choice box, an X will appear to signify your credited response. Select all answer choices that apply in order to receive credit for your response. If you want to change your answer, just click on the box a second time, and the X will disappear.

> **IMPORTANT NOTE: All of the tests covered in this book are offered in computer-delivered format only. Answer choices in this book have lettered choices A, B, C, and D for clarity, but answer choice letters will *not* appear on the actual test. On the actual computer-delivered test, you will be required to click on check boxes to select your answer for multiple-selection questions.**

Praxis English

Answer the question below by clicking on the correct responses.

Which of the following techniques should students use to avoid plagiarism?

Select **all** that apply.

- ☐ Paraphrase the author's words
- ☐ Summarize in one's own words
- ☐ Cite quotations
- ☐ Enclose borrowed words in quotation marks

◄━━ Previous   Question 2 of 130   Next ━━►

On multiple-selection questions, there may be more than one credited response. Be sure to select all that apply in order to receive credit for the question.

2. Highlight Sentence(s)

In this selected-response question type, you will read a passage and then be directed to highlight a sentence to signify your credited response. Clicking on any word in the sentence will highlight the entire sentence. If you change your mind, just click again, and the highlight will disappear. You may be asked to highlight one or two sentences, so be sure to read the directions carefully.

Praxis English

Question 10 is based on the following excerpt from an inaugural address.

   I am certain that my fellow Americans expect that on my induction into the presidency I will address them with a candor and a decision, which the present situation of our Nation impels. This is preeminently the time to speak the truth, the whole truth, frankly and boldly. Nor need we shrink from honestly facing conditions in our country today. This great nation will endure as it has endured, will revive and will prosper. So, first of all, let me assert my firm belief that the only thing we have to fear is fear itself—nameless, unreasoning, unjustified terror, which paralyzes needed efforts to convert retreat into advance.

Answer the question below by clicking on the correct sentence in the passage.

Highlight one sentence that contains the rhetorical device *ethos*.

◄━━ Previous   Question 3 of 130   Next ━━►

---

3. Parts of a Graphic

Similar to highlight the sentence(s), you will highlight a portion of text, which appears in a table or a grid.

Praxis English

Answer the question below by clicking on the correct response in the table.

Select the literary movement for Jane Austen's *Pride and Prejudice*.

Literary Period				
Movement	**Formal Characteristic**	**Representative Author(s)**	**Representative Work**	**Time**
Modern	Open form, free verse	T. S. Eliot	"The Waste Land"	1900–1940
Realist	Objective, various voices	Twain	*The Adventures of Huckleberry Finn*	1855–1900
Romantic	Imagination, transcendence	Wordsworth, Coleridge	*Lyrical Ballads*	1780–1830
Renaissance	Order, humanism, imitation	Shakespeare	*Hamlet*	Late 14th–16th century

◀ **Previous**   **Question 4 of 130**   **Next** ▶

4. Dragging and Dropping

In this selected-response question type, you will see several answer choices, which you will then drag and drop into a grid. There are typically three or four spaces in the grid to fill, so clearly there is more than one answer expected in this question type.

Praxis English

Drag and drop the following periods of American literature into the flowchart below, placing them in chronological order (oldest to most recent).

Nationalist Period	Colonial Period
Revolutionary Period	Puritan Period

```
┌────────────┐
│            │
└────────────┘
      │
      ▼
┌────────────┐
│            │
└────────────┘
      │
      ▼
┌────────────┐
│            │
└────────────┘
      │
      ▼
┌────────────┐
│            │
└────────────┘
```

◀ **Previous**   **Question 5 of 130**   **Next** ▶

5. Drop-Down Menu

This question type is easy to identify when you see a blank box with an inverted triangle in the text. Click on the inverted triangle and several possible answer choices will appear. Click on the answer choice you believe is the credited response. There may be more than one drop-down menu question in a passage.

Praxis English

The paragraphs below are incomplete. For each blank, choose the answer choice that best completes the sentence.

Five [Select... ▼] years ago, a great American, in whose symbolic shadow we stand, signed the Emancipation [Select... ▼]. This momentous decree came as a great beacon light of hope to millions of Negro slaves who had been seared in the flames of withering injustice. It came as a joyous daybreak to end the long night of captivity.

But one hundred years later, we face the tragic fact that the Negro is still not free. One hundred years later, the life of the Negro is still sadly crippled by the manacles of segregation and the chains of discrimination. One hundred years later, the Negro lives on a lonely island of [Select... ▼] in the midst of a vast ocean of material prosperity. One hundred years later, the Negro is still languished in the corners of American society and finds himself an exile in his own land. So we have come here today to dramatize an appalling condition.

| ◄ Previous | Question 6 of 130 | Next ► |

Strategies for Selected-Response Questions

Take the following systematic approach to the selected-response questions on the Praxis English Subject Assessment tests.

1. **Read the directions.** This is especially important for the multiple-selection questions, since you may have to choose more than one answer. The directions are very clear about the variation of the question (for example, drag and drop or highlight a sentence).

2. **Read the question stem.** The question stem is shown in bold in the example below.

Each of the following accurately describes common features of ballads and hymns, EXCEPT that they are

A. oral forms meant to be sung rather than read
B. written in iambic or dactylic pentameter
C. usually written in quatrains
D. rhyming

---

3. **Read all the answer choices.** Don't be too quick to select the answer choice you think is correct without carefully considering all the answer choices. Remember, one key thing that the test assesses is your critical reasoning skills, so each test question has at least one "distracter." A distracter is an answer choice that appears correct in some way—either it's related to the topic, it has a similar spelling or meaning, or it is almost correct, but not as good as the credited response. The credited response is the answer choice that will get you the points on the Praxis English Subject Assessment tests, so clearly this is the one you want!

4. **Use the process of elimination.** Mentally cross out any answer choices that you know are incorrect. If you do not know the correct answer, try to narrow it down.

   For a single-selection question, if you can use the process of elimination to narrow it down to two answer choices, you have a one in two chance of choosing the right one. If you simply guess, you have a one in four chance. Your odds are clearly better when you use the process of elimination!

5. **Select your answer or answers.** Because you can skip questions or mark questions to review on the Praxis English Subject Assessment tests, it is important to choose your "best guess" response and then use the computer navigation features to MARK the question and return to it later, if time permits. In other words, it's best to not skip a question. Give each question your best answer, and then move on.

A Few More Tips

- Remember, your goal is to pass the Praxis English Subject Assessment test, not to compete with another's score or to set test-taking records. Norm-referenced tests are designed for you not to know all the answers. Be prepared for several difficult questions, and do not worry about your score as you work.

- Don't let difficult words or unfamiliar passages throw you. Use the context of the question to help you infer the answer on difficult test questions.

- You can mark a difficult question and choose to return to it later to make your final decision on the answer. In other words, you can skip the ones you're having difficulty with, but be sure to click on the REVIEW button to see which questions you've marked or not answered.

- Remember that there are no patterns to the order in which questions are posed or to the credited responses.

- There is no penalty for guessing. Don't leave any questions blank! Remember to use the process of elimination if you have the time to do so.

- Monitor your testing time. Don't rely on the proctor or your general sense of time. There is a clock on your computer screen, and when there are 5 minutes remaining the time will blink. You are allowed to wear a traditional watch with no computer or calculator functionality.

- Read all the answer choices before choosing the credited response.

- If time permits, check your answers. To do this, check RETURN and REVIEW. It's okay to change your answer if you have taken the time to analyze the question and determined that your initial thought was incorrect.

- When you are done, press CONTINUE. If time runs out, the test session will end on its own. You will then be asked to REPORT your test score or CANCEL your test score. I recommend that you REPORT your score, even if you are not confident about your test performance. My rationale for this advice is that you've paid money for this session, and school districts and teacher licensing boards do not look at the number of times you took a test; rather, they look only for the passing score. The one exception to this advice is if you know you had extreme difficulties that prohibited you from finishing more than half the test.

- The Educational Testing Service (ETS) has an online demonstration to help you practice maneuvering in the computer format. You may find this very helpful in understanding the newer selected-response question types and feeling more confident with the on-screen view and navigation tools. The demo can be found at http://www.ets.org/s/praxis/flash/cbt/praxis_cdt_demo_web1.html.

Practice: Apply the Strategies

Now is your chance to practice the strategies for the selected-response questions. Remember to read the directions and question stem first, skim all the answer choices, and use the process of elimination to get to the credited response. After you complete these questions, review the answers and explanations, paying particular attention to the types of questions you got correct and the types you got incorrect.

Note: The practice questions reflect the four broad categories tested on each of the Praxis English Assessment tests—Reading and Literature; Language Use, Vocabulary, and Linguistics; Writing, Speaking, and Listening; and English Language Arts Instruction—to help you diagnose any strengths or weaknesses in your English content knowledge. You will find chapters 3–6 of this book particularly helpful in closing any gaps in content knowledge that you may discover.

Questions

Directions: For questions 1–12, choose the one best response. For questions 13 and 14, follow the directions supplied with the question and select the best response(s).

1. Phrases such as "physical persuasion" and "downsizing" are known as

   A. personification
   B. metaphors
   C. similes
   D. doublespeak

2. Which of the following sentences contains the correct use of the word *whom/whomever*?

   A. When lifesaving gear is scarce, the fishermen must give the resources to whomever has the best chance of surviving.
   B. Matthew was a young man whom knew his goals and future plans.
   C. Whom will be invited?
   D. You will student teach with our finest English teacher, whom you will meet later in the day.

3. Language minority students who experience academic difficulties because of a lack of proficiency in English are more likely to experience which of the following?

   I. Assignment in special education
   II. Single-parent families
   III. Inclusion in a "tracked" program of bilingual learners
   IV. Low intelligence scores on tests

   A. I, II, IV
   B. I, III, IV
   C. I, III
   D. II, III, IV

4. Each of the following phrases is an example of onomatopoeia EXCEPT

   A. kicking and screaming
   B. mooing and baaing
   C. beep, beep
   D. drip, drop, drip, drop

Questions 5 and 6 are based on the following excerpt from Edgar Allan Poe's poem "The Raven."

> Once upon a midnight dreary, while I pondered, weak and weary,
> Over many a quaint and curious volume of forgotten lore,—
> While I nodded, nearly napping, suddenly there came a tapping,
> As of some one gently rapping, rapping at my chamber door.
> (5) "'Tis some visitor," I muttered, "tapping at my chamber door—
> Only this, and nothing more."

5. The meaning of this stanza can best be interpreted as

   A. The speaker is dozing and thinking of his brother when he falls asleep.
   B. A man is reading and dozing when he is awakened by a knock on his door.
   C. A man is dreaming of his lost love.
   D. The speaker is startled by the sound of wind and then falls asleep.

6. In the passage above, lines 1 and 3 contain

   A. personification
   B. internal rhyme
   C. metaphor
   D. free verse

Question 7 is based on the following excerpt from Macbeth *by William Shakespeare.*

ACT I, SCENE I.

> *A desert place. Thunder and lightning. Enter three Witches.*
> **FIRST WITCH:** When shall we three meet again In thunder, lightning, or in rain?
> **SECOND WITCH:** When the hurlyburly's done, When the battle's lost and won.
> **THIRD WITCH:** That will be ere the set of sun.
> (5) **FIRST WITCH:** Where the place?
> **SECOND WITCH:** Upon the heath.
> **THIRD WITCH:** There to meet with Macbeth.
> **FIRST WITCH:** I come, Graymalkin!
> **SECOND WITCH:** Paddock calls.
> (10) **THIRD WITCH:** Anon.
> **ALL:** Fair is foul, and foul is fair: Hover through the fog and filthy air.

7. Which of the following literary elements is used in the passage above?

   A. Foreshadowing
   B. Metonymy
   C. Ellipsis
   D. Hyperbole

8. Which of the following authors are known for their writing during the Harlem Renaissance?

   I. John Donne
   II. Zora Neale Hurston
   III. Langston Hughes
   IV. Countee Cullen

   A. I, II, IV
   B. I, III, IV
   C. II, III, IV
   D. I, II, III

9. Mrs. Reynolds has asked her 11th-grade students to free-write in their journals for 5 minutes. Which of the following best describes this activity?

   A. Wait time
   B. Norm-referenced assessment
   C. Lecture
   D. All pupil response

Questions 10 and 11 are based on the following excerpt from The Scarlet Letter *by Nathaniel Hawthorne.*

But there was a more real life for Hester Prynne here, in New England, than in that unknown region where Pearl had found a home. Here had been her sin; here, her sorrow; and here was yet to be her penitence. She had returned, therefore, and resumed,—of her own free will, for not the sternest magistrate of that iron period would have imposed it,—resumed the symbol of which we have related so dark a tale. Never afterwards
(5)   did it quit her bosom. But ... the scarlet letter ceased to be a stigma which attracted the world's scorn and bitterness, and became a type of something to be sorrowed over, and looked upon with awe, and yet with reverence, too.

10. The "scarlet letter" is an example of which of the following literary elements?

    A.   Rhetoric

    B.   Free verse

    C.   Symbolism

    D.   Simile

11. The "..." used in the following sentence is known as which of the following?

But ... the scarlet letter ceased to be a stigma which attracted the world's scorn and bitterness, and became a type of something to be sorrowed over, and looked upon with awe, and yet with reverence, too.

    A.   Prepositional phrase

    B.   Apostrophe

    C.   Ellipsis

    D.   Coordinating conjunction

12. Which of the following is an example of holistic scoring of a student essay?

    A.   A score of 5 for exemplary content, use of conventions, and cohesiveness

    B.   A score of 4 based on the number of errors in conventions, with no consideration of content

    C.   A score of 100% based on the number of items correct

    D.   A score of 25 based on the number of points earned for correct responses

Questions 13 and 14 are based on the following excerpt from Dante's Inferno.

In the midway of this our mortal life,
I found me in a gloomy wood, astray
Gone from the path direct: and e'en to tell,
It were no easy task, how savage wild
(5)   That forest, how robust and rough its growth,
Which to remember only, my dismay
Renews, in bitterness not far from death.
Yet, to discourse of what there good befel,
All else will I relate discover'd there.

13. Which of the following correctly describes this passage from Dante's *Inferno*?

Select **all** that apply.

    A.   Poem

    B.   Sonnet

    C.   Allegory

    D.   Stanza

14. Which line can best be interpreted as the narrator has lost his way in life?

Highlight the line in the passage.

A. In the midway of this our mortal life,
B. Gone from the path direct: and e'en to tell,
C. That forest, how robust and rough its growth,
D. All else will I relate discover'd there.

Answer Key

Question	Answer	Content Category	Question Type
1.	D	Language Use, Vocabulary, and Linguistics	Complete the Statement
2.	D	Language Use, Vocabulary, and Linguistics	Which of the Following
3.	C	Language Use, Vocabulary, and Linguistics	Roman Numeral
4.	A	Language Use, Vocabulary, and Linguistics	LEAST/NOT/EXCEPT
5.	B	Reading and Literature	Text Reading Passages/Tables
6.	B	Reading and Literature	Text Complete the Statement
7.	A	Reading and Literature	Text Which of the Following
8.	C	Reading and Literature	Text Roman Numeral
9.	D	Teaching English Language Arts	Which of the following
10.	C	Writing, Speaking, and Listening	Reading Passages/Tables
11.	C	Writing, Speaking, and Listening	Which of the Following
12.	A	Writing, Speaking, and Listening	Which of the Following
13.	A and C	Reading and Literature	Multiple-Selection
14.	B	Reading and Literature	Highlight Sentence(s)

Answer Explanations

1. D. Doublespeak, also known as doubletalk, is the intentionally evasive or ambiguous use of language.

2. D. *Whom* is the direct object of the verb of the subordinate clause *will meet*. Be sure to rephrase the sentence to help you see that *whom* is the best choice: *you will meet whom*. You may have chosen choice A, which appears to be correct if *whomever* is the object of the preposition *to*. This is not correct, though, because the object of the preposition is the entire subordinate clause *whoever has the best chance of surviving*. The verb of the clause is *has,* and its subject should be *whoever*.

3. C. Students from a language minority are more likely to experience an assignment in special education (I) and placement in a program for bilingual students that "tracks" according to school performance (III). Language minority students may experience difficulties primarily because of their lack of proficiency in English, not due to learning disabilities or other special education needs.

4. A. Onomatopoeia is the use of words to imitate natural sounds, such as drip, drop, drip, drop.

5. B. This famous first stanza of the poem "The Raven" by Edgar Allan Poe is about a man who is reading and dozing when he is suddenly awakened by what he thinks is a knock on his bedroom door. The speaker then realizes that it is only the wind and continues to think about his lost love.

6. B. Lines 1 and 3 contain internal rhyme—rhyme that occurs within the line of poetry—of the words dreary, weary and napping, tapping.

7. A. This passage from *Macbeth* provides foreshadowing for the events to come in this Shakespearean tragedy.

8. **C.** Zora Neale Hurston (II), Langston Hughes (III), and Countee Cullen (IV) are all known for their contributions during the Harlem Renaissance period (1900–1940). John Donne (I) was a metaphysical poet in the 17th century.

9. **D.** A free-write is an activity that elicits an all pupil response in that all students work simultaneously and have an equal opportunity to participate.

10. **C.** The scarlet letter provides symbolism in the novel. Initially, the scarlet letter symbolizes Hester Prynne's sin, although at the story's conclusion, the letter represents an important part of her past and her identity.

11. **C.** An ellipsis (…) is used to show words have been left out of a quotation or, as in this case, to indicate the passage of time.

12. **A.** Holistic scoring of writing takes into consideration the overall piece of writing. In this example, exemplary content, use of conventions, and cohesiveness are assessed as a 5 to provide the writer with feedback on the overall effectiveness of the piece.

13. **A and C.** Some selected-response questions require more than one credited response, such as this item. In such questions, the directions will clearly state to select all responses that apply. Dante Alighieri's *Inferno*, which is the first part of *The Divine Comedy*, is an epic poem (choice A), not a sonnet (choice B), that allegorically (choice C) tells the story of a soul's journey toward God. This Italian literary work from the early 1300s is written in cantos, not stanzas (choice D).

14. **B.** At times on a selected-response item, you will be asked to highlight a sentence or line. To do so on the computer, you click on the line and it automatically highlights. For the purposes of this practice test, you had to select the line from four choices. Choice B best represents the meaning that the narrator has lost his way in life and is seeking God. This is a key line from Canto 1 of *The Divine Comedy: Inferno*.

Chapter 3

Reading and Literature

The Reading and Literature content appears on the following Praxis English Subject Assessment tests:

- Test 5038: English Language Arts: Content Knowledge
- Test 5039: English Language Arts: Content and Analysis
- Test 5047: Middle School English Language Arts
- Test 5146: Middle School: Content Knowledge—Literature and Language Studies subtest

This chapter is organized as a concise outline of the major content assessed on each of these tests. Review this outline to refresh your memory of important English content or to note any information that is unfamiliar. In addition, you will want to review "Major Works and Authors" and "Suggested References" listed in the appendix. If portions of the material are unfamiliar, you will want to study further by completing the full-length practice tests in chapters 7–10 of this book.

Identifying and Interpreting Figurative Language and Literary Terminology

This section contains an overview of figurative language and other literary terminology to help you review for the Praxis English Subject Assessment tests. This glossary may even prove helpful in your lesson planning for your first classroom!

Allegory: A story in which people (or things or actions) represent an idea or a generalization about life. Allegories usually have a strong lesson or moral.

Alliteration: Repetition of initial consonant sounds in words, such as "Peter Piper picked a peck of pickled peppers."

Allusion: A reference to a familiar person, place, thing, or event—for example, Don Juan, brave new world, Everyman, Machiavellian, utopia.

Analogy: A comparison of objects or ideas that appear, at first, to be different but are alike in some important way.

Anapestic meter: Meter that is composed of feet that are short-short-long or unaccented-unaccented-accented, usually used in light or whimsical poetry, such as a limerick. For example, the word *contradict* has three syllables, where the accent is on the third syllable.

Anaphora: A rhetorical term for the repetition of a word or a phrase at the beginning of several clauses. An example from Martin Luther King, Jr.'s "I Have a Dream" speech:

> "But **one hundred years later,** the Negro still is not free. **One hundred years later,** the life of the Negro is still sadly crippled by the manacles of segregation and the chains of discrimination. **One hundred years later,** the Negro lives on a lonely island of poverty in the midst of a vast ocean of material prosperity. **One hundred years later,** the Negro is still languishing in the corners of American society and finds himself an exile in his own land. So we have come here today to dramatize a shameful condition." (*Bold added to demonstrate the use of anaphora.*)

Anecdote: A brief story that illustrates or makes a point.

Antagonist: A person or thing working against the hero, the protagonist, of a literary work.

Anthropomorphism: A device in which the writer attributes human characteristics to an animate being or an inanimate object.

Antithesis: A contrast or opposition between two things.

Anxiety of influence: Literary critic Harold Bloom advanced this way of interpreting poetry by using Sigmund Freud's notion of the Oedipus complex to suggest that poets, filled with anxiety and no new ideas to express, struggle against the earlier influences of a previous generation of poets. While Bloom advanced the anxiety of influence when one is reading poetry, readers can also use this lens to interpret other literary works.

Aphorism: A wise saying, usually short and witty.

Apostrophe: A turn from the general audience to address a specific group of persons (or a personified abstraction) who is absent. For example, note this famous line from Shakespeare's *Hamlet*:

> HAMLET: Alas, poor Yorick! I knew him, Horatio, a fellow of infinite jest, of most excellent fancy.

Hamlet is walking with his friend Horatio in a graveyard when he sees two clowns dig up the skull of Yorick, a court jester Hamlet once knew. His address to Yorick's skull is an apostrophe in the play that signifies Hamlet's ongoing contemplation on death and decay.

Archetype: A character, plot, image, theme, or setting that appears in literature across cultures and is repeated over time.

Assonance: A repetition of the same sound in words close to one another—for example, "white stripes."

Blank verse: Unrhymed verse, most often occurring in iambic pentameter.

Cadence: The natural rhythmic rise and fall of language as it is normally spoken.

Caesura: A break in the rhythm of language, particularly a natural pause in a line of verse.

Canon: A group of literary works considered by some to be central or authoritative to the literary tradition. For example, many critics agree that the Western canon includes the literary works of Homer, Shakespeare, Hemingway, Faulkner, Frost, Dickinson, and so on.

Characterization: A method an author uses to let readers know more about the characters and their personal traits.

Cliché: An expression that has been used so often that it loses its expressive power—for example, "dead as a doornail" or "I'm so hungry, I could eat a horse."

Conceit: A specific type of metaphor or figure of speech, often elaborate, that compares two things that are very different. When reading a metaphor, the reader is aware of the dissimilarities between the two things being compared; but a conceit broadens the reader's awareness of the complexity of the things in question and often provides a clever juxtaposition. Extended metaphor is a synonym of conceit.

Consonance: Repetition of the final consonant sound in words containing different vowels—for example, "stroke of luck."

Couplet: A stanza made up of two rhyming lines.

Dactyl: A metrical foot of three syllables in which the first syllable is stressed and the next two are unstressed. Note this example of the use of dactyl meter in "Out of the Cradle Endlessly Rocking" by Walt Whitman.

> **Out** of the **cra**dle, **end**lessly **rock**ing
> **Out** of the **mock**ingbird's **throat**, the **mus**ical **shut**tle
> **Out** of the **Ninth**-month **mid**night,

Death of the author: A literary criticism that rebuts the traditional literary criticism notion that the biography of an author provides a context for interpretation of text; instead, the writing and the creator are unrelated.

Denouement: The resolution or conclusion of a story.

Dialect: A way of speaking that is characteristic of a certain region or social group.

Diction: An author's choice of words based on their clarity, conciseness, effectiveness, and authenticity. The following terms relate to diction:

- **Archaic:** Old-fashioned words that are no longer used in common speech, such as *thee, thy,* and *thou.*
- **Colloquialisms:** Expressions that usually are accepted in informal situations or regions, such as "wicked awesome."
- **Dialect:** A variation of a language used by people from a particular geographic area.
- **Jargon:** Specialized language used in a particular field or content area—for example, educational jargon includes *differentiated instruction, cooperative learning,* and *authentic assessment.*
- **Profanity:** Language that shows disrespect for others or something sacred.
- **Slang:** Informal language used by a particular group of people among themselves.
- **Vulgarity:** Language widely considered crude, disgusting, and often, offensive.

Doublespeak: Language that intentionally distorts or disguises meaning. It may take the form of a euphemism, such as "let go" for fired or "passed away" for died. Doublespeak also can disguise meaning in an intentional effort to deceive, such as vinyl is "genuine imitation leather."

End rhyme: Rhyming that occurs at the ends of lines of verse.

Enjambment: Also known as a run-on line in poetry, enjambment occurs when one line ends and continues onto the next line to complete the meaning. For example, in Thoreau's poem "My life has been the poem I would have writ," the first line is "My life has been the poem I would have writ," and the second line completes the meaning—"but I could not both live and utter it."

Epithet: A descriptive phrase or word frequently used to characterize a person or thing, such as "the father of psychology" refers to Sigmund Freud.

Euphemism: A word or phrase that substitutes for an offensive or suggestive one. Examples: "in a family way" means pregnant; "lost their lives" means killed; "I misspoke" means "I lied."

Existentialism: A philosophy that values human freedom and personal responsibility. Jean-Paul Sartre is the foremost existentialist. Other famous existentialist writers include Soren Kierkegaard ("the father of existentialism"), Albert Camus, Freidrich Nietzsche, Franz Kafka, and Simone de Beauvoir.

Flashback: A literary device in which the author jumps back in time in the chronology of a narrative.

Foil: A character who acts in contrast to another character.

Foot: A metrical foot is one stressed syllable and a number of unstressed syllables (from zero to as many as four). There are four possible metrical feet:

- Iambic: ˘ ´ (unstressed, stressed)
- Trochaic: ´ ˘ (stressed, unstressed)
- Anapestic: ˘ ˘ ´ (unstressed, unstressed, stressed)
- Dactylic: ´ ˘ ˘ (stressed, unstressed, unstressed)

In addition, there are names for the line lengths; eight feet is the typical maximum.

- One foot: Monometer

  Robert Herrick's poem "Upon His Departure Hence," which is comprised (predominantly) of iambic monometer:

  > Thus I
  > Pass by
  > And die:
  > As one,
  > Unknown,
  > And gone:
  > I'm made
  > A shade,
  > And laid
  > I' th' grave:
  > There have
  > My cave,
  > Where tell
  > I dwell,
  > Farewell.

- Two feet: Dimeter

  Excerpt from Thomas Hardy's "The Robin":

  > When up aloft
  > I fly and fly,
  > I see in pools
  > The shining sky,
  > And a happy bird
  > Am I, am I!

- Three feet: Trimeter

  Excerpt from "My Papa's Waltz" by Theodore Roethke:

  > We romped until the pans
  > Slid from the kitchen shelf;
  > My mother's countenance
  > Could not unfrown itself.

- Four feet: Tetrameter

  Excerpt from "The Road Not Taken" by Robert Frost:

  > Two roads diverged in a yellow wood,
  > And sorry I could not travel both

- Five feet: Pentameter

  Excerpt from Shakespeare's *Romeo and Juliet*:

  > But, soft! what light through yonder window breaks?
  > It is the east, and Juliet is the sun.

- Six feet: Hexameter

  Excerpt from "Adonais" by Percy Shelly:

  > He had adorn'd and hid the coming bulk of Death.

- Seven feet: Heptameter

  Excerpt from Edgar Allan Poe's "Annabel Lee":

  > It was many and many a year ago,
  >   In a kingdom by the sea,
  > That a maiden there lived whom you may know
  >   by the name of Annabel Lee;
  > And this maiden she lived with no other thought
  >   than to love and be loved by me.

- Eight feet: Octameter

  Excerpt from Edgar Allan Poe's "The Raven":

  > Once upon a midnight dreary, while I pondered, weak and weary,
  > Over many a quaint and curious volume of forgotten lore—
  >   While I nodded, nearly napping, suddenly there came a tapping
  > As of some one gently rapping, rapping at my chamber door.

Foreshadowing: A literary technique in which the author gives hints or clues about what is to come at some later point in the story.

Frame story: A literary device in which a story is enclosed in another story.

Free verse: Verse that contains an irregular metrical pattern and line length; also known as *vers libre*.

Genre: A category of literature defined by its style, form, and content. Common genres include short stories, novels, plays, poetry, biography, and so forth.

Hermeneutics: The art and science of text interpretation.

Heroic couplet: A pair of rhyming lines of poetic verse written in iambic pentameter.

Hubris: The flaw that leads to the downfall of a tragic hero; this term comes from the Greek word *hybris*, which means "excessive pride."

Hyperbole: An exaggeration for emphasis or rhetorical effect.

Idiom: An expression specific to a certain language that means something different from the literal meaning. For example, "sick as a dog" means one is very ill.

Imagery: The use of words to create pictures or arouse senses in the reader's mind.

Incongruity: The joining of opposites.

Interior monologue: A narrative technique that reveals a character's internal thoughts and memories.

Internal rhyme: A rhyme that occurs within a line of verse, not at the end of the line. For example, "While I nodded, nearly napping, suddenly there came a tapping," is an example of internal rhyme from "The Raven" by Edgar Allan Poe.

Intertextuality: The relationship between texts, especially works of literature.

Irony: The use of a word or phrase to mean the exact opposite of its literal or expected meaning. There are three kinds of irony:

- **Dramatic:** The reader sees a character's errors, but the character does not.
- **Verbal:** The writer says one thing and means another.
- **Situational:** The purpose of a particular action differs greatly from the result.

Malapropism: A type of pun or play on words that results when two words become mixed up in the speaker's mind. For example, "The police are not here to create disorder, they're here to preserve disorder," Richard Daley, former Chicago mayor.

Metaphor: A figure of speech in which a subtle or implicit comparison is made between two unlike things. Be sure to see *conceit,* which is an extended metaphor.

Meter: A rhythmical pattern in verse that is made up of stressed and unstressed syllables.

Metonymy: A figure of speech in which one word is substituted for another with which it is closely associated. For example, Hollywood is a metonym for a district in Los Angeles, which is the historical center of movie stars and U.S. film studios.

Mood: The feeling a text evokes in the reader, such as sadness, tranquility, or elation.

Moral: A lesson a work of literature is teaching.

Motif: A literary term for themes or ideas that are often repeated in a literary work. For example, a key motif in Arthur Miller's *The Crucible* is accusation and confessions.

Narration: The telling of a story.

Oedipus complex: From the Freudian theory that posits people experience a complex set of emotions based on sexual attraction, especially at a young age, to their parent of the opposite sex.

Onomatopoeia: The use of words to suggest sounds, as in "buzz," "click," or "vroom."

Oxymoron: A phrase that consists of two contradictory terms—for example, "deafening silence."

Paradox: A contradictory statement that makes sense—for example, Hegel's paradox, "Man learns from history that man learns nothing from history."

Pathetic fallacy: The attribution of human feelings and responses to inanimate things or animals.

Personification: A literary device in which animals, ideas, and things are represented as having human traits.

Poetic justice: A term that means a character gets what he or she "deserves" in the end. The purest form of poetic justice occurs when one character plots against another but ends up caught or harmed in his or her own trap. For example, poetic justice applies to Shakespeare's character Lady Macbeth. Her vices are punished by her madness as well as the loss of everything she possesses.

Point of view: The perspective from which a story is told. The possibilities include:

- **First person:** The story is told from the point of view of one character in the story.
- **Third person:** The story is told by someone outside the story.
- **Omniscient:** The narrator of the story shares the thoughts and feelings of all the characters.
- **Limited omniscient:** The narrator shares the thoughts and feelings of one character.
- **Camera view:** The narrator records the action from his or her point of view, unaware of any of the other characters' thoughts or feelings. This perspective also is known as the objective view.

Pun: A play on words based on multiple meanings or on words that sound alike but have different meanings. For example, Mark Twain's famous pun about the Nile River—"Denial ain't just a river in Egypt."

Refrain: The repetition of a line or phrase of a poem at regular intervals, particularly at the end of each stanza.

Repetition: The multiple use of a word, phrase, or idea for emphasis or rhythmic effect.

Rhetoric: Persuasive writing.

Rhetorical question: A question that is posed but does not actually require an answer.

Rhyme: The repetition of sounds in two or more words, usually at the end of a line, but not always. For example, Emily Dickinson's poem "A Word is Dead" contains end rhyme:

> A word is dead
> When it is said,
>   Some say.
> I say it just
> Begins to live
> That day.

Rhythm: The regular or random pattern of sounds in poetry.

Setting: The time and place in which the action of a fictional work takes place.

Simile: A comparison of two unlike things, usually including the word *like* or *as*.

Slant rhyme: A rhyme that is not exact, such as "Queen" and "Afternoon" in the poem below. Emily Dickinson, who penned this excerpt from her poem "Not Any Higher Stands the Grave," often used slant rhyme.

> This latest Leisure equal lulls
> The Beggar and his Queen
> Propitiate this Democrat
> A Summer's Afternoon.

Soliloquy: A long speech made in a play while no other characters are speaking. Usually, the character will be alone on the stage.

Spondee: A metrical foot consisting of two syllables, both of which are stressed.

Stanza: A division of poetry named for the number of lines it contains:

- **Couplet:** Two-line stanza
- **Triplet:** Three-line stanza
- **Quatrain:** Four-line stanza
- **Quintet:** Five-line stanza
- **Sestet:** Six-line stanza
- **Septet:** Seven-line stanza
- **Octave:** Eight-line stanza

Stream of consciousness: A style of writing that portrays the inner thoughts of a character. Stream-of-consciousness writing may not have regard for standards of language and grammar, and may contain run-on sentences, breaks in logical patterns, and so on.

Style: How the author uses words, phrases, and sentences to form ideas.

Symbol: A person, place, thing, or event used to represent something else, such as the white flag that represents surrender.

Synecdoche: A figure of speech in which a part represents the whole. For example, "hands" in this excerpt from Robert Louis Stevenson's *Treasure Island:* "Land ho! All hands on deck!"

Synesthesia: The juxtaposition of one sensory image with another that appeals to an unrelated sense. For example, in Dante's *Divine Comedy* the line "the region where the sun is silent" uses the sense of hearing combined with vision to evoke a sense of despair.

Tone: The overall feeling created by an author's use of words, such as scared, somber, intelligent, serious, etc.

Total effect: The overall impression a literary work leaves on the reader.

Transcendentalism: During the mid-19th century in New England, several writers and intellectuals worked together to write, translate works, and publish; they became known as transcendentalists. Their philosophy focused on protesting the Puritan ethic and materialism. They valued individualism, freedom, experimentation, and spirituality. Noted transcendentalists include Ralph Waldo Emerson, Nathaniel Hawthorne, Henry David Thoreau, Henry Wadsworth Longfellow, and Oliver Wendell Holmes.

Trochee: A metrical foot made up of an accented syllable followed by an unaccented syllable.

Vernacular: Language spoken by people who live in a particular region.

Verse: A metric line of poetry. A verse is named based on the kind and number of feet composing it (see *Foot*).

Voice: Distinctive features of a person's speech and speech patterns.

Identifying Patterns, Structures, and Characteristics of Literary Works

This section is designed to help you review the patterns, structures, and characteristics of literary works. The format is meant to provide a concise review. If some of this information is completely new to you, you may want to refer to the resources in the appendix to gain a more in-depth understanding of this important content. The Praxis English Subject Assessment tests are now carefully aligned to the Common Core State Standards

(CCSS) for English language arts and literacy; therefore, there is more emphasis on informational texts than ever before. You will be asked to demonstrate understanding of how textual evidence, word choice, and organizational patterns support interpretations of informational texts, which is covered in this section. Of course, you will also want to review the elements of poetry and narrative texts. In addition, you will be required to demonstrate understanding of ways authors use rhetorical strategies, structure an argument, and use techniques to appeal to target audiences in both narrative and informational texts. Because these concepts overlap with the "Rhetorical Strategies and Persuasive Techniques" section of this book, please see pages 76–78 in chapter 5 for this information.

Elements of Poetry

Ballad: A short narrative poem, often written by an anonymous author, comprising short verses intended to be sung or recited.

Canto: The main divisions of a long poem.

Dramatic monologue: A poem in which a character speaks to listeners whose response is not known. The listener may or may not be present.

Elegy: A mournful lament for the dead. Examples include William Shakespeare's "Elegy" from Cymbeline, Robert Louis Stevenson's "Requiem," and Alfred Lord Tennyson's "In Memoriam."

Epic: A long narrative poem detailing a hero's deeds. Examples include *The Aeneid* by Virgil, *The Iliad* and *The Odyssey* by Homer, *Beowulf, Don Juan* by Lord Byron, *Paradise Lost* by John Milton, *The Divine Comedy* by Dante Alighieri, and *Hiawatha* by Henry Wadsworth Longfellow.

Haiku: A type of Japanese poem that is written in English with 17 syllables divided into three lines of five, seven, and five syllables, respectively. A haiku expresses a single thought.

Limerick: A humorous verse form of five anapestic (composed of feet that are short-short-long or unaccented-unaccented-accented) lines with a rhyme scheme of AABBA.

Lyric: A short poem about personal feelings and emotions.

Narrative poem: A poem that tells a story.

Octave: An eight-line poem, or the first eight lines of a Petrarchan (or Italian) sonnet.

Ode: A lyric poem on a serious subject, written in dignified language.

Pastoral: A poem that depicts life in an idyllic, idealized way.

Sestina: A poem with six stanzas of six lines and a final triplet, all stanzas having the same six words at the line ends in six different sequences that follow a fixed pattern.

Sonnet: A 14-line poem, usually written in iambic pentameter, with a varied rhyme scheme. The two main types of sonnet are the Petrarchan (or Italian) and the Shakespearean (or English). A Petrarchan sonnet opens with an octave that states a proposition and ends with a sestet that states the solution. A Shakespearean sonnet includes three quatrains and a couplet.

Villanelle: A 19-line poem consisting of five tercets (three-line stanzas) with the rhyme scheme ABA and a final quatrain (four-line stanza) of ABAA.

Elements of Prose

Fiction (or Narrative)

Absurdist: A genre of literature, most often used in novels, plays, or poems, that focuses on the experiences of characters in a situation where they cannot find any inherent purpose in life, most often represented by ultimately meaningless actions and events.

Active voice: The voice used to indicate that the grammatical subject of the verb is performing the action or causing the event denoted by the verb. Here is an example of a sentence written in the active voice: Tory ate Pad Thai for dinner.

Fable: A short story or folktale, frequently involving animals, that contains a moral, which may be expressed explicitly at the end as a maxim. Examples of Aesop's fables include *The Country Mouse and the Town Mouse, The Tortoise and the Hare,* and *The Wolf in Sheep's Clothing.*

Fairy tale: A narrative that is made up of fantastic characters and creatures, such as witches, goblins, and fairies, and may begin with the phrase "Once upon a time …" Examples include *Rapunzel, Cinderella, Sleeping Beauty,* and *Little Red Riding Hood.*

Fantasy: A genre that uses magic and other supernatural forms as a primary element of plot, theme, and/or setting. Examples include J. R. R. Tolkien's *The Lord of the Rings,* C. S. Lewis' *The Chronicles of Narnia,* and William Morris' *The Well at the World's End.*

Farce: A type of comedy in which silly, often stereotyped characters are involved in far-fetched situations.

Folktale: A narrative form such as an epic, legend, myth, song, poem, or fable that has been retold within a culture for generations. Examples include *The People Could Fly* retold by Virginia Hamilton and *And the Green Grass Grew All Around: Folk Poetry from Everyone* by Alvin Schwartz.

Frame tale: A narrative technique in which the main story is composed primarily for the purpose of organizing a set of shorter stories, each of which is a story within a story. Examples include Geoffrey Chaucer's *Canterbury Tales,* Ovid's *Metamorphoses,* and Emily Brontë's *Wuthering Heights.*

Gothic: A subgenre of the Romanticism period (1800–1850), which features authors such as Poe, Shelley, and Hawthorne. Its origin is attributed to Horace Walpole, an English author who wrote *The Castle of Otranto,* also known as *A Gothic Story.* Gothic writing is characterized by dark and picturesque scenery, startling and melodramatic narrative devices, and an overall atmosphere of mystery and dread.

Historical fiction: Narrative fiction that is set in some earlier time and often contains historically authentic people, places, or events; for example, *The Three Musketeers* by Alexander Dumas.

Horror: Fiction that is intended to frighten or unsettle the reader. Horror fiction often overlaps with fantasy and science fiction. Examples include Stephen King's *The Shining,* Mary Shelley's *Frankenstein,* and Ray Bradbury's *Something Wicked This Way Comes.*

Impressionism: This type of literature records events or situations as they have been remembered. Features of this literary style include intentional ambiguity, recounting events as they occur through the narrator's eyes, not using chronological order, the need to read the entire work and to stand back and reflect in order to understand full meaning, and developing the setting with emphasis on the emotional landscape. Authors known for using this type of writing include Joseph Conrad, Henry James, and James Joyce. *Heart of Darkness* by Joseph Conrad is a well-known example of Impressionist literature.

Legend: A narrative about human actions that is perceived by both the teller and the listeners to have taken place within human history and that possesses certain qualities that give the tale the appearance of truth or reality. Washington Irving's "The Legend of Sleepy Hollow" is a well-known example; others include *King Arthur* and *The Holy Grail.*

Magic realism: A genre developed in Latin America that blends everyday life with the magical or mystical.

Mystery: A suspenseful story that deals with a puzzling crime. Examples include Edgar Allan Poe's "The Murders in the Rue Morgue" and Charles Dickens' *The Mystery of Edwin Drood*.

Myth: Narrative fiction that usually involves gods and heroes or has a theme that expresses a culture's ideology. Myths occur in all cultures from around the world. Examples of Greek myths include Zeus and the Olympians and Achilles and the Trojan War. Roman myths include those of Hercules, Apollo, and Venus.

Naturalism: An extreme form of Realism in which the author shows the relationship between the character(s) to the environment. This often leads to the author showing the raw or ugly side of the person or relationships. Key authors and literary works include Jack London's *The Call of the Wild,* Edith Wharton's *Ethan Frome,* and Stephen Crane's *The Red Badge of Courage*.

Novel: An extended fictional prose narrative.

Novella: A short narrative, usually between 50 and 100 pages long. Examples include George Orwell's *Animal Farm* and Franz Kafka's *The Metamorphosis*.

Parable: A short story that teaches a lesson about how to lead a good life.

Parody: A text or performance that imitates and mocks an author or work.

Picaresque novel: A novel that features a rogue main character living by his or her wits and is told in a string of loosely connected events. *The Adventures of Huckleberry Finn* by Mark Twain is one excellent example.

Quest: Literary work that features a main character seeking to find something or to achieve a goal. Over the course of the journey, the character encounters and overcomes a series of obstacles, which in turn make the character wiser and more experienced.

Realism: Literature that tries to represent life as it really is.

Romance: A novel composed of idealized events far removed from everyday life. This genre includes the subgenres gothic romance and medieval romance. Examples include Jane Austen's *Pride and Prejudice,* Charlotte Brontë's *Jane Eyre,* and contemporary author Nora Roberts' *Angels Fall*.

Satire: Literature that makes fun of social conventions or conditions, usually to evoke change.

Science fiction: Fiction that deals with the current or future development of technological advances. Examples include Kurt Vonnegut's *Slaughterhouse-Five,* George Orwell's *1984,* Aldous Huxley's *Brave New World,* and Ray Bradbury's *Fahrenheit 451*.

Short story: A brief fictional prose narrative. Examples include Shirley Jackson's "The Lottery," Washington Irving's "Rip van Winkle," D. H. Lawrence's "The Horse Dealer's Daughter," and Dorothy Parker's "Big Blond."

Slapstick: A form of low comedy that includes exaggerated and sometimes violent action. Shakespeare uses slapstick and humorous misunderstanding in his comedies *The Taming of the Shrew* and *A Midsummer Night's Dream,* for example.

Tall tale: An exaggerated, funny story that is obviously unbelievable.

Tragedy: Literature, often drama, ending in a catastrophic event for the protagonist after he or she faces several problems or conflicts.

Western: A novel set in the western United States featuring the experiences of cowboys and people living on the frontier. Examples include Zane Grey's *Riders of the Purple Sage* and *The Trail Driver,* Larry McMurtry's *Lonesome Dove,* Conrad Richter's *The Sea of Grass,* Fran Striker's *The Lone Ranger,* and Owen Wister's *The Virginian*.

Informational Texts

Advertisement: A media notice or announcement to promote a product, service, job opening, or event. Television, radio, and written advertisements for products are exceptionally noteworthy for their persuasive techniques. You will be asked to analyze and interpret the persuasive techniques used in advertisements or other media forms. Advertising techniques include bandwagon, plain folks, and testimonial.

Autobiography: A person's account of his or her own life. Famous autobiographies include Anne Frank's *The Diary of a Young Girl,* Maya Angelou's *I Know Why the Caged Bird Sings,* and *The Autobiography of Benjamin Franklin.*

Biography: An account of a person's life written by another person. Famous biographies include *Becoming Steve Jobs* by Rick Tetzeli and *Lincoln* by Gore Vidal.

Epitaph: A phrase or statement written in memory of a person, especially on a tombstone. Famous epitaphs are written for Edmond Spenser, William Shakespeare, John Donne, Robert Burns, and Benjamin Franklin.

Essay: A document organized in paragraph form that can be long or short and can be in the form of a letter, dialogue, or discussion. Examples include *Politics and the English Language* by George Orwell, *The American Scholar* by Ralph Waldo Emerson, and *Moral Essays* by Alexander Pope.

Memoir: A historical account written from personal knowledge, such as Barack Obama's *Dreams from My Father: A Story of Race and Inheritance* and Elie Wiesel's *Night.*

Periodical: A magazine or newspaper published at regular intervals. Periodicals are an excellent source of informational texts. Famous periodicals include *The New York Times, National Geographic, The Atlantic,* and *The Washington Post.*

Primary document (letter, diary, journal): An expository piece, frequently written with eloquence, that becomes part of the recognized literature of an era. Documents often reveal historical facts, the social mores of the times, and the thoughts and personality of their authors. Some documents have recorded and influenced the history of the world. Examples include the Bible, the Koran, the Constitution of the United States, and Adolf Hitler's *Mein Kampf.*

Speech: A formal address to an audience. Effective speeches use rhetorical devices, which you will want to review in chapter 5. Famous speeches you may encounter on the Praxis English Subject Assessment tests include Abraham Lincoln's "The Gettysburg Address," Martin Luther King, Jr.'s "I Have a Dream," John F. Kennedy's "Inaugural Address," and Lyndon B. Johnson's "We Shall Overcome."

Technical text: Includes charts, graphs, directions, forms, maps, and instruction manuals. On your Praxis English Subject Assessment test, you may be asked how the ideas in a technical text are connected to and distinguished from ideas in other texts.

Textbook: You may find an excerpt from a textbook on your Praxis English Subject Assessment test. The question will prompt you to analyze the text structure or use evidence from the textbook excerpt to make your points.

Website: Similar to a textbook excerpt, website questions may appear on your Praxis English Subject Assessment test. In a website question, you will be asked to cite evidence from the website to analyze and interpret this digital media format informational text. In addition, you will be asked to evaluate this source as quality or not. Websites come in two broad types: static and interactive. Static sites seek to capture information and do not allow direct engagement with the audience. Interactive sites such as wikis and blogs are part of the Web 2.0 group and allow interaction among the writers and the participants. The extension of a website—the last letters that come after the period—are a key way to evaluate the purpose of a website. For example, a ".edu" extension means that the site comes from an education source, whereas a ".com" extension signals that the site is linked to a for-profit business.

Historical, Cultural, and Critical Contexts of Texts

It is important to know the historical and cultural contexts of texts to be able to apply your knowledge of the various schools of writers, to associate works with certain authors, to identify the period within which an author wrote or a piece was written, and to identify representative works from a period. In this section, I have organized a comprehensive list of representative authors and works organized by world literature, British literature, and American literature time periods.

World Literature Timeline

Beginnings–100 C.E. Ancient World Literature

Examples: *The Epic of Gilgamesh,* Hebrew scriptures, teachings of Confucius, Buddhist texts, creation myths, Homer's *The Iliad,* Sophocles' *Oedipus Rex,* Aristophanes' *Lysistrata,* Aristotle's *Organum,* Virgil's *The Aeneid,* Ovid's *Metamorphoses,* and Plato's *The Republic.*

100 C.E.–1650 Medieval and Early Modern World

Examples: The New Testament of the Bible (Near East) and The Qu'ran (The Koran, Arabia), Dante's *Inferno* (Italy), *The Song of Roland* (France), Robert the Monk's writings about the Crusades (France), Shikubu's *The Tale of Genji* (Japan), Petrarch's *Canzoniere* (Italy), Machiavelli's *The Prince* (Italy), Martin Luther's *Speech at the Diet of the Worms* (Germany), and de Cervantes' *Don Quixote* (Spain).

1650–1800

Examples: Equiano's *The Interesting Narrative of the Life of Olaudah Equian* (Africa), Descartes' *Discourse on Method* (France), Voltaire's *Candide* (France), Swift's *Gulliver's Travels,* Basho's *The Narrow Road of the Interior* (Japan), Celebi's *The Book of Travels* (Istanbul), Molière's *Tartuffe* (France).

19th Century

Examples: Rousseau's *Confessions* (France), Goethe's *Faust* (Germany), Hugo's *Odes and Ballads* (France), Pushkin's *The Queen of Spades* (Russia), Dostoevsky's *Notes from Underground* and *Crime and Punishment* (Russia), Tolstoy's *War and Peace* and *Anna Karenina* (Russia), Ibsen's *Hedda Gabler* (Norway), Chekov's *The Cherry Orchard* (Russia).

20th Century

Examples: Tagore's *Punishment and Gitanjall* (India), Ichiyo's *Child's Play* (Japan), Strindberg's *The Ghost Sonata* (Sweden), Joyce's *Dubliners* (Ireland), Kafka's *The Metamorphosis* (Germany), Xun's *Diary of a Madman* (China), Neruda's *Residence on Earth* (Chile), Achebe's *Things Fall Apart* (Nigeria), Márquez's *One Hundred Years of Solitude* (Colombia), Heaney's *North* (Ireland), Roy's *The God of Small Things* (India).

British Literature Timeline

450–1066 Old English (Anglo-Saxon) Period

Examples: *Beowulf* (author anonymous), Bede's *Caedmon's Hymn,* and elegies "The Wife's Lament" and "The Wanderer."

1066–1500 Middle English Period

Examples: Chaucer's *Canterbury Tales*, Malory's *Le Morte d'Arthur*, the morality play *Everyman*, and lyric poetry such as "The Cuckoo Song."

1500–1660 Renaissance

1558–1603 Elizabethan Age

Examples: Shakespeare's *Twelfth Night, Much Ado About Nothing*, and *Richard III*; Marlowe's *Tamburlaine the Great, Dr. Faustus, The Jew of Malta*, and *Edward II*; and Spenser's *The Faerie Queene*.

1603–1625 Jacobean Age

Examples: Shakespeare's *The Tempest, Othello, King Lear, Hamlet, Macbeth*, and his sonnets; Donne's songs, sonnets, and elegies; Bacon's *Reports*; and Jonson's *Volpone* (or *The Fox*).

1625–1649 Caroline Age

Examples: Milton's *Paradise Lost*, Herbert's "The Temple," Herrick's "Hesperides," and Carew's "An Elegy upon the Death of the Dean of Paul's, Dr. John Donne."

1649–1660 Commonwealth Period

Examples: Hobbes' *Leviathan*, Milton's *The Tenure of Kings and Magistrates*, and Hutchinson's *Memoirs of the Life of Colonel John Hutchinson*.

1660–1785 Restoration and the 18th Century

Examples: Dryden's *The Conquest of Granada* and "Alexander's Feast," Pope's *The Rape of the Lock*, Bunyan's *Pilgrim's Progress*, Locke's *Two Treatises of Government*.

1785–1832 Romantic Period

Examples: Keats' *Lamia, Isabella, The Eve of St. Agnes, and Other Poems*, Burns' "Auld Lang Syne" and "Tam o' Shanter," Shelley's *Prometheus Unbound*, Byron's *Don Juan*, Austen's *Pride and Prejudice* and *Northanger Abbey*, Blake's *Songs of Innocence* and *Songs of Experience*, Wollstonecraft's *A Vindication of the Rights of Women*, Wordsworth's *Lyrical Ballads*, Coleridge's "The Rime of the Ancient Mariner" and "Kubla Khan," Lord Byron's "She Walks in Beauty" and "When We Two Parted," Keats' "On First Looking into Chapman's Homer," "When I have fears I may cease to be," and "Ode to a Grecian Urn."

Gothic horror, or simply Gothic, is considered a subgenre of the Romantic period and features works "The Raven" and "The Fall of the House of Usher" by Edgar Allan Poe (American), "The House of Seven Gables" by Nathaniel Hawthorne (American), and *Frankenstein* by Mary Shelley (British).

1830–1901 Victorian Age

Examples: Tennyson's *Poems*; Dickens' *Great Expectations* and *The Pickwick Papers*; Robert Browning's *Men and Women*; Elizabeth Barrett Browning's *Aurora Leigh* and *Sonnets from the Portuguese*; Charlotte Brontë's *Jane Eyre*; Emily Brontë's *Wuthering Heights*; Eliot's *The Mill on the Floss* and *Middlemarch*; Carroll's *Alice's Adventures in Wonderland*; Stevenson's *Doctor Jekyll and Mr. Hyde*; Kipling's *Plain Tales from the Hills*; Hardy's *Tess of the D'Urbervilles, Wessex Poems*, and *Jude the Obscure*; Wilde's *The Importance of Being Earnest* and *The Picture of Dorian Gray*; Shaw's *Mrs. Warren's Profession*; Conrad's *Lord Jim*.

1848–1860 Pre-Raphaelites

Examples: Dante Gabriel Rossetti's *The House of Life*, Christina Rossetti's *The Goblin Market*.

1900–20th Century

Examples: Hardy's "On the Western Circuit" and "The Convergence of the Twain"; Shaw's *Pygmalion*; Eliot's "The Love Song of J. Alfred Prufrock"; Lawrence's *Women in Love;* Yeats' "Lapis Lazuli," "Byzantium," and "In the Seven Woods"; Woolf's *Mrs. Dalloway;* Orwell's *1984;* Rushdie's *The Satanic Verses;* Beckett's *Waiting for Godot*.

American Literature Timeline

1625–1660 Puritan Period

Example: *The Scarlet Letter* by Nathaniel Hawthorne.

1630–1760 Colonial Period

Examples: Williams and Hooker's *Bay Psalm Book*, Franklin's *Poor Richard's Almanack*, Bradstreet's *The Tenth Muse Lately Sprung Up in America*, and Edwards' *The Freedom of the Will*.

1760–1787 Revolutionary Period

Examples: The Declaration of Independence; Jefferson's *Summary View of the Rights of British America;* Freneau's *The British Prison Ship*, "The Wild Honeysuckle," and "The Indian Burying Ground"; Tyler's *The Contrast* (the first comedy performed in early American theater); and Brown's *The Power of Sympathy* (the first American novel).

1828–1836 Nationalist Period

Examples: Cooper's *Leatherstocking Tales*, which included *The Deerslayer, The Last of the Mohicans, The Pathfinder, The Pioneers*, and *The Prairie;* Emerson's *Nature*, "The Over-Soul," "Compensation," and "Self-Reliance"; Irving's "Rip van Winkle" and "The Legend of Sleepy Hollow" in *The Sketch Book of Geoffrey Crayon, Gent.;* Poe's *The Raven and Other Poems* and *Tales of the Grotesque and Arabesque;* and Longfellow's *Evangeline, Hiawatha, The Courtship of Miles Standish*, and *Tales of a Wayside Inn*, which included "Paul Revere's Ride."

1830–1860 American Renaissance Period

Examples: Dickinson's poems "Life," "Love," and "Time and Eternity"; Melville's *Moby-Dick;* Whitman's "O Captain! My Captain!" and *Leaves of Grass;* and Thoreau's *Walden*.

Fireside Poets (19th century): A group of poets from Boston, including Henry Wadsworth Longfellow, Oliver Wendell Holmes, and others. Their poems were often read by the fireside for family entertainment and were memorized by students in school.

Realism (19th century): A style of writing that strives to depict life accurately without idealizing or romanticizing it. Authors of this period include Mark Twain and Stephen Crane.

Transcendentalism (19th century): A movement in the Romantic tradition that advanced the idea that every individual can reach ultimate truths through spiritual intuition. Key authors include Ralph Waldo Emerson and Henry David Thoreau.

1900–1945 Modern Period

Examples: London's *White Fang* and *The Call of the Wild;* Frost's "Nothing Gold Can Stay," "The Road Not Taken," and "Stopping by Woods on a Snowy Evening"; James' *Daisy Miller* and *Washington Square;* and Parker's *Enough Rope* and *Death and Taxes.*

Harlem Renaissance (1920s): A cultural movement led by African-American writers, musicians, and artists located in Harlem, New York. Key contributors include Langston Hughes and Countee Cullen.

Naturalism (early 20th century): A literary movement that claimed to portray life exactly as if it were being examined through a scientist's microscope. Writers include Theodore Dreiser, Jack London, and John Steinbeck.

Surrealism (1920s): A movement in art and literature that started in Europe to replace conventional realism with the full expression of the unconscious mind. The poet T. S. Eliot was influenced by surrealism.

1945–Present Contemporary Period

Examples: Miller's *The Crucible* and *Death of a Salesman;* Morrison's *Beloved;* Salinger's *The Catcher in the Rye;* Updike's *Rabbit, Run;* Plath's *The Bell Jar;* and Vidal's *Lincoln.*

The Beat Generation (1950s): A group of American writers, including Alan Ginsberg and Jack Kerouac. This generation was known for its nonconformity, experimentation with drugs, interest in Eastern religions, and rejection of materialism.

Confessional School (1950s): A group of poets who wrote in the 1950s, including Sylvia Plath, Robert Lowell, and Anne Sexton.

Literary Theories

Literary theories provide a means to interpret texts using different lenses or perspectives. One is not better than another, yet together they provide the reader deeper enjoyment and newfound critical understanding. On the Praxis English Subject Assessment tests, you will need to be familiar with various literary theories to interpret and critique texts and will be asked to recognize ways literary theories are used by teachers of English language arts.

Deconstruction/Post-Structuralism

Deconstructionists believe that we can never know the true meaning of a text because a text is not a discrete whole; rather, it contains contradictions and irreconcilable meanings. In other words, any text has more than one interpretation; therefore, any interpretive reading can only go to a certain point. This is known as an *aporia* in the text. Deconstructive reading is called *aporetic.* Meaning is made possible by the relations of a word to other words within the vast network of structures that is language.

Feminist Criticism

Society is viewed as *patriarchal*, which privileges cultural and economic access to men and denies women from realizing their potential. The woman is seen as the "other," and the man is viewed as the dominating "subject." As you read or teach the text, consider the gender/orientation of the characters, sexual stereotypes that are contradicted or reinforced, and the power relations and roles of sexuality and gender. Also think of the opposite gender's reaction or interpretation.

Historical Criticism/Post-Colonial

The time period and events of the author's time are central to understanding the text. Focus on the social, economic, political, cultural, and intellectual climate of the time. Consider to what degree Western literature is privileged and think how other cultures are depicted by the author. This lens examines issues of colonization and imperialism, rejects underrepresented people as "others," and honors the fact that people may exist in two cultures at the same time.

Marxist Criticism

Society is viewed by social class and assumes that each society's concepts, beliefs, and values are affected by economic and class structures. Examine the following as you read: Who has the power and money; what happens as a result of differences in social class; the author's social class; the dominant economic or social issues of the author's time period.

Modernism/Post-Modernism

Experimental forms of literary works are honored. Traditional forms such as chronological plots and closed endings are rejected. Multiple allusions are used to honor the past, which Modernists feel is lost. Post-Modernists value the same principles but celebrate literary forms that use fragmentation and do not long for the past. This view requires one to discover the ironies in the text and to honor both the classics and popular literature. Look for a mix of genre and form to analyze why the author uses fragmentation.

Narratology/Archetypal Criticism

Character types include the caregiver, trickster, hero/heroine, villain, orphan, jester, etc. Actions in stories include the villain's efforts to create a situation in which the hero must come to the rescue, the hero is tested, the villain is defeated, the hero returns, etc.

New Criticism/Structuralism

Common Core State Standards in English Language Arts and Literacy, as well as the Educational Testing Service Praxis English Subject Assessment test-writers, love this form of criticism! The text is viewed as existing independently, and a close reading of the text reveals meaning. Background knowledge and outside sources are not used when interpreting the text. As you read or teach a text, you would examine the interaction of words, figures of speech, and symbols and analyze how structure is established to create unity and meaning.

Psychoanalytic Criticism

Text is viewed as an expression of the feelings, thoughts, and desires of the author. Examine the text for imagery or symbols of repression or expression; consider the psychological theories exhibited by the characters, such as denial, guilt, morality, sexuality, obsessive compulsive, sociopathic, etc.

Reader-Response Criticism

This criticism examines the reader's activity while reading a literary work. Meaning is made through both an aesthetic and efferent response to text. An aesthetic response demonstrates how the text makes the reader feel, think, and make connections. An efferent response elicits the facts of the text (e.g., plot, character, setting, events in a narrative; key points in an informational text).

Teaching Reading

Teaching reading across all content areas, including English, is a hot-button issue in schools today. Students not only need to learn how to read, but also must read to learn. Secondary English teachers must be well-versed in teaching strategies to help students read and interpret texts. In this section, you will find an explanation of the key components and research-based teaching strategies for teaching reading in the secondary English classroom.

Fostering Reading Appreciation and Motivation to Learn

Below are research-based ways to foster reading appreciation and student motivation to learn.

- Using trade books, electronic texts, and the Internet
- Using nonprint materials such as film, music, art, and advertisements
- Teaching students to improve their personal and professional digital literacy
- Creating authentic literacy experiences
- Connecting students' prior knowledge and interests with texts
- Reading aloud excerpts to students
- Selecting quality texts and other lesson materials

Teaching Comprehension

There are several research-based strategies to teach reading comprehension that you'll want to know for the Reading and Literature section of your test.

Activating Prior Knowledge

Creating an anticipatory set, also known as set induction, is an activity at the start of a lesson that is used to set the stage for learning, motivate students, and activate prior knowledge. For example, a lesson on *To Kill a Mockingbird* might begin with primary-source documents of trials set during the civil rights movement. Other methods for activating prior knowledge in a lesson include:

- Using a concrete experience or object
- Pretesting
- Discussions
- Anticipation guides

Comprehension Strategies

You will need to know the commonly used research-based strategies for reading instruction, which follow below. It is important to note that you will need to identify the strategy, cite textual evidence to evaluate use of the strategy, or determine how ideas are connected in the passage.

- Identifying important information
- Predicting and verifying
- Summarizing and note-taking
- Identifying cause and effect
- Making inferences
- Synthesizing
- Visualizing

Metacognition

Metacognition is a person's ability to think about and regulate his or her own thinking. On your test, you will be expected to not only know what metacognition is, but also to identify ways to foster metacognition and self-regulation in your students.

- Ask students what they do before, during, and after reading.
- Teach students effective strategies to use before, during, and after reading in your content area.
- Ask students to support their statements or responses with examples and text citations—ask why.
- Encourage students to ask and create questions rather than just respond to the teacher's questions.
- Allow time in class to discuss not only the content of your course, but also the thinking processes students are using.
- Model your own metacognition using the think-aloud teaching method.
- Explicitly ask students to reflect on and self-assess their thinking and learning.

Modeling

In this strategy, the teacher or a capable peer shares his or her thinking while reading.

- Teachers and capable peers should model their comprehension processes in either oral or written form.
- The teacher thinks or talks aloud to share his or her thought process while reading.
- Reciprocal teaching is a method in which two students take turns reading aloud, asking one another questions, clarifying understanding, and making predictions. In this way, students model their thinking and comprehension process collaboratively.
- ReQuest (reciprocal questioning) is very similar to reciprocal teaching, but the teacher works with the whole class taking turns reading aloud, etc.

Questioning

Teachers should use questions and teach students to ask questions at a variety of levels. It is important to note that not only the teacher should be asking the questions, but also students should generate their own questions while reading. Bloom's Taxonomy, detailed below, is a helpful construct to guide the formulation of questions.

- **Knowledge:** Remember; recognize; recall who, what, where.
- **Comprehension:** Interpret, retell, organize, and select facts.
- **Application:** Subdivide information and show how it can be put back together; how this is an example of that.
- **Analysis:** What are the features of … ? How does this compare with … ?
- **Synthesis:** Create a unique product that combines ideas from the lesson. What would you infer from … ?
- **Evaluation:** Make a value decision about an issue in the lesson. What criteria would you use to assess … ?

Scaffolding

Scaffolding involves an adult or a capable peer providing structural supports to a student in a learning situation. The more capable the student becomes with a certain skill or concept, the less instructional scaffolding the adult or peer needs to provide. Scaffolding might take the form of a teacher reading aloud a portion of the text and then asking the student to repeat the same portion, for example.

Differences between Nonfiction Narrative and Informational Texts

Nonfiction narrative texts such as an autobiography or a personal essay use storytelling elements to inform and describe, whereas informational texts such as in a textbook or on a website inform the reader using clear patterns of organization and different text features, detailed below.

Narrative Text Story Elements

A narrative text is a story typically comprised of the following elements that tells the sequence of events in a fictional or nonfictional account. Students need to be able to identify patterns of stories and be able to analyze this type of text to determine literal and figurative meanings, make inferences, and determine the textual evidence that supports interpretation.

Character: A person or being in a narrative.

- **Antagonist:** A person who opposes or competes with the main character; often the villain in the story.
- **Protagonist:** The main character or hero of a written work.

Conflict: Opposing elements or characters in a plot. Possibilities include:

- **Person versus person:** A character has a problem with one or more of the other characters.
- **Person versus society:** A character has a problem with an element of society: the school, an accepted way of doing things, or the law, for example.
- **Person versus self:** A character has a problem determining what to do in a situation.
- **Person versus nature:** A character has a problem with nature: natural disasters, extreme heat, or freezing temperatures, for example.
- **Person versus fate (God):** A character has to battle what appears to be an uncontrollable problem that is attributed to fate or God.

Denouement: The outcome or resolution of plot in a story.

Plot: The structure of a work of literature; the sequence of events.

Setting: The time and place in which a story occurs.

Informational Text Features

Just as students need to know elements of a narrative text, you and your students will need to know the features of an informational text. Your students may need direct instruction in the differences between reading different types of prose. Informational texts have specific text features that you will want to be able to identify, use properly, and suggest ways to teach to students.

The **copyright page** is located in the front portion of the text and lists the date(s) of publication and publisher. This is an important page to note when evaluating the accuracy of time-sensitive information.

Fonts are presented in a variety of ways (e.g., bold, italics, color, highlighted, underlined) for a purpose, such as to call attention or to distinguish chapter titles, headings, subheadings, and important terms.

The **glossary** is where readers find the definitions of terms; it is found in a back section of the text.

Images and captions are features of an informational text that contain important information that readers will not comprehend simply by reading the sentences in the text. Readers must pay careful attention to diagrams, graphs, tables, and charts and be certain to read the accompanying captions.

The **index** is located in a back section of the text and contains the page numbers where readers can locate major concepts, ideas, terms, or theories. This section is organized alphabetically.

Notes come in three types informational texts: 1) endnotes—notes listed at the end of the book or section to provide additional information or a citation of a source; 2) footnotes—similar to an endnote, but located at the bottom of the page; and 3) side notes—notes found in the margin of the page, often containing key vocabulary definitions. Endnotes and footnotes are signaled in the text with a superscript number that is raised, like this.[1] Side notes are signaled usually by bold or color font in the text and the side note is then found in a nearby margin of that same page.

References, also called the Works Cited page when using MLA format, is the section where all works used in the text are cited. This section can help one determine the quality of the research used to write the text.

The **table of contents** is located in a front portion of the text and lists the chapters, sections, and subsections in the order they are presented. Page numbers for each section and subsection are provided so that readers can quickly locate the information they seek, rather than have to read from beginning to end.

Informational Text Structures

Below are typical text structures found in informational texts, which aid reading comprehension.

- Cause/effect is commonly used in expository or persuasive texts. Paragraphs are organized by either a cause or effect first and then alternately explain reasons why something happened.

  Signal words: *therefore, consequently, leads to, causes, since, because, as a result of*

- Compare/contrast is similar to effect, with paragraphs alternating ways people, events, places, or things are similar and different.

  Signal words: *on the other hand, in contrast, instead, similar, same, both, as well as, unlike*

- Description text structure gives details about characteristics, actions, events, etc.

  Signal words: *specifically, also, in addition, for instance, such as, for example*

- Problem/solution sets up paragraphs to establish the problem and its importance, then outlines possible solutions.

  Signal words: *problem, issue, causes, as a result, solution, which leads to, so*

- Sequence structure organizes paragraphs in chronological order.

  Signal words: *first, next, last, then, finally, following, before, after*

Study Strategies and Reading to Learn

Students are asked to read increasingly complex texts as they advance in their education careers. English teachers know that most students learned to read successfully in the early grades but that they will need ongoing instruction in how to study and how to read to learn complex texts. The following researched-based strategies are commonly used in the English classroom and will be helpful to you when responding to Praxis English Subject Assessment test questions.

Active Reading

Active reading involves determining purposes for pre-reading, reading for understanding during reading, and then evaluating success post-reading. Strategies active readers employ include, but are not limited to, highlighting or making margin notes, writing examples or connections in the margins, checking for understanding after reading for a period of time, and writing a brief summary after reading or explaining what you read to another person.

Anticipation Guides

An anticipation guide is a lot like a pretest, although there are no right or wrong answers. An anticipation guide provides students with an opportunity to respond to and discuss a series of open-ended questions or opinion questions that address various themes, vocabulary words, and concepts that will appear in an upcoming text.

Close Reading

Close reading involves reading and re-reading portions of text to determine the deeper layers of meaning in a text. Readers create a detailed and careful analysis of the text's meaning through the analysis of word choice, themes, main ideas, and text organization. One might also use multiple literary theories (see pages 51–52 in this chapter), such as the feminist or Marxist lens, to derive deeper meaning during close reading.

Graphic Organizers

A graphic organizer is a note-taking guide used before, during, or after reading a text. Here are some examples:

- Concept map
- Semantic feature analysis
- Matrix
- Venn diagram
- Cause and effect
- Cycle map
- Sequence
- Problem and solution
- Continuum

Note-Taking

Common approaches to note-taking include the double-entry page and SQ3R (survey, question, read, recite, review).

On a double-entry notebook page, the student draws a line down the middle of the page. On the left side, he or she takes notes from the reading or lecture. After the reading or lecture, the student re-reads the notes and writes his or her reactions, reflections, and connections in the right-hand column next to the corresponding information on the left.

The SQ3R method for note-taking while reading a text is widely used in schools today. The steps are as follows:

1. Survey: The student previews the chapter to assess the organization of the information.
2. Question: The student examines the chapter's headings and subheadings and rephrases them into questions.
3. Read: The student reads one section of the chapter at a time selectively, primarily to answer the questions.
4. Recite: The student answers each question in his or her own words and writes the answers in his or her notes. The student repeats this note-taking sequence for each section of the chapter.
5. Review: The student immediately reviews what has been learned.

Skimming

Skimming is a way to read a text to get a general sense of it, which is helpful to reveal story informational text structures.

Chapter 4

Language Use, Vocabulary, and Linguistics

The Language Use, Vocabulary, and Linguistics content appears on the following Praxis English Subject Assessment tests:

- Test 5038: English Language Arts: Content Knowledge
- Test 5039: English Language Arts: Content and Analysis
- Test 5047: Middle School English Language Arts
- Test 5146: Middle School: Content Knowledge—Literature and Language Studies subtest

This chapter is organized as a concise outline of the major content assessed on each of these tests. Review this outline to refresh your memory of important English content. If portions of the material are unfamiliar to you, study further by completing the full-length practice tests in chapters 7–10 of this book and by using the suggested resources in the appendix.

Principles of Language Acquisition and Development

Social, Cultural, and Historical Influences

Linguistics is the formal study of the structures and processes of a language. Linguists strive to describe language acquisition and language in general. There are several key areas of study in this field:

- **Phonetics:** The study of the sounds of language and their physical properties
- **Phonology:** The analysis of how sounds function in a language or dialect
- **Morphology:** The study of the structure of words
- **Semantics:** The study of the meaning in language
- **Syntax:** The study of the structure of sentences
- **Pragmatics:** The role of context in interpreting meaning

We understand language acquisition and development through several frameworks, including:

- **Sociolinguistics:** The study of language as it relates to society, including race, class, gender, and age
- **Ethnolinguistics:** The study of language as it relates to culture; frequently associated with minority linguistic groups within the larger culture
- **Psycholinguistics:** The study of language as it relates to the psychological and neurobiological factors that enable humans to learn language

The Role and Nature of Language, Dialects, and Diction

A key difference between language and dialect is that language is made up of several dialects. Language and dialect can be difficult to distinguish, and often are differentiated with respect to status or power.

A **dialect** is a variation of a language used by people who live in a particular geographical area, cultural group, or time period. It is a complete system of verbal (and sometimes written) communication with its own vocabulary and grammar. Dialects, particularly those spoken by a large number of people, can have subdialects. **Diction** is the choice of words or phrases in writing or speech.

Standard dialects are supported by institutions, such as governments and schools. In English, for example, standard dialects include Standard American English, Standard Indian English, and Standard British English.

Subdialects of Standard American English include African American Vernacular English (also known as Black English or Ebonics), Southern American English, Hawaiian English, Spanglish, and Appalachian English.

In the English classroom, dialects play an important role in understanding literature, composition, and rhetoric. Students learn to read dialects such as Southern American English in *The Adventures of Huckleberry Finn;* they learn to write in Standard American English and in other dialects they may speak or try to imitate; and they learn to speak in Standard American English for certain audiences and in other dialects for other audiences, such as peers, dramatic performances, and debates.

Historical and political influences on language acquisition: Some experts view every language as a dialect of an older communication form. For example, they regard the Romance languages (French, Spanish, and Portuguese, among others) as dialects of Latin. Political relationships also influence views of a language as either a new entity or a dialect. For example, English is thought to have two primary dialects—American English and British English—because the United States and Great Britain are close political allies.

Pidgins and creoles: Pidgins are contact languages. They are co-created and change between people who speak different languages but need some way to communicate to engage in trade or work. For example, many English language pidgins were spoken by African slaves who were then shipped to the United States and the West Indies. A pidgin becomes a creole when it is learned as a first language of a new generation of people. One example of a creole is Afrikaans, which is made up of Dutch, English, and Bantu.

Regionalism: This linguistic term is for words, expressions, or pronunciations preferred by people in a particular geographic area. For example, you might hear "y'all" instead of "all of you" when visiting the Southern part of the U.S., and when visiting Rhode Island, you may be surprised to learn that a water fountain is called a "bubbla'."

History and Development of the English Language

Linguistic Change

English is derived from Anglo-Saxon, which is a dialect of West Germanic, although English today contains words with roots from many languages, including Chinese, Hebrew, and Russian. The most common root words are of Anglo-Saxon descent, although more than half the words in English either come from the French or have a French cognate (a word with a common origin). Scientific words in English often have Greek or Latin roots. The Spanish language is found in many English words, especially in terms originating in the southwestern United States.

Etymology and the Process of Word Formation

Etymology is the study of the history and origin of words. Some words are derived from other words and other languages. Key parts of words and origins of words include:

- Language origin of the word (for example, *elaborate* is derived from the Latin *elaborare,* which means "to work out")
- Affixes, prefixes, and suffixes
- Compound words
- Slang words that become common language
- Common words that become slang (for example, *copper* is slang for *police officer*)
- Portmanteau words, which are words that have been melded together, such as *Ebonics*—ebony + phonics
- Taboo words that become euphemisms

Traditional Grammar

Syntax and Sentence Structure

Kinds of Sentences

A **declarative** sentence makes a statement and tells about a person, place, thing, or idea.

> *Example:* Tory is my daughter.

An **interrogative** sentence asks a question.

> *Example:* Is that my son Jimmy?

An **imperative** sentence issues a command.

> *Example:* Please clear the dinner table.

An **exclamatory** sentence communicates strong ideas or feelings.

> *Example:* That was a great shot!

A **conditional** sentence expresses wishes or conditions contrary to fact.

> *Example:* If you were to hang onto the basketball rim, then you could experience the glory of every NBA player.

Sentence Types

A **simple** sentence can have a single subject or a compound subject and a single predicate or a compound predicate. It can contain one or more phrases. The distinguishing factor is that a simple sentence has only one independent clause, and it has no dependent clauses.

- **Single subject, single predicate:** My dog growls.
- **Compound subject, single predicate:** My dog and my cat growl.
- **Compound subject, compound predicate:** My dog and my cat growl and appear agitated.
- **Independent clause with two phrases:** I must have vicious pets from the pound in my town.

A **compound** sentence is made up of two independent clauses. The clauses must be joined by a semicolon or by a comma and a coordinating conjunction.

> My dog growls at the mailman, but my cat growls at her littermate.
> My dog growls at the mailman; my cat growls at her littermate.

A **complex** sentence has one independent clause and one or more dependent clauses.

> When you pass the Praxis English Subject Assessment test [dependent clause], you'll enjoy a career in teaching [independent clause].
> You will get a teaching job [independent clause], even though it will be challenging [dependent clause].

A **compound/complex** sentence has two or more independent clauses and one or more dependent clauses.

> I just earned my teaching degree [independent clause], and I plan to get a teaching job [independent clause] because I need a career [dependent clause].

Effective Sentences

Effective sentences are clear and concise. In addition, effective sentences use imagery, precise language, and rhythm. Ineffective sentences often contain one or more of the following problems.

- Unnatural language, such as **clichés** or **jargon.**

  Example: What goes around comes around.

  More effective: A person's actions will have consequences.

- **Nonstandard language** or **unparallel construction.**

  Example of nonstandard language: I ain't mad atcha'.

  Corrected: I am not mad at you.

  Example of unparallel construction: After the Praxis English Subject Assessment test, I will go shopping, celebrating, and eat dinner.

  Corrected: After the Praxis English Subject Assessment test, I will shop, celebrate, and eat dinner.

- Errors such as **pronoun referent** problems.

  Example: Tory, Kelly, and I watched a movie, but she didn't like it.

  Corrected: Tory, Kelly, and I watched a movie, but Tory didn't like it.

- Short, stilted sentences; **run-on sentences;** or **sentence fragments.**

  Example of a run-on sentence: Katherine, a newly licensed English teacher, has job interviews at Portsmouth Middle and South Kingstown High, but will move to Massachusetts if she does not get a teaching position this summer.

  Corrected: Katherine, a newly licensed English teacher, has job interviews at Portsmouth Middle and South Kingstown High. If she does not get a teaching position this summer, she will move to Massachusetts.

  Example of a sentence fragment: In the beginning.

  Corrected: In the beginning of the movie, Mr. Keating recites poetry.

- A **dangling modifier** is a word or phrase that modifies a word not clearly stated in the sentence. A modifier describes, clarifies, or gives more detail about a concept.

  Example: Stuffed with dressing and surrounded by vegetables, Aunt Linda served the Thanksgiving turkey.

  Corrected: Aunt Linda served the Thanksgiving turkey, which was stuffed with dressing and surrounded by vegetables.

- In **passive voice,** the grammatical subject of the verb is the recipient of the action denoted by the verb.

  Example: The basketball was shot by the player.

  More effective (active voice): The player shot the basketball.

- A **split infinitive** occurs when the writer puts an adverb between the two parts of the infinitive form of a verb.

  Example: to meekly say

  Corrected: to say meekly

Parts of Speech

Nouns

Types of nouns:

- **Common nouns** do not name specific people, places, or things. Common nouns are not capitalized.

  Examples: person, animal, car

- **Proper nouns** name particular people, places, or things. Proper nouns are capitalized.

  Examples: President Obama, Chicago, Judaism

- **Concrete nouns** name a thing that is tangible (it can be seen, heard, touched, smelled, or tasted). They are either proper or common.

  Examples: dog, school, football

- **Abstract nouns** name an idea, condition, or feeling (in other words, something that is not concrete).

  Examples: ideals, justice, Americana

- **Collective nouns** name a group or unit.

  Examples: gaggle, herd, community

Number of nouns:

- **Singular:** book, library, child, bacterium, man
- **Plural:** books, libraries, children, bacteria, men

Gender of nouns:

- **Masculine:** father, brother, uncle, men, bull
- **Feminine:** mother, sister, aunt, women, cow
- **Neuter:** window, shrub, door, college, car
- **Indefinite:** chairperson, politician, president, professor, flight attendant

Case of nouns:

- A **nominative case** noun can be the subject of a clause or the predicate noun when it follows the verb "to be."
- A **possessive case** noun shows possession or ownership.
- An **objective case** noun can be a direct object, an indirect object, or an object of a preposition.

Verbs

Types of verbs:

- **Transitive verbs** require direct objects—words or word groups that complete the meaning of a verb by naming a receiver of the action.

  Subject   Verb   Direct object

  Example: The secondary English student <u>learns</u> the methods of the master teacher.

- **Intransitive verbs** require no objects or complements.

  Example: An airplane <u>flew</u> overhead.

- **Linking or connecting verbs** connect the subject and the subject complement (an adjective, noun, or noun equivalent)

  Example: It <u>was</u> rainy.

- An **auxiliary or helping verb** comes before another verb.

  Example: She <u>must have</u> passed the Praxis English Subject Assessment test.

Verb tenses:

- **Present tense** is used to describe situations that exist at the present time.

  Example: Celia and Tory <u>attend</u> Curtis Corner Middle School.

- **Past tense** is used to describe what happened in the past.
  Example: They <u>attended</u> Wakefield Elementary School.

- **Future tense** is used to express action that will take place in the future.
  Example: Next year, they <u>will attend</u> Broad Rock High School.

- **Present perfect tense** is used when action began in the past but continues into the present.
  Example: Annie <u>has attended</u> a charter school for two years.

- **Past perfect tense** is used to express action that began in the past and happened prior to another past action.
  Example: Dr. Hicks <u>had</u> never <u>seen</u> such high student test scores until she implemented the intervention.

- **Future perfect tense** is used to express action that will begin in the future and will be completed in the future.
  Example: By this time next year, Tory and Celia <u>will have graduated</u> eighth grade.

Verbs with other functions:

- An **infinitive phrase** is usually made up of *to* and the base form of a verb, such as *to order* or *to abandon*. It can function as an adjective, adverb, or noun.
- A **participle** is a verb form that usually ends in *–ing* or *–ed*. Participles operate as adjectives but also maintain some characteristics of verbs. You might think of a participle as a verbal adjective. Examples include *barking* dog and *painted* fence.
- A **gerund phrase** is made up of a present participle (a verb ending in *–ing*) and always functions as a noun.
  Example: <u>Gardening</u> is my favorite leisure activity.

Pronouns

There are three types of pronouns:

- **Simple:** I, you, he, she, it, we, they, who, what
- **Compound:** Itself, myself, anybody, someone, everything
- **Phrasal:** Each other, one another

Pronoun antecedents:

An **antecedent** is the noun to which a pronoun refers. Each pronoun must agree with its antecedent.

> *Example:* <u>Jimmy</u> is playing in a basketball tournament tomorrow. <u>He</u> hopes to play well.

Classes of pronouns:

- **Personal pronouns** take the place of nouns.
  Example: Coach Spence changed <u>his</u> starting lineup and won the game.

- **Relative pronouns** relate adjective clauses to the nouns or pronouns they modify.
  Example: A basketball player <u>who</u> plays with intensity and skill gets a place in the starting lineup.

- **Indefinite pronouns** usually refer to unnamed or unknown people or things.
  Example: Perhaps you know <u>somebody who</u> can slam-dunk a basketball.

- **Interrogative pronouns** ask questions.
  Example: <u>Who</u> are you and <u>why</u> do you play basketball?

- **Demonstrative pronouns** point out people, places, or things without naming them.
  Example: <u>This</u> should be an easy win. <u>They</u> are undefeated.

Modifiers

Modifiers are words, clauses, or phrases that limit or describe other words or groups of words.

Adjectives describe or modify nouns or pronouns.

  Examples: big, blue, old, tacky, shiny

Adverbs describe four different things:

- **Time:** tomorrow, monthly, momentarily, presently
- **Place:** there, yonder, here, backward
- **Manner:** exactly, efficiently, clearly, steadfastly
- **Degree:** greatly, partly, too, incrementally

Phrases and Clauses

Phrases are groups of related words that operate as a single part of speech, such as verb, verbal, prepositional, appositive, or absolute phrases. For example, "in the doghouse" is a prepositional phrase.

Clauses are groups of related words that have both a subject and a predicate. For example, "I have a tendency to procrastinate when I have a high-stakes assignment" contains the clause "I have a tendency to procrastinate" and the subordinate clause "when I have a high-stakes assignment."

Punctuation

There are various forms of punctuation and guidelines for using punctuation correctly. Below you will find a brief overview of the rules that guide the use of proper punctuation.

- A **comma** is used between two independent clauses, to separate adjectives, to separate contrasted elements, to set off appositives, to separate items in a list, to enclose explanatory words, after an introductory phrase, after an introductory clause, to set off a nonrestrictive phrase, to ensure clarity, in numbers, to enclose titles, in a direct address, to set off dialogue, to set off items in an address, and to set off dates. Clearly, commas have several uses and rules that make their use a challenge for writers!
- A **period** is used at the end of a sentence, after an initial or abbreviation, or as a decimal point.
- A **question mark** is used at the end of a direct or indirect question and to show uncertainty.
- A **semicolon** is used to separate groups that include commas and to set off independent clauses.
- An **exclamation point** is used to express strong feeling.
- An **apostrophe** is used in contractions, to form plurals, to form singular possessives, to form plural possessives, in compound nouns, to show shared possession, and to express the possessive form of quantities of time or amount.
- A **dash** is used for emphasis, to set off interrupted speech, to set off an introductory series, and to indicate a sudden break.
- **Parentheses** are used to set off explanatory information within a sentence and to set off full sentences.
- **Brackets** are used to set off added words, editorial corrections, and clarifying information.
- A **hyphen** is used between numbers, between fractions, in a special series, to create new words, and to join numbers.
- A **colon** is used after a statement that introduces a quotation, an example, a series, or an explanation.

Semantics

As mentioned earlier in this chapter, **semantics** is the study of the meaning in language.

Ambiguity occurs when there are two or more possible meanings to a word or phrase.

Connotation refers to the associations that are connected to a certain word or the emotional suggestions related to that word.

Denotation is the literal or primary meaning of a word, in contrast to the feelings or ideas that the word suggests.

Doublespeak is language that is intended to be evasive or to conceal. The term began to be used in the 1950s and is similar to newspeak, a term coined by George Orwell in the novel *1984.* Doublespeak is related to euphemism but is distinguished by its use by government, military, and business organizations.

> *Example:* "Downsized" actually means fired or loss of a job.

A **euphemism** is a socially accepted word or phrase used to replace unacceptable language, such as expressions for bodily functions or body parts. Euphemisms also are used as substitutes for straightforward words to tactfully conceal or falsify meaning.

> *Example*: My grandmother <u>passed away</u> last April.

Jargon is the specialized language of a particular group or culture. Education-related jargon includes words and phrases such as *rubric, tuning protocol,* and *deskilling.*

Vocabulary

Vocabulary is the body of words used in a language. On the Praxis English Subject Assessment tests, you will be asked to understand vocabulary in the context of a literary or informational text. You will need to distinguish meaning among commonly misspelled or mistaken words, figures of speech, or idioms.

Commonly misspelled or mistaken words include the following:

its and it's	eminent and imminent
their, there, and they're	principle and principal
saw and seen	lie, lay
further and farther	right, write, and rite
affect and effect	sight, site, and cite
less and fewer	

If this is an area of weakness for you, be sure to check a writing/grammar handbook for more examples.

Figures of speech, such as hyperbole, irony, and simile, are addressed more extensively in chapter 3 of this book. Following are a few more that are specific to language.

- **Understatement:** An expression or phrase that emphasizes an idea by describing it in restrained terms. For example, in Shakespeare's *Romeo and Juliet,* Mercutio is mortally wounded and states, "ay, ay, a scratch, a scratch … " This is also known as a **meiosis,** a witty understatement that diminishes or dismisses someone or something.
- **Local color:** The use of language and details that are common in specific regions of a country or geographical location. Mark Twain and Henry James are two authors who used local color to capture the dialect, expressions, and routines of people from specific regions.

- **Sarcasm:** The use of irony or false praise to make fun of someone or something. For example, Oscar Wilde wrote, "Some cause happiness wherever they go; others whenever they go."

Idioms are expressions that are not easily understood through the literal meaning of the words. For example, "it's raining cats and dogs" means that it is raining heavily, or "get Miss Maudie's goat" in *To Kill a Mockingbird* means to make Miss Maudie angry. You'll want to review more idioms using a reputable online resource if this is an area in which you need work.

Teaching Language and Vocabulary

You will want to be able to recognize and evaluate several of the commonly used research-based approaches to support language acquisition and vocabulary development for diverse learners, including English language learners (ELLs), students with learning disabilities, and students living in poverty. Bilingual education studies have demonstrated that ELLs acquire vocabulary and language more effectively when taught in both English and the first language. English language learners also benefit from explicit instruction of the components of literacy, such as phonemic awareness, phonics, and vocabulary. Some commonly used approaches include:

- Linking vocabulary with text themes or concepts, rather than teaching vocabulary or language in isolation
- Providing time to read and discuss quality texts
- Teaching students the role of "Word Finder" in a literature circle, which involves assigning one student to look for new or challenging vocabulary words in the text
- Teaching discipline-specific vocabulary
- Teaching students structural cues such as common prefixes, suffixes, and roots
- Teaching students how to effectively use context cues to identify the meanings of words and phrases
- Using graphic organizers to help students see relationships among vocabulary words

Digital vs. Print Texts

In chapter 3, we examined informational features of print texts. Digital texts share some of these same features, such as references, use of fonts for emphasis, and a table of contents. The key difference is that print texts have a static, sequential layout, whereas digital texts have an interactive, dynamic layout.

Dictionary: Stand-alone website or interactive hyperlink built into the text to help the reader know the meaning, derivation, pronunciation, and other features of a word.

Electronic menus: The table of contents of an electronic text is found in the electronic menu. This is typically in a drop-down menu from the top of the page or located on the left or right of the text in a "frame." The electronic menu guides the reader to see the organization of the text and helps one find information by clicking or selecting a link.

Glossary: A list of terms used in the digital text usually embedded in the text rather than at the end as in the print text. Terms are hyperlinked so that readers can find definitions as needed.

Hyperlinks: Interactive elements of a text, caption, video, or graphic that allow the reader to navigate to find additional information.

Icons: A symbol or picture that provides a link or shortcut for users. Common icons in digital texts include symbols for sound (a speaker), moving forward or backward (arrows), and help (question mark).

Pages: There are no pages in e-books or digital texts. The content flows from one screen to another, and may be formatted to meet the reader's individual needs or wants, such as font size, color, and background shading.

Pronunciation or speech features: A unique feature of digital texts that allows users to hear the definition of a term or to listen to portions or the entire text. Rate of speech, language, accent, and voice of speaker are all features that can be adjusted.

Spell check: Digital texts have a built-in spell check that highlights words that may be spelled incorrectly.

Thesaurus: Like spell check, the thesaurus is a hyperlink or electronic menu item. The thesaurus provides alternate terms with similar meaning to the word one is examining.

Translation: Unlike print texts, the reader can change the language of a digital text. While there may be issues with the translation, this is a unique and important feature of digital texts.

URL: Uniform Resource Locator or URL is an Internet address. It is important to note website domain extensions such as .edu (education), .com (commercial business), .net (network), and .org (organization) to check the reliability and accuracy of information, although one must also check the date and creator of a website.

Word count and tools features: The electronic menu allows readers to check how many words are being read/used, how difficult the text is to read according to commonly used readability formulas, and to find a word or phrase (shortcut: Ctrl-F).

Chapter 5

Writing, Speaking, and Listening

The Writing, Speaking, and Listening content appears on the following Praxis English Subject Assessment tests:

- Test 5038: English Language Arts: Content Knowledge
- Test 5039: English Language Arts: Content and Analysis
- Test 5047: Middle School English Language Arts
- Test 5146: Middle School: Content Knowledge—Literature and Language Studies subtest

This chapter is organized as a concise outline of the major content assessed on each of these tests. Review this outline to refresh your memory of important English content. If portions of the material are unfamiliar to you, study further by completing the full-length practice tests in chapters 7–10 and by using the suggested resources in the appendix.

Teaching Writing

The Common Core State Standards (CCSS) for English Language Arts and Literacy grades 6–12 require teachers to be prepared to teach several different writing activities. While you will want to be familiar with each of the types of activities below, the CCSS emphasize persuasive, argumentative, essay, and research writing.

- **Personal writing:** Students can express their innermost thoughts, feelings, and responses through a variety of personal writing, including journal writing, autobiographies, diaries, reflective essays, logs, blogs, personal narratives, and personal essays.
- **Workplace writing:** Middle- and secondary-level students must learn how to prepare resumes, cover letters, job applications, and business letters.
- **Subject writing:** In subject writing activities, middle- and secondary-level students write interviews, accounts, profiles, or descriptions to capture the meaning of the subject being written about.
- **Creative writing:** Creative writing provides students with the opportunity to play with language, express emotions, articulate stories, or develop a drama for others to enjoy.
- **Persuasive writing:** In this genre of writing, students learn rhetorical strategies to persuade others, such as writing editorials, arguments, commentaries, or advertisements.
- **Scholarly writing:** Essays, research papers, and bibliographies are the most prevalent types of scholarly writing in middle- and secondary-level classrooms.

Types of Source Materials for Writing

Your students will need to know which sources to use to support their writing and also evaluate sources. Below are several types of source material for writing.

- **Reference works:** Dictionaries, encyclopedias, writers' reference handbooks, books of lists, almanacs, thesauruses, books of quotations, and so on.
- **Internet:** Each of the types of reference works above is available online. In addition, writers can use search engines or portals (sites that list many resources and websites) to gather ideas and information.
- **Student-created sources:** Examples of student-created resources include a student's personal dictionary of words to know or spell, note cards, graphic organizers, oral histories, and journals.
- **Other sources:** Film, art, media, and so on.

Stages of the Writing Process

The stages of the writing process are recursive; in other words, they recur and repeat. You will want to know the following six stages for your Praxis English Subject Assessment test and also be able to identify ways to help your students prewrite, revise, and publish writing.

1. **Prewriting** (also called planning or rehearsal): This stage of the writing process involves gathering and selecting ideas. English teachers can help students prewrite in several ways: by creating lists, researching, brainstorming, reading to discover more about the author's style, discussing the topic, collecting memorabilia or clips from other texts, and free-writing.

2. **Drafting:** In this stage, students begin writing, connecting, and developing ideas. Drafts often contain main points, a thesis, relevant support, and elaboration. Depending on the purpose for writing and the audience for the piece, there may be a few drafts or many.

3. **Revising:** This stage of the writing process involves rewriting, or "re-seeing." At this point, the student looks at the piece again, either alone or with the help of a teacher or capable peer. The student strives to ensure that the reader is able to understand the piece of writing. In the revising stage, emphasis is placed on examining sentence structure, word choice, voice, and organization of the piece.

4. **Editing:** This stage involves checking for style and conventions—spelling, grammar, usage, and mechanics. At this point in the writing process, the student ensures that errors in conventions will not be intrusive when others read the piece of writing.

5. **Publishing:** This is the "going public" stage. A student can share his or her writing with a larger audience in many ways. Teachers can encourage students to publish their writing in newsletters, online publications, performances, brochures, and magazines.

6. **Evaluating:** In this stage, the student looks back at his or her work and self-evaluates. The audience also evaluates the effectiveness of the writing.

Stages of the Research Writing Process

The stages of the research writing process include each of the stages of the writing process discussed in the last section. However, there are some differences, as described below.

1. **Prewriting** involves identifying a general topic of interest or one that is determined by the test or teacher, listing key words to use in the search for information, and then accessing reputable sources, either online or print. Next, the student creates source cards, note cards with a list of your references. This prewriting process helps the student focus on the topic. The student then writes a statement of purpose, identifies questions and organizes questions with similar headings, and returns to more sources and makes additional source cards.

2. **Drafting** begins with the student making an outline of the headings for each of the source cards. Some sources will be used; others may be deleted at this point. The student can change the statement of purpose from the prewriting stage to a draft thesis statement and begin to write the body of the research paper using source cards and notes. Students need to be sure to both paraphrase and include an in-text citation or use a direct quote with an in-text citation as they use source material. They should also be sure to write an introduction and conclusion. Research papers also include a title page and works cited or references section, which follows a specific format, typically Modern Language Association (MLA) in a middle school or high school English course.

3. **Revising** and the remaining stages of the research writing process are the same as the general writing process in the last section. Revising should be particularly focused on the organization of the paragraphs and the conciseness of sentences.

4. **Editing** should include additional focus on ethical citation of sources and accuracy of works cited.

5. **Publishing** typically involves submitting a research paper to the English or Humanities teacher in hard copy and sometimes using an electronic submission tool such as TurnItIn.com to check for plagiarism.

6. **Evaluating** involves self-assessment and audience feedback on the effectiveness of the writing.

Evaluating Print or Digital Source Materials

Students must evaluate sources carefully to ensure that each source is reliable, worthwhile, and accurate. The following general guidelines will help students determine whether print sources (such as journal articles) and nonprint sources (such as Internet sources) are reliable.

1. **Check the basic information about the source, such as author, year published, and publisher.** Review this initial information to check for credibility, evidence of bias, conflict of interest or other agendas, and accuracy. Is your source peer-reviewed or edited by others? Have other works by this author proven to be credible and accurate?

2. **If your source initially appears reliable, take time to read a portion of the material.** Use the following questions to guide your next level of review: Is the writing style factual, credible, and free of errors in conventions? Who is the intended audience, or is this piece written for a different purpose other than yours? Is the coverage of the content thorough and accurate for your purposes? Have other people read the source and found it credible, accurate, and helpful?

3. **Check digital sources.** Digital sources require the same checks for basic information as in step 1 above, but require additional evaluation for the following:

   Purpose: What is the motivation for the source—promotional, educational, entertainment?

   Authority: Is the author identifiable? If yes, what is the author's background, and are the author's sources cited? If no, what agency or organization has created this online source? What is the organization's history, political view, or purpose?

   Currency: When was the source last updated or revised? This information is usually at the bottom of the home page.

   Reliability: Does the source appear to be credible? Do most of the website links work? Do you think that this source will still be available in the future, based on your review of the authority and currency of the source?

   Coverage: Is the source completed or under construction? What key information is omitted?

MLA and APA Citations

Take a look at the following citation for a book in both the Modern Language Association (MLA) and the American Psychological Association (APA) formats.

> **MLA:** Salinger, J. D. *The Catcher in the Rye.* New York: Little, Brown, and Company, 1945. Print.
>
> **APA:** Salinger, J. D. (1945). *The Catcher in the Rye.* New York: Little, Brown and Company.

As you can see, MLA and APA formats require slightly different ways to document a source. Each format has specific rules for citing books, journals, and periodicals; in-text citations; and more. Middle school and secondary school students must be taught how to use appropriate formats and the proper way to cite the words or ideas of others. The following websites contain in-depth information about MLA and APA formats, the most common formats used for secondary-level writing:

- https://www.mla.org/
- http://www.apa.org/

Avoiding plagiarism is an important topic in American schools; teaching students to cite sources responsibly is often the role of the English teacher. Students should be taught how to paraphrase a source, cite a source, and quote a source directly.

Instructional Practices and Key Terms

English teachers are required to provide students with the opportunity to express their thoughts through writing in a variety of forms, such as argument, persuasive, creative, and research. In this section, we will review key terms and instructional practices related to teaching writing in the middle school classroom.

Argument: The Common Core State Standards (CCSS) call for increased attention on teaching argument writing. The parts of an argument include a claim, evidence to support the claim, the warrant that explains how the evidence supports the claim, support for the warrant, and qualifications or counterarguments that refute competing claims.

Conventions: Conventions include spelling, grammar, punctuation, capitalization, and paragraphing.

Portfolio: A portfolio is a compilation of a student writer's work for evaluation. Some portfolios are comprised solely of works self-selected by the student; others contain a combination of self-selected and required work. Portfolios help teachers and the student assess a writer's growth over time.

Stages of writing: The stages of writing include prewriting, drafting, revising, editing, and publishing. The stages are recursive, which means repeating or reoccurring. Of course, not all writing moves from the prewriting to the drafting stage; not all writing moves from the drafting to the publishing stage. Here is a description of each stage:

1. **Prewriting:** Writers think about a topic, gather information, establish purposes for writing, consider the audience for the piece, make preliminary notes or lists, and prepare to write. Teaching techniques for prewriting include brainstorming, outlining, free writing, researching, interviewing, clustering ideas using a graphic organizer, and asking 5W and 1H (who, what, where, when, why, and how) questions.

2. **Drafting:** Writers begin composing either on paper or by using an electronic device. Attention is on the ideas and content, not the specific form or conventions, such as spelling or grammar. This stage may move the writer back to prewriting for some time or require multiple copies of drafts before advancing to other stages.

3. **Revising:** Writers re-read and re-see the draft in progress, either alone or with the help of a peer, teacher, or group of writers. Emphasis of this stage is still on the ideas and the clarity of content. Writers may also want to begin to work on the form and organization of the piece to ensure that the audience understands the purpose of the writing. They may need to return to other drafts, cut and paste passages, improve word choice, and so on by returning to the drafting stage.

4. **Editing:** This stage is also known as proofreading. Here writers work on conventions, such as spelling, grammar, and punctuation. Writers will also want to check for proper formatting and style, such as paragraphs or MLA citations.

5. **Publishing:** Writers often select just a few pieces to move to the publishing stage. Publishing in this context simply means "going public" with a written work. A final copy of the written work is composed and shared. Student writers can go public by posting the work on a bulletin board, sharing the piece with classmates, sending the work to a student newspaper or publication, sending the work to another (such as a grandparent or the principal), displaying the work in the school or local library, or entering the writing in a contest.

Types of writing: Choosing the type of writing helps the writer narrow the topic, set the purposes for writing, determine the style of writing (formal or informal), and select the tone (argumentative, objective, supportive). Types of writing emphasized in schools today include essays (personal, cause/effect, persuasive), argument, informative or explanatory, research reports, journals, response to text, and poetry.

Writing workshop: When an English teacher uses the writing workshop method, he or she structures the instructional time in the following way.

- Mini-lesson, led by the teacher or a capable student, based on individual and group instructional needs.
- Status of the class, in which the teacher asks each student to provide a brief update on what he or she will be working on during the workshop.

- Time for writing, in which students work alone, with a partner, or with the teacher to advance through the stages of the writing process. The teacher often confers with students during this time. Students also might participate in a peer revising or editing conference.
- Sharing, in which the teacher selects one or a few students to share aspects of their writing.

Teaching Speaking and Listening

Presentation Formats

As the final step of the composition and rhetoric processes, students go public with their ideas. There are many ways for students to present their writing and ideas. Below, you'll find a few common ways to help your students make effective presentations in your English classroom.

- Performing speeches, plays, videos, or Readers' Theater productions
- Delivering a speech, participating in a debate, or giving a PowerPoint presentation
- Creating booklets, brochures, family scrapbooks, or personal websites
- Publishing a school newspaper, student magazine, or portfolio of work
- Submitting work for publication beyond the classroom in a literary magazine for young adults, in the local newspaper, in a professional publication for writers, in a contest, or for an online publication

Effective Speaking and Listening Techniques

The English Language Arts Common Core State Standards include speaking and listening standards to guide your instruction. Below you will find key techniques for effective speaking and listening.

Speaking and Discussion Skills

- Come to any discussion or speech prepared.
- Focus the speech on one topic.
- Follow rules for collegial discussions; set specific goals and deadlines.
- Pose and respond to specific questions or prompts with elaboration and detail, citing texts as appropriate.
- Review key ideas expressed and demonstrate understanding of multiple perspectives.
- Interpret information presented in various media and formats, then explain how it contributes to the discussion or topic.
- Present an argument using specific claims, evidence, and effective rhetorical devices.
- Include multimedia components in presentations to clarify information.
- Adapt speech to a variety of contexts to demonstrate command of formal English when required or as appropriate.

Listening Skills

- Pay attention to nonverbal cues.
- Face the speaker and maintain eye contact.
- Be attentive.
- Be open-minded.
- Evaluate the speaker's point of view.
- Don't interrupt.
- Wait for speaker to pause before you start speaking.

- Check for understanding; ask good questions.
- Try to feel what the speaker is feeling.
- Provide regular feedback to the speaker.
- Delineate a speaker's argument and specific claims.

Methods to Teach and Evaluate Speaking and Listening

On your Praxis English Subject Assessment test, you may be asked to identify a few methods to teach and evaluate speaking and listening. Several key methods to help you prepare for your test and for your classroom are given below.

- **Debate:** This staple of the English classroom requires two oppositional sides to prove that one viewpoint is better than the other. The CCSS emphasize argument, so this is an important format to teach your students. Listeners strive to find flaws in the logic of the argument and to find rebuttals for the opposing side's argument.

- **Dialogue:** Classroom dialogue requires students to work collaboratively, to listen to multiple perspectives, and to build on the points of others to reach high levels of critical thinking and understanding.

- **Fishbowl:** Fishbowl is a technique in which a small subset of the class sits in a circle in the center of the class and engages in dialogue. The rest of the class listens to and observes the "fishbowl"; from time to time, the teacher pauses the discussion to seek the listeners' content and to process feedback on the fishbowl discussion. The teacher then seeks new members to join the fishbowl and continue the dialogue.

- **Inside circle/outside circle:** The teacher divides the class in half, and students form two circles facing one another—an inside circle and an outside circle. Students discuss with the person facing them, and after some time, the teacher asks one circle to move left or right so that students can continue the discussion with a different partner.

- **Panel:** A panel discussion requires students to listen to four or five classmates or guest speakers on a specific theme or topic. Panelists must be "experts" on the topic, which may require research prior to the discussion.

- **Performance:** Performances can be scripted, like a play, or impromptu, like a classroom reenactment of a scene from Shakespeare. In addition to plays and reenactments, other structures to teach performance include Readers' Theater, Digital Storytelling, and Spoken Word.

- **Presentation:** Presentations require students to inform, demonstrate, explain, or persuade an audience. Typical formats include senior project presentations (individual presents to audience), Book Talk (individual presents short talk either face-to-face or digitally), and Newscast (team of presenters share information either face-to-face or using video).

- **Socratic Seminar:** This great discussion structure shifts the center of conversation from the teacher to the students. Students sit in a whole group circle and talk collaboratively on a topic. The teacher needs to spend time setting up the norms of the Socratic Seminar, such as asking probing questions, paraphrasing, listening and speaking courteously, no raising hands, and ensuring that all students engage in the discussion. The teacher does speak, usually at the beginning and the end of the seminar, and strives to ask thought-provoking questions.

- **Speech:** Classroom speeches can be prepared or extemporaneous; very brief and informal or several minutes and formal. Technology might be used to add visual appeal and to enhance audience engagement. Sample speech formats include Book Talk, How to, Important Memory, and Keynote Speech.

- **TED talk:** TED talks are delivered without notes, from memory, and are approximately 18 minutes long. Slides or visuals are displayed behind the orator. This type of talk requires much rehearsal, and the slides must be of high quality, free of errors, and visually stimulating.

- **Think-Pair-Share:** This informal, impromptu classroom conversation structure requires a student to gather his or her own thoughts individually and then pair with a nearby classmate and share thoughts on the topic.

Understanding and Analyzing Rhetorical Features in Writing and Speaking

In this final section of the chapter, we will examine rhetorical features in writing and speaking. Argument and persuasive techniques are one of the key shifts required of the CCSS. You will want to study this section not only for your Praxis English Subject Assessment test, but also for your own English classroom!

Audience and Purpose

Successful writers know the importance of writing for a specific audience and a specific purpose. Imagine you're writing a personal letter to a former teacher or mentor. Then imagine the differences between that letter and a letter that you write to your prospective employer or to your best friend. The words you choose, the style of writing you employ, and the formality of your letter format all depend on knowing your audience. In middle school and high school English classrooms, teachers should provide students with a variety of opportunities to practice writing for different purposes and for specific audiences. Here are a few prompts to get your students thinking about audience and purpose in your writing classroom.

- Besides you (the English teacher), who is the intended or imaginary audience of the piece?
- What is the background knowledge of the audience? What kinds of information will you need to provide to communicate your message clearly?
- How might this piece of writing be used beyond the classroom? Will it be helpful in some other real-life context, such as for a local nonprofit agency or to persuade readers of a local newspaper?
- What is the purpose of this writing assignment? Be sure to consider your educational reason for assigning the task and your students' purpose for writing. For example, is the purpose to persuade, to entertain, or to inspire?
- What voice should the writer use to communicate most effectively? For example, is the purpose a formal piece, or would the local dialect or informal language be more effective?

Organization of the Passage

Writing requires organization. There are several general ways to organize passages that will help your students communicate effectively.

- **Chronologically:** The writer shows order of time or the steps in a process.
- **Classification:** The writer explains the relationships between terms or concepts.
- **Illustration:** The topic sentence is stated and then followed by the details.
- **Climax:** The details are stated first, followed by the topic sentence.
- **Location:** The writer describes a person, place, or thing and organizes the description in a logical manner.
- **Comparison:** The writer demonstrates similarities and differences between two or more subjects.
- **Cause and effect:** The writer shows the relationship between events and their results.

Types of Discourse

Discourses, according to Foucault, a preeminent researcher on discourse, are systems of thought that "systematically construct the subjects and worlds of which they speak." Discourse can be classified into four general categories:

- **Exposition:** Speech or written form in which one explains or describes. Definitions and comparative analysis of ideas are examples.
- **Narration:** Speech or written form that includes drama, stories, and folklore.

- **Description:** Speech or written form that uses the senses to describe something. For example, novels, essays, or a speech about a childhood recollection may contain descriptive discourse.
- **Argument:** Speech or written form that debates or argues a topic in a logical way. The typical argument essay format is the five-paragraph essay, although longer essay formats may be required of students. Since this form is likely to be emphasized on your test and in your future classroom because of current national standards, let's be sure you know key components of an argument. According to the Online Writing Lab (OWL) at Purdue University, well-written argument essays or speeches contain the following:
  - Well-defined thesis statement and an explanation why this topic is important (exigence)
  - Body paragraphs that include well-researched evidence to support the thesis (warrants) and counterpoints and why these views are wrong
  - Clear transitions between paragraphs
  - Thoughtful inclusion of ethos (an appeal to ethics), logos (an appeal to logic, facts), or pathos (an appeal to emotion)
  - A conclusion that advances the thesis based on the evidence provided

Rhetorical Strategies and Persuasive Techniques

Rhetorical strategies and persuasive techniques are found in speeches, writing, and multiple media formats. The CCSS have renewed the need for English teachers to be prepared to teach rhetorical strategies in writing arguments, persuasive essays, and speeches. Below you will find key strategies and techniques to guide you on your Praxis English Subject Assessment test and in your classroom.

- **Ad hominem** is a technique in an argument used to counter a position using feelings or prejudice, not facts, reason, or logic. Technically, an ad hominem argument directly attacks another person, not that person's position.
- **Analogies** are comparisons of two ideas that have the same relationship.
- **Appeal to authority** is a type of persuasion in logic in which an expert or knowledgeable other is cited for the purpose of strengthening the argument.
- **Appeal to emotion** is a type of argument in which the author appeals to the reader's emotion (fear, security, pity, flattery) to prove the argument.
- **Association** links a product, idea, or service with something the members of the target audience already like or desire, such as fun, security, intimacy, or success.
- **Bandwagon** tries to appeal to people's desire to not be left out and sends the message that "everyone is doing it." One technique closely associated with bandwagon is majority belief, such as "American people believe…," which of course cannot be known by the speaker. In a live audience situation or public event such as a rally or fundraiser, group dynamics build on the bandwagon technique to persuade people to "go along with the crowd."
- **Beautiful people,** a common technique in advertisements, employs good-looking models (some of whom are celebrities) to get our attention and persuade us that if we use this product we may even look as good as these beautiful people.
- **The big lie** is a misrepresentation of facts or gross distortion used as a propaganda technique by an official body or politician.
- **Brand new** persuades the audience that this brand new, "shiny" reason, issue, or product is one that we must agree upon or possess.
- **Bribery** is a persuasive technique that offers you something extra, such as buying a makeup product and getting a free gift with purchase, which is truly not "free," as the cost of the gift is covered in the price.
- **Card stacking** is a persuasive technique in which one side of an issue is advanced and the other is repressed.
- **Charisma** occurs when the persuader appears firm, strong, confident, and even bold. People tend to follow charismatic leaders even when they disagree with their positions on issues.
- **Counterpoint** uses contrasting ideas to communicate a message.

- **Diction** is a person's choice of words based on their clarity, conciseness, effectiveness, and authenticity.

- **Euphemism** uses an indirect or milder word or phrase when referring to something embarrassing or unpleasant, such as "passed away" for "died."

- **Explicit claims or facts** share information directly, clearly, or factually so we believe we have the information we need to make a decision.

- **Extended metaphor** is a metaphor (a comparison of two unlike things) used throughout a work or over a series of lines in prose or poetry.

- **Extrapolation** is a technique that works by ignoring how complex something is and predicts an outcome we hope will be true because we want to believe it.

- **False statements** or **fallacious reasoning** is an error in reasoning, not in grammar or usage. Examples include *slippery slope, red herring*, and *straw man,* which are defined in this section.

- **Fear** is a persuasive technique that uses something feared or disliked by the intended audience to advance a solution. For example, bad breath is used to persuade one to purchase gum.

- **Flattery** praises or acknowledges so that the audience feels accepted and persuaded.

- **Foreshadowing** is a technique in which the writer or speaker gives hints or clues about what is to come at some later point in the piece.

- **Glittering generalities** use words like "justice," "freedom," and "democracy" in vague ways. Since these are positive concepts that everyone would support, this technique helps the audience accept an argument.

- **Humor** appeals to emotion that builds rapport between the speaker and the listener. In addition, humor is one way an orator or writer can establish ethos (a persuasive appeal) between the speaker and listener.

- **Hyperbole** is an exaggerated claim or statement that's not meant to be taken literally and is used to make a point, such as "I have a ton of homework."

- **Intensity** in advertisements or speeches is a persuasive technique that includes superlatives (greatest, lowest prices, fastest), comparatives (better than, fewer calories, improved), and exaggeration.

- **Irony** uses a word or phrase to mean the exact opposite of its literal or expected meaning.

- **Juxtaposition** places normally unassociated ideas, words, or phrases next to one another to create an effect of surprise and wit.

- **Nostalgia** looks back at an earlier time in history, when life was supposedly simpler, better, and desired.

- **Point of view** identifies the perspective from which a piece is written. First-person point of view is told from the view of one of the characters. Third-person point of view is told by someone outside the story. Third-person point of view can be told from three different views: 1) omniscient, in which the narrator shares the thoughts and feelings of all the characters; 2) limited omniscient, in which the narrator shares the thoughts and feelings of only one character; and 3) camera view, in which the storyteller records the action from his or her point of view, unaware of any of the other characters' thoughts or feelings, as if creating a film of the event.

- **Praise** uses positive messages to recognize or influence others.

- **Quotations** are used as a rhetorical device to establish the writer or orator as a knowledgeable person. This is an appeal to the mind, also known as *logos.*

- **Red herring** may either be a logical fallacy or a literary device that leads the audience or reader toward a false conclusion.

- **Repetition** (of language, words, sounds, or images) is used within a speech or advertisement to advance the point and make it memorable.

- **Rhetorical questioning,** also known as *erotema,* is a question that is posed but is not intended to be answered. Instead, the purpose is often to affirm or deny a point strongly.

- **Rule of three** is a rhetorical device in which the writer or speaker uses three successive words to express a central point (e.g., "Veni, vidi, vici," Julius Caesar) or three parallel elements (words or phrases) (e.g., "Be sincere, be brief, be seated," Franklin D. Roosevelt).

- **Sarcasm** is the use of what appears to be positive feedback or cutting wit to mock someone.

- **Satire** uses humor, irony, exaggeration, or ridicule to expose and criticize human vices or folly, usually with the purpose of improving something in society.

- **Scapegoating** finds something or someone to blame for current issues or problems.

- **Selection of detail** is a person's choice of specific events, words, incidents, anecdotes, etc., which are used to make or create a narrative/scene.

- **Slippery slope** is also known as "thin edge of the wedge," "domino fallacy," "absurd extrapolation," and "camel's nose." A relatively insignificant event is suggested, then a more significant event follows, until the "the next thing you know," the ultimate, most significant event is reached. The logic is fallacious and unwarranted, and often each step leading to the most significant event becomes more and more improbable.

- **Straw man** is a common technique in an argument in which the speaker or writer gives the impression of arguing against the opponent's position, while actually refuting an argument that was not suggested by the opponent.

- **Style** encompasses the way an author or orator uses words, phrases, and sentences to formulate ideas. In addition, style is thought of as the ways one person's work is distinguished from the work of others.

- **Testimonials** are used in the media or in speeches to persuade us about the value or quality of a product or idea. The people sharing the testimonial are sometimes scientific experts, celebrities, or plain folks. Key to this technique's success is the authenticity of the person sharing the testimonial and making us believe the person really uses this product or believes deeply in this idea.

  - **Scientific experts:** Experts offer evidence to unequivocally convince the target audience that there is proof to support use of the product or point being made. The expert will often use charts or graphs and wear a lab coat to appeal to our trust in scientists and science.

  - **Celebrities:** A famous person is used to get our attention, build appeal for the idea or product, and gain our favor.

  - **Plain folks:** The opposite approach of using celebrities, this technique uses a regular person to endorse the product to appeal to our sense of pride, patriotism, or home. This technique is often used in truck advertisements and political campaigns to strengthen the "authentic" image of the product or person.

- **Tone** is the overall feeling created in a piece of writing or speech. The tone of a piece can be humorous, satiric, serious, morose, etc.

- **Understatement** is a figure of speech used to intentionally make a situation seem less important than it really is, which often has an ironic effect.

- **Warm and fuzzy** is a technique that appeals to emotions and uses sentimental images and pleasant words/ voice to evoke feelings of comfort.

Chapter 6

English Language Arts Instruction

The English Language Arts Instruction content category on the Praxis English Subject Assessment tests requires that you know the key theories, theorists, terms, and methods related to teaching English in middle school classrooms today. You will be expected to apply your knowledge in this category to only one English Subject Assessment test:

- Test 5047: Middle School English Language Arts

This chapter is organized into eight sections that correspond to the specific content categories you'll find on the Middle School English Language Arts (5047) test.

Language Acquisition and Vocabulary Development for Diverse Learners

In this section, we will first examine terms related to English language learners and diverse learners. Then we will review key research-based teaching methods that assist our students in the acquisition of language and vocabulary.

Diverse Learners

English language learner (ELL), English as a second language (ESL), and primary language not English (PLNE): These terms are used to describe students who are learning English as a second (or third or fourth) language. Teachers of bilingual and multilingual students can support English language acquisition and learning in several important ways, including building on students' culture, supporting students' proficiency in their native language, giving students time to learn English (two years for conversational English, seven years for academic English), and offering opportunities for students to work and talk in small groups.

Family culture: According to researcher Luis Moll, families can provide valuable funds of knowledge for teachers to tap into and use for successful lessons. Communicating with families, knowing the school community, and appreciating the differences and similarities among family cultures will help teachers offer instruction that meets the needs of all students.

Linguistic patterns: Many students' first language is not English; furthermore, students within the same school district may speak various dialects. Students whose first language is not English or who use a dialect that is not Standard American English (SAE) benefit when a teacher views these differences as sources of enrichment in the classroom. Students who are new to speaking English may experience a period of silence and may prefer listening in the classroom, which is to be expected and respected. Language is always used in a social context; therefore, students who have linguistically diverse language patterns may "code switch." In other words, a student may use a certain dialect on the playground and another in the classroom. One dialect, African American Vernacular English (AAVE), or Ebonics, is spoken by many African Americans. The best method for teaching students who speak AAVE became a political controversy in the 1990s. Teaching techniques similar to those used with students whose primary language is not English appear to be most successful for students who speak in dialects of Standard American English.

Multiculturalism: Students come from a wide variety of cultures. Successful teachers help students define and understand their own cultures to deal with mutual misconceptions and inform future lesson planning. Sometimes a family's expectations may differ from a teacher's expectations for a student. Making positive connections between schoolwork and home life can support students' success.

Teachers must understand that culture is complex and multidimensional. In her work starting in the early 1990s, researcher Nitza Hidalgo offers three levels of culture—concrete, behavioral, and symbolic—to help us more deeply understand the cultural backgrounds of our students and their families, and to build a sense of relatedness and respect in the classroom.

- **Concrete:** This level of culture is the most visible and tangible. It includes surface-level aspects such as clothes, music, games, and food.
- **Behavioral:** This level of culture is defined by our social roles, language, and approaches to nonverbal communication that help us situate ourselves organizationally in society (for example, gender roles, family structure, and political affiliation).
- **Symbolic:** This level of culture involves our values and beliefs. It is often abstract, yet it is a key to how we define ourselves (for example, customs, religion, and mores).

Vocabulary and Language Instruction

Middle school students benefit from direct language and vocabulary instruction as well as indirect methods. In this section, we will review several research-based methods that will aid in the instruction of diverse learners.

Indirect Methods

Context clues: Teaching students to use context—the words around the spoken or printed word—is an effective indirect method for students to learn language and vocabulary. Students can read, re-read, or just leave an unfamiliar word out to try to determine its meaning.

Opportunities to speak and listen: Students need ample opportunities to speak and listen in pairs, small groups, and with the whole class. Structures like Think-Pair-Share or Turn and Talk are easy ways to encourage students to talk with their peers.

Reading: There is ample research to support that reading increases students' vocabulary. Students can read "just right" texts independently, and they can also increase word knowledge by listening to a challenging text that is read aloud.

Word wall: A word wall is a collection of words, usually listed alphabetically, which is posted on a large wall in the classroom. Students and the teacher refer to the words in discussions and in writing.

Direct Methods

Graphic organizers: Also known as visual structures, graphic organizers are note-taking guides to help students capture, organize, and remember new terms and concepts. One favorite is the Word Map, which has the new term in the center and boxes surrounding the term that require students to define the word, the classification, and qualities of the term, and give examples.

Key-word method: This is a favorite method and has a strong research base. The teacher pre-teaches an important or challenging word prior to reading through the use of a word clue in the form of an image or a word that is part of the definition. The key word provides a cognitive clue to help the learner remember the word.

Root analysis: Many words in the English language are derived from Latin or Greek roots. Breaking a word into its prefix, suffix, and root word helps students learn new vocabulary, which ideally is applied more and more independently in reading and speech.

Vocabulary self-collection strategy: In this small-group activity, students and the teacher share two words they think may be new or difficult to define. Individuals discuss what they think the word might mean and why it is an important one to learn, and then the small group decides on five to eight words they would like to study and learn over the course of the week. Students practice the words in multiple contexts over time and discuss the words' histories, antonyms, and synonyms.

Word sorts: This research-based word study activity focuses students' attention on key features of words, such as their sounds, patterns, and meaning(s). There are two types of word sorts—open and closed. Students categorize and actively manipulate words in open word sorts. In closed word sorts, the teacher clarifies the process for defining the words and then engages students in critical thinking as they examine word structure, key concepts, or sight vocabulary.

Speaking and Listening Instruction

Middle school students should have multiple opportunities to practice speaking and listening in the English classroom. For example, students can engage in discussions, participate in literature circles or debates, analyze famous speeches online, and make presentations to the class. These methods are also shared in chapter 5.

- **Debate:** This staple of the English classroom requires two oppositional sides to prove that one viewpoint is better than the other. The CCSS emphasize argument, so this is an important format to teach your students. Listeners strive to find flaws in the logic of the argument and to find rebuttals for the opposing side's argument.

- **Dialogue:** Classroom dialogue requires students to work collaboratively, to listen to multiple perspectives, and to build on the points of others to reach high levels of critical thinking and understanding.

- **Fishbowl:** Fishbowl is a technique in which a small subset of the class sits in a circle in the center of the class and engages in dialogue. The rest of the class listens to and observes the "fishbowl"; from time to time, the teacher pauses the discussion to seek the listeners' content and process feedback on the fishbowl discussion. The teacher then seeks new members to join the fishbowl and continue the dialogue.

- **Inside circle/outside circle:** The teacher divides the class in half, and students form two circles facing one another—an inside circle and an outside circle. Students discuss with the person facing them, and after some time, the teacher asks one circle to move left or right so that students can continue the discussion with a different partner.

- **Panel:** A panel discussion requires students to listen to four or five classmates or guest speakers on a specific theme or topic. Panelists must be "experts" on the topic, which may require research prior to the discussion.

- **Performance:** Performances can be scripted, like a play, or impromptu, like a classroom reenactment of a scene from Shakespeare. In addition to plays and reenactments, other structures to teach performance include Readers' Theater, Digital Storytelling, and Spoken Word.

- **Presentation:** Presentations require students to inform, demonstrate, explain, or persuade an audience. Typical formats include senior project presentations (individual presents to audience), Book Talk (individual presents short talk either face-to-face or digitally), and Newscast (team of presenters share information either face-to-face or using video).

- **Socratic Seminar:** This great discussion structure shifts the center of conversation from the teacher to the students. Students sit in a whole-group circle and talk collaboratively on a topic. The teacher needs to spend time setting up the norms of the Socratic Seminar, such as asking probing questions, paraphrasing, listening and speaking courteously, no raising hands, and ensuring all students engage in the discussion. The teacher does speak, usually at the beginning and the end of the seminar, and strives to ask thought-provoking questions.

- **Speech:** Classroom speeches can be prepared or extemporaneous; very brief and informal or several minutes and formal. Technology might be used to add visual appeal and to enhance audience engagement. Sample speech formats include Book Talk, How to, Important Memory, and Keynote Speech.

- **TED talk:** TED talks are delivered without notes, from memory and are approximately 18 minutes long. Slides or visuals are displayed behind the orator. This type of talk requires much rehearsal, and the slides must be of high quality, free of errors, and visually stimulating.

- **Think-Pair-Share:** This informal, impromptu classroom conversation structure requires a student to gather his or her own thoughts individually and then pair with a nearby classmate and share thoughts on the topic.

Information and Communication Technology Instruction

The National Council of Teachers of English (NCTE) emphasizes the importance of information and communication technologies in the teaching of English today. In the 21st-century classroom, students will use computers and handheld devices, such as smartphones and tablets, to learn. Below you will find key terms and instructional practices to teach students to be "digitally literate."

Blog: A blog is a website that is regularly updated by an individual or a small group. Blogs are written in an informal, conversational style, which makes them a great space for student or teacher writing.

Evernote: This free app is a productivity tool where students and teachers can bookmark or "clip" websites, make notes and organize in notebooks, and tag information with key words to aid in searching and recalling information gathered. For a small fee, Evernote Premium also allows people to share notebooks, which is especially helpful for teachers in providing research or background information and helpful for students in group projects.

Google: Google has many features—too many to list here—so we'll focus on the key uses of Google in the classroom. As you know, Google is a search engine and one of the first ways students typically search for information. It's important to teach students about the difference between advertisement sites, which tend to be the first one or two entries of information presented, and the list of all other websites that can be from a variety of sources that are not advertisers. After the advertisements come the top websites that match the key words searched. Students may not realize that at the top of the Google main page is a menu of items: Web, News, Images, Videos, Maps, More, and Search Tools. You will want to teach your students how to use these menus more effectively and how to refine a search. Google Apps and Google Classroom are also major features you will want your students to become familiar with. Google Apps such as Gmail, Drive, Docs, Sheets, and Slides are free productivity tools that allow teachers and students to share information and co-create texts. Google Classroom is free to educators with school access to Google Education and allows you to set up a paperless classroom, lets students know when assignments are due, and provides access to grades instantaneously.

Information literacy: In today's technology-filled world, information literacy is a crucial skill students will need to gain knowledge. You will need to teach students what information is needed and then how to locate, evaluate, effectively use and store, and then communicate information accurately and ethically.

Podcast: Podcasts are digital audio files available on the Internet. Podcasts are often updated regularly and can be automatically downloaded to one's computer when they are available. This technology is a great classroom tool for learning new information or for students to co-create their own knowledge and then share with others. One of my favorite podcasts is National Public Radio's *This American Life,* which I often use in my middle-level and college classrooms.

Presentation software: Your students will need to know how to use presentation software to make an effective presentation in your classroom as well as in their future workplace. Applications such as PowerPoint, Prezi, and Google Slides are usually readily available in classrooms to support students in sharing visual, audio, and video content professionally and creatively.

Skype, FaceTime, or Google Hangouts: These tools allow your students to see and hear others using the Internet and a webcam. You could set up a conversation with a classroom of students halfway around the world or invite an expert to "meet" with your students online.

Twitter: Twitter is a mini-blog in which people communicate using only 140 characters. While many students use Twitter for only social reasons, you can tap into this innovative technology to keep your students engaged and up-to-date on current assignments, current events, and issues of importance. Twitter also offers a means to stay connected with families and help students recall information to share at home. By creating a hashtag specific to your classroom or project, students can co-create and then follow along in the unit of study.

Webquest: A webquest is an online lesson format in which all of the information in a unit of study is embedded in an inquiry-oriented experience. Students often work with partners or small groups to engage in a webquest to learn in a nonlinear, interactive format.

Wiki: A wiki is a website that is co-constructed with members of the space. Wikipedia is the most famous wiki; it is a portal of information that users update and change together over time. It is important for your middle-level students to understand that using Wikipedia to conduct research requires fact checking to evaluate the accuracy of the information.

Grouping and Differentiated Instruction

English teachers know and use these research-based teaching methods to group students and differentiate instruction. It's important to know that teachers also combine several methods during a lesson, particularly if they are teaching in a longer block schedule. No one instructional strategy is better than others; it's important to know several student-directed and teacher-directed methods to find which works best for your students.

Teacher-Directed Methods

Computer-delivered and online instruction: As the name implies, computer-delivered and online instruction involve the use of a computer in the delivery of instruction. There are many formats for computer-based and online instruction, such as drill and practice, tutorials, simulations, instructional games, and problem-solving. Commonly used software programs for middle school English language arts are READ 180 and Accelerated Reader. Online tutorial programs and videos are readily available to teachers of middle-level students.

Direct instruction: One version of direct instruction involves a highly scripted lesson that requires students to achieve mastery of the material. Typically the lesson comes from a curriculum provided by the school district, and teachers are expected to follow the lesson plan materials as written with no modifications. Another type of direct instruction, which is also known as mastery teaching, has the teacher carefully planning instruction. During the opening of the lesson, the teacher plans for the anticipatory set, which activates or develops students' prior knowledge and gets them ready to learn. Next, the teacher teaches students how to learn the new information through a carefully planned instructional sequence with clear models or examples. The teacher then has students work in pairs or small groups to experience guided practice. The teacher monitors student work and understanding, stopping to re-teach or correct misunderstandings as needed. Finally, the teacher individually assesses student learning and provides further individual practice as needed.

Lecture: This familiar method works best when the teacher organizes the lecture information and plans for creative and engaging ways to gain and maintain student attention. Lectures are more appropriate with upper-grade-level students, although brief lectures can be effective with middle school students.

Mastery learning: The teacher introduces new concept(s) using a brief lecture or demonstration lesson, and then gives an ungraded assignment or quiz to assess students' mastery of the information. Then the teacher offers enrichment to the students who have mastered the new information and remediation to the students who have not. The teacher then gives a final test. If the mastery learning approach is effective, all students should receive high scores, typically 80% or higher.

Student-Directed Methods

Ad hoc, small group work: In this teaching method, the teacher allows students to form their own small groups to complete a short-term task.

Cooperative learning: The teacher selectively places students in groups. In most cooperative learning structures, the students are grouped heterogeneously. In a few cooperative learning structures, such as Student Teams Achievement Divisions (STAD), students are placed in homogeneous groups to compete, but earn group rewards for a heterogeneously grouped team. In essence, cooperative learning is designed to foster collaboration among peers so that all students achieve academic excellence. Successful cooperative learning structures contain the following essential elements.

- Positive interdependence, in which students encourage teammates to complete tasks well
- Individual accountability, in which each group member is individually assessed by the teacher
- Simultaneous management, in which materials and tasks are provided to the groups in an efficient way so that little or no class time is wasted and all students can be actively engaged in the task. For example, the teacher can predetermine group membership and place a notecard with the names of group members at the assigned seats for the group.

Inquiry learning: In direct opposition to the lecture method, inquiry learning begins with the teacher or a student leader asking thought-provoking questions and engaging students in discussion and investigation. This method is also known as discovery learning.

Literature circle: A literature circle is a structure to support student-directed discussion about literature. The literature circle may be heterogeneously or homogeneously grouped. The students all read the same selection independently and then get together to discuss the piece. Students prepare for the discussion by actively reading with a role in mind, such as Discussion Director, Connector, Word Finder, Character Sketcher, or Summarizer. During the discussion, each student offers contributions to the discourse based on their various roles and their ideas about the literature.

Reciprocal teaching: This method requires students to work in pairs to read new material. One student acts as the reader and the other student actively listens, then the students switch roles. There are four steps the student pair engages in: 1) preview/predict; 2) question; 3) clarify for understanding; 4) summarize.

Text Selection

English language arts teachers are required to use certain texts, such as a literature anthology, but will need to know how to supplement required texts to actively engage students in reading literature, poetry, and informational texts. Some texts in middle school classrooms today still come in the traditional printed book format, but more and more only a digital format is offered or the reading is done completely online. The following aspects of texts will help guide your selection of rigorous, quality, and grade-appropriate texts for your students.

Qualitative assessment: Teachers must use their professional judgment to determine if a text is of high quality and right for students. Qualitative assessment of a text includes reading to check for the text meaning or purpose, the knowledge demands, as well as the structure and language conventions.

Quantitative assessment: Also known as determining the readability or difficulty level of a text, quantitative assessment is typically computer generated, although a teacher can calculate some readability formulas, such as the Fry method. Features of the text, such as word length, sentence length, and word frequency, are measured. Common quantitative measures of text difficulty include Lexile and Flesch-Kincaid.

Reader-task considerations: The teacher knows his or her students, so reader-task considerations are an important third component to determining if the text is "just right." One needs to consider the reader's motivation, knowledge, and experiences. Cultural considerations must also be taken into account. Task considerations involve determining if the text fits the purpose of the instruction, offers quality and complexity, and is free from bias and inaccuracies.

Reading Instruction

Below you will find key reading terms and instructional practices that middle-level classroom teachers will want to know.

Comprehension strategy instruction: In most teaching circumstances, the majority of students will know how to read at grade level but may need to learn strategies to help them read to learn, particularly when reading nonfiction texts. English teachers can facilitate student comprehension by explicitly teaching comprehension strategies using a variety of texts. Key comprehension strategies include identifying important information, summarizing, sequencing, comparing and contrasting, envisioning character change, and predicting/verifying.

Fluency methods: Fluency is the ability to read with expression and ease, without halting to sound out words or figure out the text's meaning. English teachers can promote fluency by using methods such as echo reading (repeat-reading after another capable reader), choral reading (performing a text simultaneously with other readers), and Readers' Theater (performing parts of a text, much like a play, with emphasis on reading with expression rather than on props, scenery, or movement).

Metacognition: A person's ability to think about his or her own thinking, metacognition (meta = between; cognition = thinking) requires self-awareness and self-regulation of thinking. A student who demonstrates a high level of metacognition is able to explain his or her own thinking and describe which strategies he or she uses to read or solve a problem.

Reading workshop: In the reading workshop method, an English teacher plans for reading instruction by using the following structure.

- Mini-lesson on reading skills or strategies, such as identifying main ideas, led by the teacher or a capable student, based on individual and group instructional needs.
- Status of the class, in which the teacher asks each student to provide a brief update on what he or she will be working on during the workshop.
- Time for reading, in which students work alone or with the teacher in a small group to advance skills, knowledge, and appreciation. The teacher often confers with students during this time. Students also might participate in a peer-group conversation about their reading.
- Sharing, in which the teacher selects one or a few students to share aspects of their reading.

Scaffolding: These are instructional supports provided to a student by an adult or a more capable peer in a learning situation. Scaffolding might take the form of a teacher reading aloud a portion of the text and then asking the student to repeat the same sentence, for example. The more capable a student becomes with a certain skill or concept, the less instructional scaffolding the adult or peer needs to provide.

Schema: These are concepts in the mind about events, scenarios, actions, or objects that have been acquired from past experience. The mind loves organization and must find previous events or experiences with which to associate information, or the information may not be learned. Teachers can activate schema by asking students to recall previous experiences or can develop schema be providing concrete experiences to help students connect what they know to what they are learning.

Teaching literary response and analysis: Students have multiple opportunities to respond to quality literature and analyze the meaning of what they are reading. English teachers often ask students to provide both an efferent (factual) response and an aesthetic (emotive) response to what they have read.

Transfer: This is the ability to apply a lesson learned in one situation to a new situation—for example, a student who has learned to read the word *ambivalent* in a book at school and understands the word *ambivalent* successfully in a conversation between family members.

Writing Instruction

English teachers are required to provide students with the opportunity to express their thoughts through writing in a variety of forms, such as argument, persuasive, creative, and research. In this section, we will review key terms and instructional practices related to teaching writing in the middle school classroom. These methods are also shared in chapter 5.

Argument: The Common Core State Standards (CCSS) call for increased attention on teaching argument writing. The parts of an argument include a claim, evidence to support the claim, the warrant that explains how the evidence supports the claim, support for the warrant, and qualifications or counterarguments that refute competing claims.

Conventions: Conventions include spelling, grammar, punctuation, capitalization, and paragraphing.

Portfolio: A portfolio is a compilation of a student writer's work for evaluation. Some portfolios are comprised solely of works self-selected by the student; others contain a combination of self-selected and required work. Portfolios help teachers and the student assess a writer's growth over time.

Stages of writing: The stages of writing include prewriting, drafting, revising, editing, and publishing. The stages are recursive, which means repeating or reoccurring. Of course, not all writing moves from the prewriting to the drafting stage; not all writing moves from the drafting to the publishing stage. Here is a description of each stage:

1. **Prewriting:** Writers think about a topic, gather information, establish purposes for writing, consider the audience for the piece, make preliminary notes or lists, and prepare to write. Teaching techniques for prewriting include brainstorming, outlining, free writing, researching, interviewing, clustering ideas using a graphic organizer, and asking 5W and 1H (who, what, where, when, why, and how) questions.

2. **Drafting:** Writers begin composing either on paper or by using an electronic device. Attention is on the ideas and content, not the specific form or conventions, such as spelling or grammar. This stage may move the writer back to prewriting for some time or require multiple copies of drafts before advancing to other stages.

3. **Revising:** Writers re-read and re-see the draft in progress, either alone or with the help of a peer, teacher, or group of writers. Emphasis of this stage is still on the ideas and the clarity of content. Writers may also want to begin to work on the form and organization of the piece to ensure that the audience understands the purpose of the writing. They may need to return to other drafts, cut and paste passages, improve word choice, and so on by returning to the drafting stage.

4. **Editing:** This stage is also known as proofreading. Here writers work on conventions, such as spelling, grammar, and punctuation. Writers will also want to check for proper formatting and style, such as paragraphs or MLA citations.

5. **Publishing:** Writers often select just a few pieces to move to the publishing stage. Publishing in this context simply means "going public" with a written work. A final copy of the written work is composed and shared. Student writers can go public by posting the work on a bulletin board, sharing the piece with classmates, sending the work to a student newspaper or publication, sending the work to another (such as a grandparent or the principal), displaying the work in the school or local library, or entering the writing in a contest.

Types of writing: Choosing the type of writing helps the writer narrow the topic, set the purposes for writing, determine the style of writing (formal or informal), and select the tone (argumentative, objective, supportive). Types of writing emphasized in schools today include essays (personal, cause/effect, persuasive), argument, informative or explanatory, research reports, journals, response to text, and poetry.

Writing workshop: When an English teacher uses the writing workshop method, he or she structures the instructional time in the following way.

- Mini-lesson, led by the teacher or a capable student, based on individual and group instructional needs.
- Status of the class, in which the teacher asks each student to provide a brief update on what he or she will be working on during the workshop.
- Time for writing, in which students work alone, with a partner, or with the teacher to advance through the stages of the writing process. The teacher often confers with students during this time. Students also might participate in a peer revising or editing conference.
- Sharing, in which the teacher selects one or a few students to share aspects of their writing.

Assessment of Student Progress

Authentic assessments: Authentic assessments include anecdotal records of student behavior, portfolios, checklists of student progress, performance-based assessments, and student-teacher conferences. Alternative assessments can be contrasted with traditional assessments. Alternative assessments provide a view of a student's process and product, which is closely related to the instructional activity. Traditional assessments usually provide a view only of the product of the learning, such as the score on a test, and may not be as closely related to classroom instruction.

Criteria and rubrics: English teachers provide clear criteria for assignments to ensure that students understand the requirements of the task. A rubric is aligned with the criteria for the assignment to clearly delineate how the assignment will be scored.

Formal assessments: Formal assessment techniques include quizzes, tests, projects, and norm-referenced testing. These are often also known as traditional assessments.

Formative assessments: Formative assessments include teacher observations and student work. This type of assessment is meant to inform daily instruction, re-teaching, and positively affect student achievement.

Informal assessments: Informal assessment techniques include observation, checklists, homework checks, and class and group participation.

Standardized tests: This assessment format requires all test-takers to complete the same questions from a common test-bank. That test is scored in the same way so that results can be compared with the results of other test-takers.

Summative assessments: This type of assessment is used to measure student progress at the end of a phase of instruction. Examples include tests, projects, and performances.

Chapter 7
English Language Arts: Content Knowledge (5038)

This chapter includes one full-length practice test for the Praxis English Language Arts: Content Knowledge (5038) test. This practice test will give you a sense of the format of the test and help you determine which content areas you need to study. You also may want to practice your pacing while taking this full-length practice test. Remember, you will have a total of 150 minutes to complete it.

After you complete the practice test, score your answers and use the explanations to assess content areas to study in chapters 3–5 of this book. Note that the English Language Arts Instruction content in chapter 6 is not assessed on this test.

It's time to set yourself up in a quiet place with no interruptions, get your pencils ready, take a look at the clock, and begin your practice test.

IMPORTANT NOTE: For ease of studying, all questions on this practice test are single-selection multiple-choice.

Answer Sheet

1 Ⓐ Ⓑ Ⓒ Ⓓ	46 Ⓐ Ⓑ Ⓒ Ⓓ	91 Ⓐ Ⓑ Ⓒ Ⓓ
2 Ⓐ Ⓑ Ⓒ Ⓓ	47 Ⓐ Ⓑ Ⓒ Ⓓ	92 Ⓐ Ⓑ Ⓒ Ⓓ
3 Ⓐ Ⓑ Ⓒ Ⓓ	48 Ⓐ Ⓑ Ⓒ Ⓓ	93 Ⓐ Ⓑ Ⓒ Ⓓ
4 Ⓐ Ⓑ Ⓒ Ⓓ	49 Ⓐ Ⓑ Ⓒ Ⓓ	94 Ⓐ Ⓑ Ⓒ Ⓓ
5 Ⓐ Ⓑ Ⓒ Ⓓ	50 Ⓐ Ⓑ Ⓒ Ⓓ	95 Ⓐ Ⓑ Ⓒ Ⓓ
6 Ⓐ Ⓑ Ⓒ Ⓓ	51 Ⓐ Ⓑ Ⓒ Ⓓ	96 Ⓐ Ⓑ Ⓒ Ⓓ
7 Ⓐ Ⓑ Ⓒ Ⓓ	52 Ⓐ Ⓑ Ⓒ Ⓓ	97 Ⓐ Ⓑ Ⓒ Ⓓ
8 Ⓐ Ⓑ Ⓒ Ⓓ	53 Ⓐ Ⓑ Ⓒ Ⓓ	98 Ⓐ Ⓑ Ⓒ Ⓓ
9 Ⓐ Ⓑ Ⓒ Ⓓ	54 Ⓐ Ⓑ Ⓒ Ⓓ	99 Ⓐ Ⓑ Ⓒ Ⓓ
10 Ⓐ Ⓑ Ⓒ Ⓓ	55 Ⓐ Ⓑ Ⓒ Ⓓ	100 Ⓐ Ⓑ Ⓒ Ⓓ
11 Ⓐ Ⓑ Ⓒ Ⓓ	56 Ⓐ Ⓑ Ⓒ Ⓓ	101 Ⓐ Ⓑ Ⓒ Ⓓ
12 Ⓐ Ⓑ Ⓒ Ⓓ	57 Ⓐ Ⓑ Ⓒ Ⓓ	102 Ⓐ Ⓑ Ⓒ Ⓓ
13 Ⓐ Ⓑ Ⓒ Ⓓ	58 Ⓐ Ⓑ Ⓒ Ⓓ	103 Ⓐ Ⓑ Ⓒ Ⓓ
14 Ⓐ Ⓑ Ⓒ Ⓓ	59 Ⓐ Ⓑ Ⓒ Ⓓ	104 Ⓐ Ⓑ Ⓒ Ⓓ
15 Ⓐ Ⓑ Ⓒ Ⓓ	60 Ⓐ Ⓑ Ⓒ Ⓓ	105 Ⓐ Ⓑ Ⓒ Ⓓ
16 Ⓐ Ⓑ Ⓒ Ⓓ	61 Ⓐ Ⓑ Ⓒ Ⓓ	106 Ⓐ Ⓑ Ⓒ Ⓓ
17 Ⓐ Ⓑ Ⓒ Ⓓ	62 Ⓐ Ⓑ Ⓒ Ⓓ	107 Ⓐ Ⓑ Ⓒ Ⓓ
18 Ⓐ Ⓑ Ⓒ Ⓓ	63 Ⓐ Ⓑ Ⓒ Ⓓ	108 Ⓐ Ⓑ Ⓒ Ⓓ
19 Ⓐ Ⓑ Ⓒ Ⓓ	64 Ⓐ Ⓑ Ⓒ Ⓓ	109 Ⓐ Ⓑ Ⓒ Ⓓ
20 Ⓐ Ⓑ Ⓒ Ⓓ	65 Ⓐ Ⓑ Ⓒ Ⓓ	110 Ⓐ Ⓑ Ⓒ Ⓓ
21 Ⓐ Ⓑ Ⓒ Ⓓ	66 Ⓐ Ⓑ Ⓒ Ⓓ	111 Ⓐ Ⓑ Ⓒ Ⓓ
22 Ⓐ Ⓑ Ⓒ Ⓓ	67 Ⓐ Ⓑ Ⓒ Ⓓ	112 Ⓐ Ⓑ Ⓒ Ⓓ
23 Ⓐ Ⓑ Ⓒ Ⓓ	68 Ⓐ Ⓑ Ⓒ Ⓓ	113 Ⓐ Ⓑ Ⓒ Ⓓ
24 Ⓐ Ⓑ Ⓒ Ⓓ	69 Ⓐ Ⓑ Ⓒ Ⓓ	114 Ⓐ Ⓑ Ⓒ Ⓓ
25 Ⓐ Ⓑ Ⓒ Ⓓ	70 Ⓐ Ⓑ Ⓒ Ⓓ	115 Ⓐ Ⓑ Ⓒ Ⓓ
26 Ⓐ Ⓑ Ⓒ Ⓓ	71 Ⓐ Ⓑ Ⓒ Ⓓ	116 Ⓐ Ⓑ Ⓒ Ⓓ
27 Ⓐ Ⓑ Ⓒ Ⓓ	72 Ⓐ Ⓑ Ⓒ Ⓓ	117 Ⓐ Ⓑ Ⓒ Ⓓ
28 Ⓐ Ⓑ Ⓒ Ⓓ	73 Ⓐ Ⓑ Ⓒ Ⓓ	118 Ⓐ Ⓑ Ⓒ Ⓓ
29 Ⓐ Ⓑ Ⓒ Ⓓ	74 Ⓐ Ⓑ Ⓒ Ⓓ	119 Ⓐ Ⓑ Ⓒ Ⓓ
30 Ⓐ Ⓑ Ⓒ Ⓓ	75 Ⓐ Ⓑ Ⓒ Ⓓ	120 Ⓐ Ⓑ Ⓒ Ⓓ
31 Ⓐ Ⓑ Ⓒ Ⓓ	76 Ⓐ Ⓑ Ⓒ Ⓓ	121 Ⓐ Ⓑ Ⓒ Ⓓ
32 Ⓐ Ⓑ Ⓒ Ⓓ	77 Ⓐ Ⓑ Ⓒ Ⓓ	122 Ⓐ Ⓑ Ⓒ Ⓓ
33 Ⓐ Ⓑ Ⓒ Ⓓ	78 Ⓐ Ⓑ Ⓒ Ⓓ	123 Ⓐ Ⓑ Ⓒ Ⓓ
34 Ⓐ Ⓑ Ⓒ Ⓓ	79 Ⓐ Ⓑ Ⓒ Ⓓ	124 Ⓐ Ⓑ Ⓒ Ⓓ
35 Ⓐ Ⓑ Ⓒ Ⓓ	80 Ⓐ Ⓑ Ⓒ Ⓓ	125 Ⓐ Ⓑ Ⓒ Ⓓ
36 Ⓐ Ⓑ Ⓒ Ⓓ	81 Ⓐ Ⓑ Ⓒ Ⓓ	126 Ⓐ Ⓑ Ⓒ Ⓓ
37 Ⓐ Ⓑ Ⓒ Ⓓ	82 Ⓐ Ⓑ Ⓒ Ⓓ	127 Ⓐ Ⓑ Ⓒ Ⓓ
38 Ⓐ Ⓑ Ⓒ Ⓓ	83 Ⓐ Ⓑ Ⓒ Ⓓ	128 Ⓐ Ⓑ Ⓒ Ⓓ
39 Ⓐ Ⓑ Ⓒ Ⓓ	84 Ⓐ Ⓑ Ⓒ Ⓓ	129 Ⓐ Ⓑ Ⓒ Ⓓ
40 Ⓐ Ⓑ Ⓒ Ⓓ	85 Ⓐ Ⓑ Ⓒ Ⓓ	130 Ⓐ Ⓑ Ⓒ Ⓓ
41 Ⓐ Ⓑ Ⓒ Ⓓ	86 Ⓐ Ⓑ Ⓒ Ⓓ	
42 Ⓐ Ⓑ Ⓒ Ⓓ	87 Ⓐ Ⓑ Ⓒ Ⓓ	
43 Ⓐ Ⓑ Ⓒ Ⓓ	88 Ⓐ Ⓑ Ⓒ Ⓓ	
44 Ⓐ Ⓑ Ⓒ Ⓓ	89 Ⓐ Ⓑ Ⓒ Ⓓ	
45 Ⓐ Ⓑ Ⓒ Ⓓ	90 Ⓐ Ⓑ Ⓒ Ⓓ	

Practice Test 5038

Time: 150 minutes
130 questions

Directions: Each of the questions or statements below is followed by four suggested answers or completions. In each case, select the answer that is best.

1. The following literary works were written during which period in British literature?

   Isabella by Keats
   Prometheus Unbound by Shelley
   Don Juan by Byron

   A. Renaissance
   B. Romantic
   C. Modern
   D. Harlem

Questions 2 and 3 are based on the following excerpt from a Robert Frost poem.

Two roads diverged in a yellow wood,
And sorry I could not travel both
And be one traveler, long I stood
And looked down one as far as I could
To where it bent in the undergrowth;

2. Which of the following is the correct title of the poem from which this excerpt is taken?

   A. "The Long and Winding Road"
   B. "The Road Less Traveled"
   C. "Life Is a Road"
   D. "The Road Not Taken"

3. Which of the following describes the rhyme scheme and meter of this excerpt?

   I. ABAAB
   II. Iambic pentameter
   III. Couplet
   IV. Trochaic septameter

   A. I
   B. I, II
   C. I, IV
   D. All of the above

GO ON TO THE NEXT PAGE

Questions 4–6 are based on this opening scene from Shakespeare's Macbeth.

FIRST WITCH: When shall we three meet again?
In thunder, lightning, or in rain?

SECOND WITCH: When the hurleyburley's done,
When the battle's lost and won.

THIRD WITCH: That will be ere the set of sun.

FIRST WITCH: Where the place?

SECOND WITCH: Upon the heath.

THIRD WITCH: There to meet with Macbeth.

FIRST WITCH: I come, Graymalkin.

ALL: Paddock calls. Anon!
Fair is foul, and foul is fair.
Hover through the fog and filthy air.

4. Who or what is Graymalkin in this scene?

  A. A sentry
  B. One of the witches
  C. A familiar in the form of a toad
  D. An evil servant in the form of a cat

5. Which of the following is synonymous with the word *heath*?

  A. Moor
  B. Desert
  C. Valley
  D. Mountain

6. What does the term *ere* mean in the line "That will be ere the set of the sun"?

  A. Before
  B. After
  C. During
  D. Until

GO ON TO THE NEXT PAGE

Questions 7 and 8 are based on the following excerpt from Alfred Lord Tennyson's poem "The Lady of Shallot."

On either side the river lie
Long fields of barley and of rye,
That clothe the wold and meet the sky;
And thro' the field the road runs by
To many-tower'd Camelot;
And up and down the people go,
Gazing where the lilies blow
Round an island there below,
The island of Shallot.

7. Which of the following best describes the versification of the lines above?

   A. Iambic pentameter
   B. Iambic tetrameter
   C. Anapestic pentameter
   D. Anapestic tetrameter

8. This poem contains an allusion to Malory's *Le Morte d'Arthur*. Which of the following words in this excerpt alludes to this work from the Middle English period?

   A. Island
   B. Lilies
   C. Wold
   D. Camelot

Questions 9 and 10 are based on the following excerpt from a poem written by Thomas Gray.

Here rests his head upon the lap of Earth
A youth to Fortune and to Fame unknown.
Fair Science frowned not on his humble birth,
And Melancholy marked him for her own.

Large was his bounty, and his soul sincere,
Heaven did a recompense as largely send:
He gave to Misery all he had, a tear,
He gained from Heaven ('twas all he wish'd) a friend.

No farther seek his merits to disclose,
Or draw his frailties from their dread abode
(There they alike in trembling hope repose),
The bosom of his Father and his God.

9. The title of this poem is _____.

   A. "When Lilacs Last in the Dooryard Bloom'd"
   B. "To my Lord"
   C. "O Captain! My Captain!"
   D. "Elegy Written in a Country Churchyard"

10. Thomas Gray's poem is mourning the loss of _____.

   A. the President of the United States
   B. a way of life
   C. a close personal friend
   D. W. B. Yeats

GO ON TO THE NEXT PAGE

11. Which of the following best describes the writing process?

    A. Stagelike

    B. Developmental

    C. Exclusionary

    D. Recursive

Questions 12 and 13 are based on the following poem, "A Birthday," by Christina Rossetti.

My heart is like a singing bird
    Whose nest is in a watered shoot;
My heart is like an apple-tree
    Whose boughs are bent with thick-set fruit;
My heart is like a rainbow shell
    That paddles in a halcyon sea;
My heart is gladder than all these,
    Because my love is come to me.

Raise me a dais of silk and down;
    Hang it with vair and purple dyes;
Carve it in doves and pomegranates,
    And peacocks with a hundred eyes;
Work it in gold and silver grapes,
    In leaves and silver fleurs-de-lys;
Because the birthday of my life
    Is come, my love is come to me.

12. Which of the following best describes the theme of this poem?

    A. Love can be fraught with peril and delight.

    B. Dreams really do come true.

    C. The natural world can enhance self-expression.

    D. Good things come to those who wait.

13. During which literary time period did Rossetti write?

    A. Pre-Raphaelite

    B. Modern

    C. The Beat Generation

    D. Renaissance

14. Which of the following authors is associated with the Victorian period of British literature?

    A. Shakespeare

    B. Whitman

    C. Dickens

    D. Emerson

GO ON TO THE NEXT PAGE

Questions 15–17 are based on the following excerpt from Nathaniel Hawthorne's "Young Goodman Brown."

Young Goodman Brown came forth at sunset into the street at Salem village; but put his head back, after crossing the threshold, to exchange a parting kiss with his young wife. And Faith, as the wife was aptly named, thrust her own pretty head into the street, letting the wind play with the pink ribbons of her cap while she called to Goodman Brown.

"Dearest heart," whispered she, softly and rather sadly, when her lips were close to his ear, "prithee put off your journey until sunrise and sleep in your own bed to-night. A lone woman is troubled with such dreams and such thoughts that she's afeard of herself sometimes. Pray tarry with me this night, dear husband, of all nights in the year."

"My love and my Faith," replied young Goodman Brown, "of all nights in the year, this one night must I tarry away from thee. My journey, as thou callest it, forth and back again, must needs be done 'twixt now and sunrise. What, my sweet, pretty wife, dost thou doubt me already, and we but three months married?"

"Then God bless you!" said Faith, with the pink ribbons; "and may you find all well when you come back."

"Amen!" cried Goodman Brown. "Say thy prayers, dear Faith, and go to bed at dusk, and no harm will come to thee."

So they parted; and the young man pursued his way until, being about to turn the corner by the meeting-house, he looked back and saw the head of Faith still peeping after him with a melancholy air, in spite of her pink ribbons.

"Poor little Faith!" thought he, for his heart smote him. "What a wretch am I to leave her on such an errand! She talks of dreams, too. Methought as she spoke there was trouble in her face, as if a dream had warned her what work is to be done tonight. But no, no; 't would kill her to think it. Well, she's a blessed angel on earth; and after this one night I'll cling to her skirts and follow her to heaven."

15. Based on your reading of the excerpt above, which of the following best describes the role of the character Faith in this short story?

   A. To contrast the role of men and women in society
   B. To represent the stability of home
   C. To acknowledge religion
   D. To suggest the frailty of women

16. In a short story such as "Young Goodman Brown," brief _____ prose is used to give readers a glimpse of an event or life experience.

   A. theatrical
   B. poetic
   C. nonfiction
   D. fictional

17. Nathaniel Hawthorne wrote during which literary period?

   A. Medieval
   B. Transcendental
   C. Romantic
   D. Victorian

18. Which of the following names the "legend" of Washington Irving's "The Legend of Sleepy Hollow"?

   A. Satchmo
   B. Rip van Winkle
   C. Tam O'Shanter
   D. The Headless Horseman

GO ON TO THE NEXT PAGE

19. Each of the following novels is correctly paired with its author EXCEPT

A. *Peyton Place,* Hawthorne
B. *Pride and Prejudice,* Austen
C. *Waiting for Godot,* Beckett
D. *The Catcher in the Rye,* Salinger

20. Of the following lines, which ones contain alliteration?

I. If ever man were loved by wife, then thee;
II. Or all the riches that the East doth hold
III. Then while we live, in love let's so persevere
IV. That when we live no more, we may live ever

A. I
B. I, II
C. I, II, III
D. All of the above

Questions 21–25 are based on the following excerpt from the final chapter of Charles Dickens' Great Expectations.

Estella was the next to break the silence that ensued between us.

"I have very often hoped and intended to come back, but have been prevented by many circumstances. Poor, poor old place!"

The silvery mist was touched with the first rays of the moonlight, and the same rays touched the tears that dropped from her eyes. Not knowing that I saw them, and setting herself to get the better of them, she said quietly:

"Were you wondering, as you walked along, how it came to be left in this condition?"

"Yes, Estella."

"The ground belongs to me. It is the only possession I have not relinquished. Everything else has gone from me, little by little, but I have kept this. It was the subject of the only determined resistance I made in all the wretched years."

"Is it to be built on?"

"At last it is. I came here to take leave of it before its change. And you," she said, in a voice of touching interest to a wanderer, "you live abroad still?"

"Still."

"And do well, I am sure?"

"I work pretty hard for a sufficient living, and therefore—Yes, I do well."

"I have often thought of you," said Estella.

"Have you?"

"Of late, very often. There was a long hard time when I kept far from me, the remembrance of what I had thrown away when I was quite ignorant of its worth. But, since my duty has not been incompatible with the admission of that remembrance, I have given it a place in my heart."

"You have always held your place in my heart," I answered.

And we were silent again, until she spoke.

"I little thought," said Estella, "that I should take leave of you in taking leave of this spot. I am very glad to do so."

"Glad to part again, Estella? To me, parting is a painful thing. To me, the remembrance of our last parting has been ever mournful and painful."

"But you said to me," returned Estella, very earnestly, "'God bless you, God forgive you!' And if you could say that to me then, you will not hesitate to say that to me now—now, when suffering has been stronger than all other teaching, and has taught me to understand what your heart used to be. I have been bent and broken, but—I hope—into a better shape. Be as considerate and good to me as you were, and tell me we are friends."

GO ON TO THE NEXT PAGE

"We are friends," said I, rising and bending over her, as she rose from the bench.

"And will continue friends apart," said Estella.

I took her hand in mine, and we went out of the ruined place; and, as the morning mists had risen long ago when I first left the forge, so the evening mists were rising now, and in all the broad expanse of tranquil light they showed to me, I saw no shadow of another parting from her.

21. Dickens' concluding line of *Great Expectations* includes imagery of evening mists, tranquil light, and no shadow when Estella parted from Pip. Which of the following best summarizes the author's meaning in the closing of the novel?

    A. Pip will always regret losing Estella.

    B. The dark mists, the evening, and the shadow signify the anger Pip still holds for Estella.

    C. Pip is at peace with his relationship with Estella and can let her go.

    D. Pip had great expectations for his home and Estella that never came to fruition.

22. The house that is referred to in this excerpt is known as _____ House in *Great Expectations*.

    A. Tara

    B. Satis

    C. Havisham

    D. Bleak

23. This final chapter of *Great Expectations* is best known as which of the following?

    A. Denouement

    B. Climax

    C. Suspense

    D. Plot

24. Which of the following is the correct MLA-format citation for the book *Great Expectations*?

    A. Dickens, C. Great expectations. New York: Random House, 1907. Print.

    B. Dickens, C. (1907). Great Expectations. New York: Random House. Print.

    C. Dickens, Charles. *Great Expectations*. New York: Random House, 1907. Print.

    D. Dickens, Charles. *Great expectations*. New York; Random House, 1907. Print.

25. Which of the following is the correct APA-format citation for the book *Great Expectations*?

    A. Charles Dickens, Great Expectations. New York: Random House, 1907.

    B. Dickens, C. (1907). *Great expectations*. New York: Random House.

    C. Dickens, C. (1907). *Great Expectations*. New York: Random House

    D. Dickens, Charles. (1907). *Great expectations*. New York: Random House.

26. Which of the following lines from a Robert Louis Stevenson poem do NOT contain an example of onomatopoeia?

    I. The squalling cat and the squeaking mouse,

    II. The howling dog by the door of the house,

    III. The bat that lies in bed at noon,

    IV. All love to be out by the light of the moon.

    A. II, III, IV

    B. III, IV

    C. I, II

    D. All of the above

GO ON TO THE NEXT PAGE

Questions 27 and 28 are based on the following excerpt from a Shakespearean work, which you will be asked to identify below.

> I have heard that guilty creatures sitting at a play
> Have, by the very cunning of the scene,
> Been struck so to the soul that presently
> They have proclaimed their malefactions.

27. Which of the following Shakespearean tragedies, identified by the excerpt above, contains a play within a play in which the villainous king is invited to *The Mousetrap* to see a reenactment of the murder of his brother?

   A. *Hamlet*
   B. *Macbeth*
   C. *Julius Caesar*
   D. *King Richard III*

28. Which villainous character from this work is meant to proclaim his "malefactions"?

   A. Polonius
   B. Macbeth
   C. Claudius
   D. Caesar

Questions 29–31 are based on the following excerpt from the Declaration of Independence.

When in the Course of human events, it becomes necessary for one people to dissolve the political bands which have connected them with another, and to assume among the powers of the earth, the separate and equal situation to which the Laws of Nature and of Nature's God entitle them, a decent respect to the opinions of mankind requires that they should declare the causes which impel them to the separation.

29. Which of the following authors wrote the first draft of the Declaration of Independence?

   A. George Washington
   B. Thomas Jefferson
   C. Patrick Henry
   D. John Hancock

30. Which of the following best describes the meaning of the phrase "to dissolve the political bands which have connected them with another"?

   A. To seek a resolution to the political nature of a conflict
   B. To sever political ties with England
   C. To seek a change in the political structure of the homeland
   D. To seek religious freedom

31. The phrase "a decent respect to the opinions of mankind" works persuasively because it appeals to the reader's sense of _____.

   A. audience
   B. propriety
   C. rationale
   D. manhood

GO ON TO THE NEXT PAGE

Questions 32–34 are based on the following passage from Gulliver's Travels *by Jonathan Swift.*

We arrived at Lisbon, Nov. 5, 1715. At our landing, the captain forced me to cover myself with his cloak, to prevent the rabble from crowding about me. I was conveyed to his own house; and at my earnest request, he led me up to the highest room backwards. I conjured him to "conceal from all persons what I had told him of the Houyhnhnms; because the least hint of such a story would not only draw numbers of people to see me, but probably put me in danger of being imprisoned, or burnt by the Inquisition." The captain persuaded me to accept a suit of clothes newly made; but I would not suffer the tailor to take my measure; however, Don Pedro being almost of my size, they fitted me well enough. He accoutred me with other necessaries, all new, which I aired for twenty-four hours before I would use them.

32. Which of the following best describes this excerpt from *Gulliver's Travels*?

   A. Realistic fiction
   B. Lyrical poetry
   C. Prose in comparison-and-contrast structure
   D. Prose in chronological sequence

33. Which of the following best describes the meaning of the phrase "would not suffer the tailor to take my measure"?

   A. Because of Gulliver's personality, he does not have the patience for the tailor.
   B. Due to Gulliver's size, the tailor would not be equipped to prepare a suit for Gulliver.
   C. Gulliver did not want the tailor to go to the trouble of measuring him.
   D. The tailor would suffer if he took Gulliver's measurement.

34. In which of the following periods was *Gulliver's Travels* written and first published?

   A. Early 1600s
   B. Early 1700s
   C. Early 1800s
   D. Early 1900s

35. If a student makes several errors like those in the following sentence, the teacher should plan for more instruction in _____.

One sunny morning sixty-seven years ago Southern New England was going well until everything changed.

   A. verb tense
   B. syntax
   C. paraphrasing
   D. comma usage

36. Each of the following pairs are homophones, EXCEPT

   A. sell/cell
   B. read/read
   C. waist/waste
   D. witch/which

37. Which of the following is the best example of a rhetorical question?

   A. Can you help me locate the main office?
   B. Do you need anything else to help make your lesson more effective?
   C. Do we really expect that schools will be funded by property taxes alone?
   D. Do you think you will pass the Praxis English Subject Assessment test?

GO ON TO THE NEXT PAGE

38. One phonological feature of African American Vernacular English (also known as Black English) is _____.

    A. the use of sporting expressions such as "bowled over" to mean "taken by surprise" and "football" to mean "soccer"

    B. the pronunciation of the final -ng in one-syllable words: *sing* becomes *sin* or *ring* becomes *rin*

    C. the pronunciation of the final -ng in two-syllable words: *wedding* becomes *weddin* or *nothing* becomes *nuffin*

    D. the use of the word *ja* in place of the word *yes,* as in, "You're alright, ja?"

39. In the quote "To err is human; to forgive divine," which of the following rhetorical devices is used?

    A. Persuasion

    B. Rhetorical question

    C. Parallel structure

    D. Emotive language

40. Abraham Lincoln is credited as having said, "You can fool some of the people all of the time, and all of the people some of the time, but you cannot fool all of the people all of the time." Which of the following rhetorical devices was President Lincoln using?

    A. Simile

    B. Hyperbole

    C. Metaphor

    D. Repetition

Questions 41 and 42 are based on this excerpt from "O Captain! My Captain!" by Walt Whitman.

O Captain! my Captain! our fearful trip is done,
The ship has weather'd every rack, the prize we sought is won,
The port is near, the bells I hear, the people all exulting,
While follow eyes the steady keel, the vessel grim and daring;
But O heart! heart! heart!
O the bleeding drops of red,
Where on the deck my Captain lies,
Fallen cold and dead.

41. In the first line of this stanza, which poetic device is used?

    A. Apostrophe

    B. Rhyme

    C. Hubris

    D. Irony

42. Who is memorialized in this Whitman poem?

    A. Lincoln

    B. Keating

    C. Browning

    D. Washington

GO ON TO THE NEXT PAGE

43. During which period did the British Romantics such as Keats, Shelley, and Byron write?

    A. 1660–1700

    B. 1780–1840

    C. 1880–1930

    D. 1900–2000

Questions 44–46 are based on this excerpt from William Shakespeare's "Sonnet 18."

Shall I compare thee to a summer's day?
Thou art more lovely and more temperate:
Rough winds do shake the darling buds of May,
And summer's lease hath all too short a date:
Sometime too hot the eye of heaven shines,
And often is his gold complexion dimm'd;
And every fair from fair sometime declines,
By chance, or nature's changing course untrimm'd;
But thy eternal summer shall not fade,
Nor lose possession of that fair thou ow'st,
Nor shall death brag thou wander'st in his shade,
When in eternal lines to time thou grow'st;
So long as men can breathe, or eyes can see,
So long lives this, and this gives life to thee.

44. Which of the following is another name for this Shakespearean sonnet?

    A. Ode

    B. Elegy

    C. Epic poem

    D. Lyric poem

45. Which of the following describe the metrics of Shakespeare's "Sonnet 18"?

    I. 14 lines

    II. Iambic pentameter

    III. Approximately 10 syllables per line

    IV. Rhyming couplet

    A. I

    B. II

    C. I, II, III

    D. All of the above

46. Which of the following best describes this sonnet's rhyme scheme?

    A. BABA; DCDC; FEFE; GG

    B. ABAB; CDCD; EFEF; GG

    C. AABB; CCDD; EEFF; GG

    D. Three quatrains and two couplets

GO ON TO THE NEXT PAGE

Questions 47 and 48 are based on the following excerpt from Don Quixote.

So then, his armour being furbished, his morion turned into a helmet, his hack christened, and he himself confirmed, he came to the conclusion that nothing more was needed now but to look out for a lady to be in love with; for a knight-errant without love was like a tree without leaves or fruit, or a body without a soul. As he said to himself, "If, for my sins, or by my good fortune, I come across some giant hereabouts, a common occurrence with knights-errant, and overthrow him in one onslaught, or cleave him asunder to the waist, or, in short, vanquish and subdue him, will it not be well to have some one I may send him to as a present, that he may come in and fall on his knees before my sweet lady, and in a humble, submissive voice say, 'I am the giant Caraculiambro, lord of the island of Malindrania, vanquished in single combat by the never sufficiently extolled knight Don Quixote of La Mancha, who has commanded me to present myself before your Grace, that your Highness dispose of me at your pleasure'?"

47. The phrase "for a knight-errant without love was like a tree without leaves or fruit, or a body without a soul" includes which of the following literary devices?

    A.   Rhetorical question
    B.   Personification
    C.   Paradox
    D.   Simile

48. Who is the author of *Don Quixote*?

    A.   Escobar
    B.   Achebe
    C.   Cervantes
    D.   More

Question 49 is based on this haiku by Raizan.

You rice-field maidens!
The only things not muddy
Are the songs you sing.

49. Haiku is often written in 17 syllables with three lines divided into _____.

    A.   5, 7, 5 syllables
    B.   3, 7, 7 syllables
    C.   5, 7, 5 words
    D.   5, 7, 7 words

50. Which of the following is best described as a cliché?

    A.   You can't teach an old dog new tricks.
    B.   My grandmother passed away last April.
    C.   The Holocaust victims were executed in a concentration camp.
    D.   Agent Orange was a chemical used during the Vietnam War.

GO ON TO THE NEXT PAGE

Questions 51 and 52 are based on the following Thomas Hardy poem, "To a Lady."

Now that my page upcloses, doomed, maybe,
Never to press thy cosy cushions more,
Or wake thy ready Yeas as heretofore,
Or stir thy gentle vows of faith in me:

Knowing thy natural receptivity,
I figure that, as flambeaux banish eve,
My sombre image, warped by insidious heave
Of those less forthright, must lose place in thee.

So be it. I have borne such. Let thy dreams
Of me and mine diminish day by day,
And yield their space to shine of smugger things;
Till I shape to thee but in fitful gleams,
And then in far and feeble visitings,
And then surcease. Truth will be truth alway.

51. The poet's use of the word *upcloses* indicates which of the following meanings?

    A. His feelings have died.
    B. He is up close and personal with this woman.
    C. His book is complete.
    D. His relationship is coming to an end.

52. Which of the following rhetorical devices does Hardy use in the last line of this poem?

    A. Rhetorical question
    B. Repetition
    C. Extended metaphor
    D. Contrast

53. Which of the following lines contains an allusion?

    A. Men are April when they woo, December when they wed.
    B. Knaves and robbers can obtain only what was before possessed by others.
    C. Town Manager Kern is a "man for all seasons."
    D. The couple had a bliss-filled marriage.

GO ON TO THE NEXT PAGE

Questions 54 and 55 are based on the following excerpt from The Scarlet Letter.

The effect of the symbol—or rather, of the position in respect to society that was indicated by it—on the mind of Hester Prynne herself, was powerful and peculiar. All the light and graceful foliage of her character had been withered up by this red-hot brand, and had long ago fallen away, leaving a bare and harsh outline, which might have been repulsive, had she possessed friends or companions to be repelled by it.

54. Which of the following best describes the main conflict in *The Scarlet Letter*?

    A. Person versus nature

    B. Person versus person

    C. Person versus society

    D. Person versus fate

55. Which of the following authors wrote *The Scarlet Letter*?

    A. Edwards

    B. Emerson

    C. Hawthorne

    D. Miller

Questions 56 and 57 are based on this final scene from Henrik Ibsen's play A Doll's House.

NORA: That's right. Now it is all over. I have put the keys here. The maids know all about everything in the house—better than I do. Tomorrow, after I have left her, Christine will come here and pack up my own things that I brought with me from home. I will have them sent after me.

HELMER: All over! All over!—Nora, shall you never think of me again?

NORA: I know I shall often think of you, the children, and this house.

HELMER: May I write to you, Nora?

NORA: No—never. You must not do that.

HELMER: But at least let me send you—

NORA: Nothing—nothing—

HELMER: Let me help you if you are in want.

NORA: No. I can receive nothing from a stranger.

HELMER: Nora—can I never be anything more than a stranger to you?

NORA: *(Taking her bag)* Ah, Torvald, the most wonderful thing of all would have to happen.

HELMER: Tell me what that would be!

NORA: Both you and I would have to be so changed that—. Oh, Torvald, I don't believe any longer in wonderful things happening.

HELMER: But I will believe in it. Tell me! So changed that—?

NORA: That our life together would be a real wedlock. Goodbye. *(She goes out through the hall.)*

GO ON TO THE NEXT PAGE

HELMER: *(Sinks down on a chair at the door and buries his face in his hands)* Nora! Nora! *(Looks around, and rises.)* Empty. She is gone. *(A hope flashes across his mind.)* The most wonderful thing of all—?

(The sound of a door shutting is heard from below.)

56. Ibsen's play *A Doll's House* popularized which of the following types of drama?

    A. Realist

    B. Romantic

    C. Existentialist

    D. Neoclassical

57. The character Nora possesses which of the following character traits at some point in the play?

    I. Silly

    II. Feminist

    III. Serious

    IV. Open-minded

    A. I, II

    B. I, III

    C. III, IV

    D. All of the above

58. From which of the following works by the playwright Oscar Wilde is the excerpt below?

Morning-room in Algernon's flat in Half-Moon Street. The room is luxuriously and artistically furnished. The sound of a piano is heard in the adjoining room.

(Lane is arranging afternoon tea on the table, and after the music has ceased, Algernon enters.)

ALGERNON: Did you hear what I was playing, Lane?

LANE: I didn't think it polite to listen, sir.

ALGERNON: I'm sorry for that, for your sake. I don't play accurately—anyone can play accurately—but I play with wonderful expression. As far as the piano is concerned, sentiment is my forte. I keep science for Life.

LANE: Yes, sir.

ALGERNON: And, speaking of the science of Life, have you got the cucumber sandwiches cut for Lady Bracknell?

LANE: Yes, sir. *(Hands them on a salver.)*

ALGERNON: *(Inspects them, takes two, and sits down on the sofa.)* Oh! … by the way, Lane, I see from your book that on Thursday night, when Lord Shoreman and Mr. Worthing were dining with me, eight bottles of champagne are entered as having been consumed.

LANE: Yes, sir; eight bottles and a pint.

ALGERNON: Why is it that at a bachelor's establishment the servants invariably drink the champagne? I ask merely for information.

    A. *An Ideal Husband*

    B. *Flowers for Algernon*

    C. *The Importance of Being Earnest*

    D. *Utopia*

GO ON TO THE NEXT PAGE

Questions 59 and 60 are based on this final excerpt from "The Fall of the House of Usher."

From that chamber, and from that mansion, I fled aghast. The storm was still abroad in all its wrath as I found myself crossing the old causeway. Suddenly there shot along the path a wild light, and I turned to see whence a gleam so unusual could have issued; for the vast house and its shadows were alone behind me. The radiance was that of the full, setting, and blood-red moon which now shone vividly through that once barely-discernible fissure of which I have before spoken as extending from the roof of the building, in a zigzag direction, to the base. While I gazed, this fissure rapidly widened—there came a fierce breath of the whirlwind—the entire orb of the satellite burst at once upon my sight—my brain reeled as I saw the mighty walls rushing asunder—there was a long tumultuous shouting sound like the voice of a thousand waters—and the deep and dank tarn at my feet closed sullenly and silently over the fragments of the "House of Usher."

59. Which literary device is used in the excerpt above?

    A. Epitaph
    B. Cliché
    C. Euphemism
    D. Personification

60. Who is the author of "The Fall of the House of Usher"?

    A. Poe
    B. Wilde
    C. Dickens
    D. Hardy

Questions 61 and 62 are based on the following excerpt from the play Pygmalion *by George Bernard Shaw.*

THE FLOWER GIRL: *(To Pickering, as he passes her)* Buy a flower, kind gentleman. I'm short for my lodging.

PICKERING: I really haven't any change. I'm sorry. *(He goes away.)*

HIGGINS: *(Shocked at girl's mendacity)* Liar. You said you could change half-a-crown.

THE FLOWER GIRL: *(Rising in desperation)* You ought to be stuffed with nails, you ought. *(Flinging the basket at his feet)* Take the whole blooming basket for sixpence.

(The church clock strikes the second quarter.)

HIGGINS: *(Hearing in it the voice of God, rebuking him for his Pharisaic want of charity to the poor girl)* A reminder. *(He raises his hat solemnly; then throws a handful of money into the basket and follows Pickering.)*

THE FLOWER GIRL: *(Picking up a half-crown)* Ah—ow—ooh! *(Picking up a couple of florins)* Aaah—ow—ooh! *(Picking up several coins)* Aaaaaah—ow—ooh! *(Picking up a half-sovereign)* Aasaaaaaaaaah—ow—ooh!!!

FREDDY: *(Springing out of a taxicab)* Got one at last. Hallo! *(To the girl)* Where are the two ladies that were here?

THE FLOWER GIRL: They walked to the bus when the rain stopped.

FREDDY: And left me with a cab on my hands. Damnation!

GO ON TO THE NEXT PAGE

THE FLOWER GIRL: *(With grandeur)* Never you mind, young man. I'm going home in a taxi. *(She sails off to the cab. The driver puts his hand behind him and holds the door firmly shut against her. Quite understanding his mistrust, she shows him her handful of money.)* Eightpence ain't no object to me, Charlie. *(He grins and opens the door.)* Angel Court, Drury Lane, round the corner of Micklejohn's oil shop. Let's see how fast you can make her hop it. *(She gets in and pulls the door to with a slam as the taxicab starts.)*

FREDDY: Well, I'm dashed!

61. Which of the following is the primary setting of *Pygmalion*?

    A. Contemporary France
    B. Modern-day Africa
    C. Puritan times in New England
    D. Great Britain

62. After hearing the church bell, Higgins reflects that he may have expressed a "Pharisaic want of charity" toward the Flower Girl. Which of the following best defines the word Pharisaic in this play?

    A. A member of an ancient Jewish sect
    B. Hypocritically self-righteous
    C. Pragmatic
    D. A kinglike leader of ancient Egypt

Questions 63 and 64 are based on this excerpt from T. S. Eliot's poem "The Waste Land."

April is the cruelest month, breeding
Lilacs out of the dead land, mixing
Memory and desire, stirring
Dull roots with spring rain.
Winter kept us warm, covering
Earth in forgetful snow, feeding
A little life with dried tubers.

63. T. S. Eliot wrote this poem during which of the following periods?

    A. Nationalist period (1828–1836)
    B. Modern period (1900–1945)
    C. Colonial period (1630–1760)
    D. Puritan period (1625–1660)

64. Which of the following literary works does the excerpt above allude to?

    A. *Beowulf*
    B. *The Iliad*
    C. *Canterbury Tales*
    D. *War and Peace*

GO ON TO THE NEXT PAGE

Questions 65–69 are based on the following excerpt from William Shakespeare's Hamlet.

HAMLET: O that this too too sullied flesh would melt,
Thaw, and resolve itself into a dew!
Or that the Everlasting had not fixed
His canon 'gainst self-slaughter! O God, God,
How weary, stale, flat, and unprofitable
Seem to me all the uses of this world!
Fie on't, ah fie! 'tis an unweeded garden
That grows to seed; things rank and gross in nature
Possess it merely. That it should come to this!
But two months dead, nay, not so much, not two.
So excellent a king, that was to this
Hyperion to a satyr; so loving to my mother
That he might not beteem the winds of heaven
Visit her face too roughly. Heaven and earth,
Must I remember? Why, she would hang on him
As if increase of appetite had grown
By what it fed on.

65. Which of the following best describes the phrase "'tis an unweeded garden/That grows to seed"?

    A. A simile comparing Hamlet to his mother
    B. A metaphor comparing an unweeded garden to Denmark's ruin after the death of King Hamlet
    C. A metaphor comparing Hamlet's appetite to a garden
    D. A simile comparing the king's death to heaven and hell

66. To whom is Hamlet referring in the line "But two months dead, nay, not so much, not two"?

    A. Fortinbras
    B. Queen Gertrude
    C. King Claudius
    D. King Hamlet

67. Which of the following best describes *Hamlet*?

    A. Comedy
    B. Tragedy
    C. History
    D. Sonnet

68. This excerpt from *Hamlet* uses which of the following rhetorical devices?

    A. Sarcasm
    B. Praise
    C. Appeal to emotion
    D. Counterpoints

69. Which of the following is the best interpretation of the lines "...that was to this/Hyperion to a satyr..."?

    A. It alludes to an entertainment industry giant.
    B. It alludes to an incomplete poem by Keats.
    C. It alludes to a star in the universe.
    D. It alludes to the mythical god of the sun.

GO ON TO THE NEXT PAGE

70. The author of *Beowulf* is _____.

    A. Racine

    B. Socrates

    C. Ulysses

    D. Unknown

Question 71 is based on the following excerpt from Plato's The Republic.

The result, then, is that more plentiful and better-quality goods are more easily produced if each person does one thing for which he is naturally suited, does it at the right time, and is released from having to do any of the others.

71. Which of the following best summarizes Plato's point in this passage?

    A. Each person must do the work that fits his or her own strengths.

    B. Every man for himself.

    C. A philosopher must choose wisely.

    D. A farmer's work is never done.

72. Which of the following terms can be defined as using language persuasively or impressively?

    A. Personification

    B. Rhetoric

    C. Tone

    D. Point of view

73. Which of the following lines contains a simile?

    A. Mine eyes have seen the glory of the coming of the Lord:

    B. Woodman, spare that tree! Touch not a single bough!

    C. Away to the window I flew like a flash.

    D. My candle burns at both ends; it will not last the night;

74. The following poem by Edward Lear is known as a _____.

There was a Young Lady whose eyes,
Were unique as to colour and size;
When she opened them wide,
People all turned aside,
And started away in surprise.

    A. ballad

    B. canto

    C. ode

    D. limerick

75. Which of the following authors wrote *The Catcher in the Rye*?

    A. Alex Haley

    B. John Updike

    C. J. D. Salinger

    D. Sylvia Plath

GO ON TO THE NEXT PAGE

76. In which of the following periods was *The Catcher in the Rye* written?

    A. 20th-century British literature

    B. Contemporary U.S. literature

    C. American Renaissance period

    D. British Victorian period

Questions 77 and 78 are based on the following excerpt from the poem "The Love Song of J. Alfred Prufrock" by T. S. Eliot.

No! I am not Prince Hamlet, nor was meant to be;
Am an attendant lord, one that will do
To swell a progress, start a scene or two,
Advise the prince; no doubt, an easy tool,
Deferential, glad to be of use,
Politic, cautious, and meticulous;
Full of high sentence, but a bit obtuse;
At times, indeed, almost ridiculous—
Almost, at times, the Fool.

I grow old...I grow old...
I shall wear the bottoms of my trousers rolled.

Shall I part my hair behind? Do I dare to eat a peach?
I shall wear white flannel trousers, and walk upon the beach.
I have heard the mermaids singing, each to each.

I do not think that they will sing to me.

77. Which of the following is the best interpretation of the poet's meaning in this excerpt?

    A. Prufrock is paralyzed to act; specifically, to eat a peach.

    B. Prufrock is contemplating murder, like Hamlet.

    C. Prufrock is afraid of growing old.

    D. Prufrock is a man in love with a mermaid.

78. Modernist poets such as T. S. Eliot expressed _____.

    A. the desire to turn to nature for inspiration

    B. the romantic hopes of poets during this time period

    C. the fundamental rights of humanity

    D. the fragile nature of the human psyche in the 20th century

79. A high school English teacher wants to effectively open a lesson on *King Lear*. Which of the following is most likely to motivate adolescent readers?

    A. An analysis of the play by a famous English author

    B. A homework assignment to read Act I

    C. A round-robin read-aloud in which students take turns reading the play without time to practice

    D. A discussion about seeking justice in students' lives, personal experiences, and world events

GO ON TO THE NEXT PAGE

80. Which of the following cognates is most DIFFERENT in meaning and usage from its original Latin root?

    A. Facile

    B. Facilitate

    C. Faction

    D. Facility

81. Which of the following are examples of correlative conjunctions?

    A. and/but

    B. not only/but also

    C. after/before

    D. since/then

82. Which of the following is an appropriate revision-stage activity during the writing process?

    A. Peer conferencing

    B. Peer editing

    C. Teacher editing

    D. Prewriting

83. Which of the following is the best definition of a writing rubric?

    A. A frame story

    B. A writing scoring guide

    C. A description of a writing assignment

    D. A part of a manuscript or book

84. Which of the following correctly cites a source using MLA-format guidelines?

    A. Golding wrote in his opening line of Lord of the Flies, "The boy with fair hair lowered himself down the last few feet of rock and began to pick his way toward the lagoon" (7).

    B. Golding wrote in his opening line of *Lord of the Flies*, "The boy with fair hair lowered himself down the last few feet of rock and began to pick his way toward the lagoon" (7).

    C. Golding wrote in his opening line of <u>Lord of the Flies</u>, "The boy with fair hair lowered himself down the last few feet of rock and began to pick his way toward the lagoon" (Golding, 7).

    D. Golding wrote in his opening line of *Lord of the Flies*, "The boy with fair hair lowered himself down the last few feet of rock and began to pick his way toward the lagoon." (Golding, 7)

85. Which of the following plays by Harold Pinter is seen as an extended metaphor for society in the 1950s, with Stanley representing "angry young men" and his antagonists representing repressive conformists?

    A. *The Birthday Party*

    B. *The Homecoming*

    C. *A Doll's House*

    D. *Waiting for Godot*

GO ON TO THE NEXT PAGE

86. Consider the following sentence:

The Commander's conceited wife rambled on about her upcoming move from one military base to another and was heard to say, "The move is eminent."

The wife's error is known as (a) _____.

   A.   cliché
   B.   slang
   C.   malapropism
   D.   metaphor

87. Which of the following authors and works represents the Colonial period of literature?

   A.   Anne Bradstreet's *The Tenth Muse Lately Sprung Up in America*
   B.   Thomas Hardy's "Winter Words"
   C.   Washington Irving's "Rip van Winkle"
   D.   Ben Franklin's "The Contrast"

88. Which of the following characters is the protagonist of the work cited?

   A.   Claudius in *Hamlet*
   B.   Nanny in *Their Eyes Were Watching God*
   C.   Chillingsworth in *The Scarlet Letter*
   D.   Odysseus in *The Odyssey*

89. Which of the following is the definition of the denouement in a literary work?

   A.   The conflict or problem
   B.   The solution or outcome
   C.   The setting, such as time and place
   D.   The plot or events in the story

90. Which of the following strategies is used in this excerpt from W. E. B. Du Bois' "Advice to a Black Schoolgirl"?

   Ignorance is a cure for nothing. Get the very best training possible and the doors of opportunity will fly open before you as they are flying before thousands of your fellows. On the other hand every time a colored person neglects an opportunity, it makes it more difficult for others of the race to get such an opportunity. Do you want to cut off the chances of the boys and girls of tomorrow?

   A.   Appeal to emotion
   B.   Appeal to authority
   C.   Extended metaphor
   D.   Counterpoints

GO ON TO THE NEXT PAGE

Questions 91–94 are based on the following excerpt from Theodore Roosevelt's speech "The Strenuous Life," given before the Hamilton Club, Chicago, Illinois, on April 10, 1899.

...I preach to you, then, my countrymen, that our country calls not for the life of ease but for the life of strenuous endeavor. The twentieth century looms before us big with the fate of many nations. If we stand idly by, if we seek merely swollen, slothful ease and ignoble peace, if we shrink from the hard contests where men must win at hazard of their lives and at the risk of all they hold dear, then the bolder and stronger peoples will pass us by, and will win for themselves the domination of the world. Let us therefore boldly face the life of strife, resolute to do our duty well and manfully; resolute to uphold righteousness by deed and by word; resolute to be both honest and brave, to serve high ideals, yet to use practical methods. Above all, let us shrink from no strife, moral or physical, within or without the nation, provided we are certain that the strife is justified, for it is only through strife, through hard and dangerous endeavor, that we shall ultimately win the goal of true national greatness.

91. Roosevelt alludes to what time period in American history in the opening lines of his speech?

    A. Western Expansion and Reform
    B. The Depression and World War II
    C. The Great War and Jazz Age
    D. Civil War

92. Roosevelt uses which of the following rhetorical devices in the following line: "If we stand idly by, if we seek merely swollen, ... if we shrink from the hard contests where men must win at hazard of their lives and at the risk of all they hold dear ..."?

    A. Rhetorical question
    B. Understatement
    C. Oxymoron
    D. Anaphora

93. Which of the following best describes the rhetorical strategy Roosevelt uses in the line "Let us therefore boldly face the life of strife, resolute to do our duty well and manfully; ..."?

    A. Alliteration
    B. Allusion
    C. Prose
    D. Appeal to emotion

94. The sentence "The twentieth century looms before us big with the fate of many nations" can be described as which of the following sentence types?

    A. Single subject, single predicate
    B. Compound subject, single predicate
    C. Independent clause with two or more phrases
    D. Compound subject, compound predicate

95. When a story is written from an omniscient point of view, which of the following statements is true?

    A. The narrator compares two unlike things.
    B. The story is told from the point of view of one of the characters.
    C. The story is told by someone outside of the story.
    D. The narrator is free to tell the story from any and all characters' points of view.

GO ON TO THE NEXT PAGE

96. A poem written in a quintet contains _____.

    A. a five-line stanza

    B. five stanzas

    C. five syllables

    D. parts for five actors

Questions 97–99 are based on a speech given on November 19, 1863, at the dedication of the National Cemetery in Gettysburg, Pennsylvania.

Four score and seven years ago our fathers brought forth on this continent, a new nation, conceived in Liberty, and dedicated to the proposition that all men are created equal.

Now we are engaged in a great civil war, testing whether that nation, or any nation so conceived and so dedicated, can long endure. We are met on a great battlefield of that war. We have come to dedicate a portion of that field, as a final resting place for those who here gave their lives that that nation might live. It is altogether fitting and proper that we should do this.

But, in a larger sense, we cannot dedicate—we cannot consecrate—we cannot hallow—this ground. The brave men, living and dead, who struggled here, have consecrated it, far above our poor power to add or detract. The world will little note, nor long remember what we say here, but it can never forget what they did here. It is for us the living, rather, to be dedicated here to the unfinished work, which they who fought here have thus far so nobly advanced. It is rather for us to be here dedicated to the great task remaining before us—that from these honored dead we take increased devotion to that cause for which they gave the last full measure of devotion—that we here highly resolve that these dead shall not have died in vain—that this nation, under God, shall have a new birth of freedom—and that government of the people, by the people, for the people, shall not perish from the earth.

97. The orator's use of the phrase "four score and seven years ago" exemplifies which of the following rhetorical features?

    A. Tone

    B. Diction

    C. Attitude

    D. Sarcasm

98. The author's description of the National Cemetery as "a final resting place" is known as a(n) _____.

    A. antithesis

    B. epistrophe

    C. euphemism

    D. metaphor

99. Who was the orator of this address?

    A. Lincoln

    B. Kennedy

    C. Roosevelt

    D. Jackson

100. Which of the following best describes the initial setting of *The Grapes of Wrath*?

    A. 1900s Industrial Revolution in the Midwestern United States

    B. 1930s Dust Bowl in the Midwestern United States

    C. 1890s Gold Rush

    D. 1930s pre–World War I England and the United States

GO ON TO THE NEXT PAGE

101. Who is the author of *The Grapes of Wrath*?

    A. Michener

    B. Hemingway

    C. Orwell

    D. Steinbeck

102. In which of the following literary periods was *Le Morte d'Arthur* written?

    A. Middle English period

    B. Elizabethan period

    C. Romantic period

    D. Victorian period

Questions 103 and 104 are based on the following excerpt from Sonnets from the Portuguese.

> Beloved, thou hast brought me many flowers
> Plucked in the garden, all the summer through,
> And winter, and it seemed as if they grew
> In this close room, nor missed the sun and showers.
> So, in the like name of that love of ours,
> Take back these thoughts which here unfolded too,
> And which on warm and cold days I withdrew
> From my heart's ground. Indeed, those beds and bowers
> Be overgrown with bitter weeds and rue,
> And wait thy weeding; yet here's eglantine,
> Here's ivy!—take them, as I used to do
> Thy flowers, and keep them where they shall not pine.
> Instruct thine eyes to keep their colours true,
> And tell thy soul, their roots are left in mine.

103. Which of the following metric is used in the sonnet above?

    A. Trochaic pentameter

    B. Iambic quintet

    C. Iambic pentameter

    D. Anapestic pentameter

104. Which of the following authors wrote *Sonnets from the Portuguese*?

    A. Emily Dickinson

    B. Elizabeth Barrett Browning

    C. T. S. Eliot

    D. George Eliot

GO ON TO THE NEXT PAGE

Questions 105 and 106 are based on the following excerpt from D. H. Lawrence's essay "Nathaniel Hawthorne and The Scarlet Letter."

Nathaniel Hawthorne writes romance.

And what's romance? Usually, a nice little tale where you have everything *As You Like It,* where rain never wets your jacket and gnats never bite your nose and it's always daisy-time. *As You Like It* and *Forest Lovers,* etc. *Morte d'Arthur.*

Hawthorne obviously isn't this kind of romanticist: though nobody has muddy boots in *The Scarlet Letter,* either.

But there is more to it. *The Scarlet Letter* isn't a pleasant, pretty romance. It is a sort of parable, an earthly story with a hellish meaning.

All the time there is this split in the American art and art-consciousness. On the top it is as nice as pie, goody-goody and lovey-dovey. Like Hawthorne being such a blue-eyed darling, in life, and Longfellow and the rest such sucking-doves. Hawthorne's wife said he 'never saw him in time,' which doesn't mean she saw him too late.

105. Hawthorne's *The Scarlet Letter* is a parable. Which of the following is the best definition of a parable?

    A. A brief story that illustrates a point

    B. A story with a contradictory message or statement

    C. A fictional work meant to tell a story

    D. A story meant to teach a moral lesson

106. Longfellow and Hawthorne were considered _____.

    A. existentialists

    B. transcendentalists

    C. communists

    D. anarchists

107. Which of the following works is from the Middle English period (1066–1550)?

    A. Chaucer's *Canterbury Tales*

    B. Shakespeare's sonnets

    C. Goethe's *Faust*

    D. Homer's *The Iliad*

108. Dorothy Parker's poem "Guinevere at Her Fireside" is from her collection of poems titled _____.

    A. *The Arthurian Legend*

    B. *Enough Rope*

    C. *Death and Taxes*

    D. *The New Yorker Collection*

109. Langston Hughes wrote his poem "Po' Boy Blues" using _____.

    A. iambic pentameter

    B. free verse

    C. authentic setting and meaning

    D. idioms and dialect from African American Vernacular English

GO ON TO THE NEXT PAGE

110. Tory participates in basketball, softball, and playing the piano.

This sentence can be improved by _____.

    A. adding "playing" before basketball
    B. deleting "playing the" and adding "lessons" after piano
    C. deleting "playing"
    D. deleting the comma after "softball"

111. Consider the following sentences:

Jimmy and Austin were the highest scorers in the basketball game. He enjoyed the recognition of his accomplishment from the coach and his teammates.

Which of the following grammatical errors is the primary problem in the second sentence above?

    A. Pronoun reference
    B. Subject-verb agreement
    C. Verb tense
    D. Coordinating pronoun

112. Sociolinguistics is the study of language as it relates to _____.

    A. semantics
    B. social skills
    C. society
    D. psychology

113. Which of the following activities is LEAST likely to occur during the publishing stage of the writing process?

    A. Examining a book to learn about the features of the publication
    B. Preparing a cover and title page
    C. Using the Internet to search for writing ideas
    D. Writing an acknowledgment section

114. In which of the following sources is a reader MOST likely to find an aphorism from Benjamin Franklin?

    A. Dictionary
    B. Bartlett's *Familiar Quotations*
    C. Encyclopedia
    D. Thesaurus

115. Which of the following is an appropriate greeting in a business letter?

    A. Dear Sir or Madam:
    B. Dear Sir or Madam,
    C. Dear Mary,
    D. Hi, Mr. Stevens:

GO ON TO THE NEXT PAGE

116. Which of the following activities is MOST likely to occur in the prewriting stage of the writing process?

    A. Listing topics

    B. Sharing a draft with a peer

    C. Reading the draft to the teacher

    D. Correcting spelling errors

117. The word *restroom* is a(n) _____ for the toilet room.

    A. elegy

    B. anapestic

    C. aphorism

    D. euphemism

118. Concrete poetry is a poetic form in which _____.

    A. formal structure is foremost

    B. stanzas and couplets are used

    C. shape and visual effects are emphasized

    D. onomatopoeia is emphasized

119. *Canto* is best defined as _____.

    A. proficient use of the dictionary

    B. an exact quotation

    C. disregard for meaning with an emphasis on pronunciation

    D. the main section of a long poem

120. The emotional atmosphere created by the author is known as the _____ of a literary work.

    A. setting

    B. mood

    C. plot

    D. denouement

121. Which of the following pairs of characters appears in Shakespeare's *A Midsummer Night's Dream*?

    A. Romeo and Juliet

    B. Hermia and Robin Goodfellow

    C. Caesar and Calpurnia

    D. Gertrude and Claudius

122. *The Giver, 1984,* and *The Lord of the Rings* can all be classified as belonging to which of the following genres?

    A. Realistic fiction

    B. Poetry

    C. Historical fiction

    D. Science fiction/fantasy

123. The setting of *Fahrenheit 451* is_____.

    A. 1984

    B. the 21st century

    C. the 24th century

    D. the 1950s

GO ON TO THE NEXT PAGE

Questions 124 and 125 are based on the poem "Jabberwocky."

'Twas brillig, and the slithy toves
    Did gyre and gimble in the wade;
All mimsy were the borogoves,
    And the mome raths outgrabe.

"Beware the Jabberwock, my son!
    The jaws that bite, the claws that catch!
Beware the Jubjub bird, and shun
    The frumious Bandersnatch!"

He took his vorpal sword in hand:
    Long time the manxome foe he sought—
So rested he by the Tumtum tree.
    And stood awhile in thought.

And as in uffish thought he stood,
    The Jabberwock, with eyes of flame,
Came wiffling through the tulgey wood,
    And burbled as it came!

One, two! One, two! And through and through
    The vorpal blade went snicker-snack!
He left it dead, and with its head
    He went galumphing back.

"And hast thou slain the Jabberwock?
    Come to my arms, my beamish boy!
O frabjous day! Callooh! Callay!"
    He chortled in his joy.

'Twas brillig, and the slithy toves
    Did gyre and gimble in the wabe;
All mimsy were the borogoves,
    And the mome raths outgrabe.

124. Who is the author of "Jabberwocky"?

    A.   e. e. cummings
    B.   Lewis Carroll
    C.   Edward Lear
    D.   Ogden Nash

125. "Jabberwocky" was written during which of the following literary time periods?

    A.   Old English
    B.   Victorian
    C.   Romantic
    D.   Contemporary

GO ON TO THE NEXT PAGE

126. Tituba, a character in Arthur Miller's play *The Crucible,* says, "My Betty be hearty soon?" Which of the following best describes Tituba's use of language?

    A. Dialect

    B. Phonology

    C. Pragmatics

    D. Grammatical error

127. The following sentence is a _____ sentence.

I look forward to teaching, and I plan to teach middle school English because I love literature.

    A. compound

    B. compound/complex

    C. complex

    D. simple

128. Which of the following best describes the beliefs of the Beat Generation in American literature?

    A. Knowledge can be arrived at not only through the senses, but also through intuition and contemplation of the internal spirit.

    B. The literary work's function is to report what happens, without comment or judgment.

    C. Literature helps identify the underlying causes for a person's actions or beliefs.

    D. Unchecked capitalism is destructive to the human spirit and antithetical to social equality.

129. Which of the following criteria should be used when evaluating Internet sources for a research paper?

    I.   Author

    II.   Accuracy

    III. Purpose of the site

    IV. Access

    A. I

    B. I, II

    C. I, II, IV

    D. All of the above

130. When a writer considers the _____ for a piece, he or she considers who else will read it and what background knowledge the reader might need to understand the point of the writing.

    A. grade

    B. publisher

    C. location

    D. audience

Answer Key

Question	Answer	Content Category	Where to Get More Help
1.	B	Reading and Literature	Chapter 3
2.	D	Reading and Literature	Chapter 3
3.	B	Reading and Literature	Chapter 3
4.	D	Reading and Literature	Chapter 3
5.	A	Reading and Literature	Chapter 3
6.	A	Language Use, Vocabulary, and Linguistics	Chapter 4
7.	B	Language Use, Vocabulary, and Linguistics	Chapter 4
8.	D	Writing, Speaking, and Listening	Chapter 5
9.	D	Writing, Speaking, and Listening	Chapter 5
10.	B	Writing, Speaking, and Listening	Chapter 5
11.	D	Writing, Speaking, and Listening	Chapter 5
12.	C	Writing, Speaking, and Listening	Chapter 5
13.	A	Reading and Literature	Chapter 3
14.	C	Reading and Literature	Chapter 3
15.	B	Reading and Literature	Chapter 3
16.	D	Reading and Literature	Chapter 3
17.	B	Reading and Literature	Chapter 3
18.	D	Reading and Literature	Chapter 3
19.	A	Reading and Literature	Chapter 3
20.	D	Reading and Literature	Chapter 3
21.	C	Language Use, Vocabulary, and Linguistics	Chapter 4
22.	B	Language Use, Vocabulary, and Linguistics	Chapter 4
23.	A	Writing, Speaking, and Listening	Chapter 5
24.	C	Writing, Speaking, and Listening	Chapter 5
25.	B	Writing, Speaking, and Listening	Chapter 5
26.	B	Writing, Speaking, and Listening	Chapter 5
27.	A	Reading and Literature	Chapter 3
28.	C	Reading and Literature	Chapter 3
29.	B	Reading and Literature	Chapter 3
30.	B	Reading and Literature	Chapter 3
31.	B	Reading and Literature	Chapter 3
32.	D	Reading and Literature	Chapter 3
33.	C	Reading and Literature	Chapter 3
34.	B	Reading and Literature	Chapter 3
35.	D	Language Use, Vocabulary, and Linguistics	Chapter 4
36.	B	Language Use, Vocabulary, and Linguistics	Chapter 4
37.	C	Writing, Speaking, and Listening	Chapter 5
38.	C	Writing, Speaking, and Listening	Chapter 5
39.	C	Writing, Speaking, and Listening	Chapter 5

continued

Question	Answer	Content Category	Where to Get More Help
40.	D	Writing, Speaking, and Listening	Chapter 5
41.	A	Writing, Speaking, and Listening	Chapter 5
42.	A	Reading and Literature	Chapter 3
43.	B	Reading and Literature	Chapter 3
44.	D	Reading and Literature	Chapter 3
45.	D	Reading and Literature	Chapter 3
46.	B	Reading and Literature	Chapter 3
47.	D	Reading and Literature	Chapter 3
48.	C	Reading and Literature	Chapter 3
49.	A	Reading and Literature	Chapter 3
50.	A	Language Use, Vocabulary, and Linguistics	Chapter 4
51.	D	Language Use, Vocabulary, and Linguistics	Chapter 4
52.	B	Writing, Speaking, and Listening	Chapter 5
53.	C	Writing, Speaking, and Listening	Chapter 5
54.	C	Reading and Literature	Chapter 3
55.	C	Reading and Literature	Chapter 3
56.	A	Reading and Literature	Chapter 3
57.	D	Reading and Literature	Chapter 3
58.	C	Reading and Literature	Chapter 3
59.	D	Reading and Literature	Chapter 3
60.	A	Reading and Literature	Chapter 3
61.	D	Reading and Literature	Chapter 3
62.	B	Writing, Speaking, and Listening	Chapter 5
63.	B	Writing, Speaking, and Listening	Chapter 5
64.	C	Language Use, Vocabulary, and Linguistics	Chapter 4
65.	B	Language Use, Vocabulary, and Linguistics	Chapter 4
66.	D	Writing, Speaking, and Listening	Chapter 5
67.	B	Writing, Speaking, and Listening	Chapter 5
68.	C	Writing, Speaking, and Listening	Chapter 5
69.	D	Reading and Literature	Chapter 3
70.	D	Reading and Literature	Chapter 3
71.	A	Reading and Literature	Chapter 3
72.	B	Reading and Literature	Chapter 3
73.	C	Reading and Literature	Chapter 3
74.	D	Reading and Literature	Chapter 3
75.	C	Reading and Literature	Chapter 3
76.	B	Reading and Literature	Chapter 3
77.	A	Reading and Literature	Chapter 3
78.	D	Reading and Literature	Chapter 3
79.	D	Language Use, Vocabulary, and Linguistics	Chapter 4
80.	C	Language Use, Vocabulary, and Linguistics	Chapter 4
81.	B	Writing, Speaking, and Listening	Chapter 5

Question	Answer	Content Category	Where to Get More Help
82.	A	Writing, Speaking, and Listening	Chapter 5
83.	B	Writing, Speaking, and Listening	Chapter 5
84.	B	Writing, Speaking, and Listening	Chapter 5
85.	A	Writing, Speaking, and Listening	Chapter 5
86.	C	Reading and Literature	Chapter 3
87.	A	Reading and Literature	Chapter 3
88.	D	Reading and Literature	Chapter 3
89.	B	Reading and Literature	Chapter 3
90.	A	Reading and Literature	Chapter 3
91.	A	Reading and Literature	Chapter 3
92.	D	Writing, Speaking, and Listening	Chapter 5
93.	D	Writing, Speaking, and Listening	Chapter 5
94.	C	Language Use, Vocabulary, and Linguistics	Chapter 4
95.	D	Language Use, Vocabulary, and Linguistics	Chapter 4
96.	A	Writing, Speaking, and Listening	Chapter 5
97.	B	Writing, Speaking, and Listening	Chapter 5
98.	C	Writing, Speaking, and Listening	Chapter 5
99.	A	Reading and Literature	Chapter 3
100.	B	Reading and Literature	Chapter 3
101.	D	Reading and Literature	Chapter 3
102.	A	Reading and Literature	Chapter 3
103.	C	Reading and Literature	Chapter 3
104.	B	Reading and Literature	Chapter 3
105.	D	Reading and Literature	Chapter 3
106.	B	Reading and Literature	Chapter 3
107.	A	Reading and Literature	Chapter 3
108.	C	Reading and Literature	Chapter 3
109.	D	Language Use, Vocabulary, and Linguistics	Chapter 4
110.	B	Language Use, Vocabulary, and Linguistics	Chapter 4
111.	A	Language Use, Vocabulary, and Linguistics	Chapter 4
112.	C	Language Use, Vocabulary, and Linguistics	Chapter 4
113.	C	Writing, Speaking, and Listening	Chapter 5
114.	B	Writing, Speaking, and Listening	Chapter 5
115.	A	Writing, Speaking, and Listening	Chapter 5
116.	A	Writing, Speaking, and Listening	Chapter 5
117.	D	Reading and Literature	Chapter 3
118.	C	Writing, Speaking, and Listening	Chapter 5
119.	D	Writing, Speaking, and Listening	Chapter 5
120.	B	Writing, Speaking, and Listening	Chapter 5
121.	B	Reading and Literature	Chapter 3
122.	D	Reading and Literature	Chapter 3
123.	C	Reading and Literature	Chapter 3

continued

Question	Answer	Content Category	Where to Get More Help
124.	B	Reading and Literature	Chapter 3
125.	B	Reading and Literature	Chapter 3
126.	A	Language Use, Vocabulary, and Linguistics	Chapter 4
127.	B	Language Use, Vocabulary, and Linguistics	Chapter 4
128.	D	Reading and Literature	Chapter 3
129.	D	Writing, Speaking, and Listening	Chapter 5
130.	D	Writing, Speaking, and Listening	Chapter 5

Answer Explanations

1. **B.** Keats, Shelley, and Byron are all Romantic period authors in British literary history.

2. **D.** This excerpt is from the first stanza of Robert Frost's famous poem "The Road Not Taken."

3. **B.** This excerpt is an example of a five-line stanza, so you can rule out choice D immediately because it is not written in couplets (III). The rhyme scheme is ABAAB (I), so choices A, B, and C are viable options. Next, you have to identify the metrical feet of the poem. An iambic metrical foot begins with an unstressed syllable followed by a stressed syllable. A trochaic metrical foot begins with a stressed syllable followed by an unstressed syllable. Each line of this excerpt begins with an unstressed syllable and contains five feet, indicating that choice B (I and II) is the credited response.

4. **D.** Graymalkin is the evil servant of the first witch. In this period, this creature was known as a "familiar," which is synonymous with "evil servant." The toad is the familiar to the second witch, and its name is Paddock.

5. **A.** A heath or moor is a large expanse of land covered with low-growing shrubs such as heather and other varieties of evergreens.

6. **A.** The word *ere* in Elizabethan English means "before."

7. **B.** Iambic tetrameter is the versification of the poem "The Lady of Shallot" by Alfred Lord Tennyson. An iamb is a metrical foot in poetry that has an unstressed first syllable followed by a stressed second syllable. Poetry written in iambic tetrameter will have four of these feet in each line. Whenever you get a question about poetic meter, first count the number of stressed syllables in a few lines, and then eliminate incorrect answers. For example, in this question, two responses (choices A and C) have the word "pentameter," which requires five stressed syllables per line; the poem in question has only four.

8. **D.** Camelot is the setting of *Le Morte d'Arthur* by Malory and cues the reader to the allusion to this famous work from the Middle English period.

9. **D.** "Elegy Written in a Country Churchyard" is a poem written by Thomas Gray (1716–1771).

10. **B.** This elegy is noteworthy in that it mourns the loss of a way of life rather than the loss of a person.

11. **D.** The writing process is a recursive process in which the writer moves through the stages of writing in a unique sequence. The term *recursive* signifies that each writer's process is not linear—going directly from one prescribed stage to another. Rather, the writing process is unique to each writer and is based on that writer's distinct needs.

12. **C.** One theme of Rossetti's poem "The Birthday" is how poetry can provide a natural outlet for one's emotions. The imagery of the "singing bird," which opens the poem, signals the song or poem is as natural as breathing.

13. **A.** Christina Rossetti (1830–1894) lived in England and wrote during the Pre-Raphaelite literary period along with writers and artists Dante Gabriel Rossetti, Thomas Woolner, Aubrey Beardsley, and Algernon Charles Swinburne. Pre-Raphaelites were influenced by the doctrines of the Pre-Raphaelite brotherhood, which called for genuine expression of ideas and the attentive study of nature.

14. **C.** Charles Dickens wrote during the Victorian period of British literary history, approximately 1840–1900. He is the author of many works, including *Great Expectations* and *Oliver Twist*.

15. **B.** The character of Faith, Young Goodman Brown's wife, represents the Puritan view of the importance of domestic life and the stability of home.

16. **D.** A short story is a brief fictional prose that succinctly portrays a life event or experience.

17. **B.** Nathaniel Hawthorne (1804–1864) was an American author who wrote during the Transcendental Movement between 1830 and 1860. Hawthorne also wrote *The Scarlet Letter*.

18. **D.** "The Legend of Sleepy Hollow," a short story whose main character is Ichabod Crane, is about the legend of a headless horseman who lost his head to a cannonball and rides to find his lost head.

19. **A.** *Peyton Place* was written by Grace Metalious in 1957, not by Hawthorne.

20. **D.** Each of the selected lines from Anne Bradstreet's poem "To My Dear and Loving Husband" contains at least one example of alliteration—the repetition of initial consonant sounds (not necessarily the same letter). Below you will see the initial consonant sounds in bold:

   I.   If ever man were loved by wife, **then** **th**ee;

   II.   Or all the riches **th**at **th**e East doth hold

   III.   Then **wh**ile **w**e **l**ive, in **l**ove **l**et's so persevere

   IV.   That **wh**en **w**e **l**ive no more, **w**e may **l**ive ever

21. **C.** The imagery of the tranquility of nightfall and Pip's not envisioning a shadow of another parting with Estella signifies his ability to let his loss of her love go and be at peace with the ending of their relationship.

22. **B.** Satis House is the mansion in which Estella lived her entire childhood with Miss Havisham, who preferred that no light enter the house.

23. **A.** The denouement of a literary work follows the events after the story's climax and serves as the conclusion. The word *denouement* is derived from the Old French term *denoer,* meaning "to untie."

24. **C.** The proper MLA citation of Dickens' *Great Expectations* is:

Dickens, Charles. *Great Expectations.* New York: Random House, 1907. Print.

25. **B.** The proper APA citation of all book titles, such as Dickens' *Great Expectations,* is:

Dickens, C. (1907). *Great expectations.* New York: Random House.

26. **B.** "The bat that lies in bed at noon," and "All love to be out by the light of the moon" are the only lines that do not contain onomatopoeia—the use of sound words to suggest meaning.

27. **A.** *Hamlet* contains at least one play within a play, the primary of which is referred to in this passage. Hamlet invites actors to perform a play he has written, called *The Mousetrap*, which contains parallels to Claudius' marriage to Hamlet's mother and Claudius' murder of his brother, King Hamlet.

28. **C.** Claudius is the villainous man who plays many roles in Hamlet's life—uncle, stepfather, king, traitor, enemy—and is the intended audience of *The Mousetrap*, the play that Hamlet consigns to be performed at the castle in an effort to expose Claudius' evil acts.

29. **B.** The Declaration of Independence was first penned by Thomas Jefferson as a member of a committee with John Adams and Benjamin Franklin.

30. B. The meaning of the phrase "to dissolve the political bands which have connected them with another" is best paraphrased in choice B: to sever political ties with England.

31. B. The author respectfully sets a purpose for this declaration based on "a decent respect to the opinions of mankind." This rhetorical strategy persuades the reader to read on and respectfully consider this declaration.

32. D. This excerpt from *Gulliver's Travels* can best be described as prose in chronological sequence. The narrator first tells the reader about his arrival in Lisbon, then his welcoming at the captain's home, and finally his efforts to be clothed properly and comfortably.

33. C. The term *suffer* is used often in *Gulliver's Travels* to express discomfort or trouble.

34. B. Jonathan Swift was born in 1667. *Gulliver's Travels* was first published anonymously in 1726.

35. D. The student's most important error is in comma usage. This issue should be the teacher's first priority; lessons on word choice and sentence construction could follow.

36. B. The words *read* and *read* are not homophones because they are not pronounced the same way. For example, consider the following sentences using *read* and *read*:

I *read* the newspaper yesterday.

I will *read* the newspaper tomorrow.

37. C. A rhetorical question is one that the speaker does not truly want answered.

38. C. African American Vernacular English (AAVE) has many features, including the pronunciation of two-syllable words that end in -*ng* as *weddin* for *wedding* or *nuffin* for *nothing*.

39. C. This quote uses parallel structure as a rhetorical device.

40. D. Lincoln, one of the United States' great orators, used repetition in this quote to make his point effectively.

41. A. In poetry, apostrophe is a literary device in which some abstraction or personification that is not physically present is addressed, as in the first lines of the poem "O Captain! My Captain!"

42. A. Whitman wrote this poem to memorialize President Abraham Lincoln.

43. B. The British Romantic period of literature was 1780–1840.

44. D. A sonnet is a lyric poem with a formal structure. Lyric poems are usually short and often personal.

45. D. This sonnet has 14 lines written in iambic pentameter, which means that each line has 10 syllables, with the stressed syllable or accent on every second syllable in a rhyming couplet.

46. B. The Shakespearean sonnet's rhyme scheme is ABAB, CDCD, EFEF, GG: three quatrains followed by one couplet.

47. D. This line from *Don Quixote* contains a simile, which is a comparison using *like* or *as*.

48. C. Miguel de Cervantes (1547–1616) wrote *Don Quixote*.

49. A. Traditional haiku poetry is made up of three lines containing 5, 7, 5 syllables.

50. A. Clichés are phrases that are used so often that they lose their expressive power.

51. D. Hardy uses the metaphor of a book and its pages to convey the message of this poem, which is that this relationship is coming to an end.

52. B. Hardy repeats the word *truth* for emphasis and persuasion.

53. C. The allusion "man for all seasons" refers to Thomas More, the author of *Utopia,* who was sent to prison and executed. He was considered a man for all seasons for courageously holding firm to his beliefs. An allusion is a reference to a familiar person, place, thing, or event.

54. C. The central conflict in *The Scarlet Letter* is best described as person versus society. Hester Prynne, the main character in the story, has a problem with an element of society; specifically, she has committed adultery and is forced to wear a scarlet letter on her dress at all times.

55. C. The author of *The Scarlet Letter* is Nathaniel Hawthorne, who completed this classic novel in 1850.

56. A. In the mid-1800s, a time of revolution in Europe, writers like Ibsen began to challenge the romantic traditions that were in vogue at the time. Ibsen, a writer from Norway, is credited with mastering and popularizing realist drama.

57. D. Nora is an immature, silly young woman at the opening of the play. By the end, she has grown into a serious, open-minded woman who rejects the traditional roles available to a woman during this time—housewife, mother, dependent.

58. C. This opening scene is from *The Importance of Being Earnest* by Oscar Wilde.

59. D. Personification is a literary device in which the author describes an inanimate object or abstraction—the storm, in this text—using human qualities or abilities, such as "fierce breath of the whirlwind" and "a long tumultuous shouting sound."

60. A. "The Fall of the House of Usher" was written by Edgar Allan Poe (1809–1849). Poe was an American author during the Romantic period, known especially for his stories of the macabre and mysterious.

61. D. *Pygmalion* takes place in Great Britain, which is signaled by the mention of Drury Lane, a famous location in Great Britain, and the mention of eightpence, a denomination of British money.

62. B. The use of the term *Pharisaic* is best defined as hypocritically self-righteous. Higgins regrets his behavior toward the lower-class Flower Girl and offers her much of the change in his pocket as a sign of his repentance.

63. B. T. S. Eliot wrote his most famous poem, "The Waste Land," during the Modern period, 1900–1945.

64. C. Eliot's description of the month of April as "cruel" is an ironic allusion to the prologue of Chaucer's *Canterbury Tales,* which describes spring as a time of rebirth and life.

65. B. In this scene, Hamlet is despondent over his father's death and his mother's hasty marriage to his uncle. Hamlet uses the metaphor of an unweeded garden to represent that Denmark is in ruin after King Hamlet's death.

66. D. Hamlet is referring to his father, King Hamlet.

67. B. *Hamlet* is one of Shakespeare's great tragedies.

68. C. This excerpt from *Hamlet* uses an appeal to emotion to convey the author's message. We are to feel pity and empathy for Prince Hamlet.

69. D. This allusion to the mythical god of the sun as compared to a cowardly beast contrasts Old King Hamlet and the new King Claudius.

70. D. The author of *Beowulf* is unknown.

71. A. Plato suggests that each person must do the work that fits his or her own strengths.

72. B. Rhetoric can be defined as the use of language in a persuasive or impressive way.

73. C. This line from Clement C. Moore's *A Visit from Saint Nicholas* contains the simile "like a flash."

74. D. This limerick by Edward Lear is a humorous verse form of five anapestic lines with the rhyme scheme AABBA.

75. C. J. D. Salinger is the author of *The Catcher in the Rye.*

76. B. *The Catcher in the Rye* was published in 1951 in the United States. It is considered contemporary U.S. literature.

77. A. Prufrock's name is meant to elicit the image of a prude in a frock who is incapable of action, specifically to eat a peach in the presence of high-society women.

78. D. Modernist poets, such as T. S. Eliot, focused on the inner, artistic, stream of consciousness mind, not the outer concrete world.

79. D. A discussion about seeking justice in students' lives, personal experiences, and world events would activate students' prior knowledge and experiences about a central theme in Shakespeare's *King Lear*.

80. C. *Faction*—a group of persons forming a cohesive, often contentious group—is the word least related to the Latin cognate *facilis,* which means "easy."

81. B. Correlative conjunctions are used only in pairs and include not only/but also, neither/nor, and either/or.

82. A. During a peer conference, students read their writing to hear their ideas aloud and receive feedback from an initial audience. This is an appropriate revision-stage activity in which students re-see their writing to potentially strengthen and change the piece.

83. B. A writing rubric is a scoring guide used to provide feedback to students and help them assess their writing.

84. B. The proper MLA citation is choice B because it contains italics for the book title and only the page number in parentheses since the author's name appears in the sentence.

85. A. *The Birthday Party*, one of Harold Pinter's most famous plays, contains an extended metaphor.

86. C. A malapropism is the unintentional misuse of a word that is confused with one that sounds similar. The correct word here is *imminent* (pending), not *eminent* (distinguished).

87. A. Anne Bradstreet's *The Tenth Muse Lately Sprung Up in America* was written in 1650, during the Colonial period.

88. D. A protagonist is the central character. Odysseus is the central character in the epic *The Odyssey*.

89. B. The denouement is the tying up of loose ends in a story, leading to the outcome or resolution.

90. A. W. E. B. Du Bois effectively uses the rhetorical device of appeal to emotion to persuade the young schoolgirl not to give up and to attend to her studies.

91. A. Theodore Roosevelt alluded to the period in American history called Western Expansion and Reform, which included the life of frontiersmen and women, who placed hard work and the needs of the nation above those of the individual.

92. D. Roosevelt's repetition of "if we stand; if we seek; if we shrink" utilizes the rhetorical strategy anaphora, which builds tension for the listener and a resulting sense of satisfaction due to the parallelism and the resolution at the end of the statement.

93. D. Roosevelt conjures the listeners' sense of pride, masculinity, and duty—all appeals to the listeners' emotions.

94. C. This sentence has one independent clause (The twentieth century looms) with three prepositional phrases (before us big; with the fate; of many nations).

95. D. In the omniscient point of view, the narrator is free to tell the story from any and all characters' perspectives.

96. A. A quintet contains a five-line stanza.

97. B. The speaker displays his diction—choice and use of words and phrases—by opening with the phrase "four score and seven years ago" rather than the date of the American Revolution in 1776.

98. C. "Final resting place" is a euphemism, a word or phrase that substitutes for a harsher or more blunt term. It is used in the place of the phrase "the battlefield where these men were killed."

99. **A.** President Abraham Lincoln (1809–1865) was the orator of the Gettysburg Address of 1863.

100. **B.** The initial setting of *The Grapes of Wrath* is the 1930s Dust Bowl in the Midwestern United States. The family then heads to California in search of a better life.

101. **D.** John Steinbeck (1902–1968) is the author of *The Grapes of Wrath*.

102. **A.** *Le Morte d'Arthur* was written in the mid-1400s, during the Middle English period (1066–1550).

103. **C.** This is an English sonnet, which is traditionally written in iambic pentameter.

104. **B.** Elizabeth Barrett Browning wrote *Sonnets from the Portuguese,* a collection of 44 love sonnets to her husband, Robert Browning.

105. **D.** A parable is a story meant to teach a moral lesson. Hester Prynne's scarlet letter is meant to symbolize shame, but she integrates it into who she is, empowering her to find her own identity and inner strength.

106. **B.** Transcendentalist authors like Longfellow and Hawthorne were dedicated to the belief that the divine can be found everywhere.

107. **A.** Chaucer's *Canterbury Tales* is from the Middle English period of British literature.

108. **C.** "Guinevere at Her Fireside" is from *Death and Taxes*, which is perhaps the most famous collection of poetry by Dorothy Parker.

109. **D.** Hughes captured the beauty of African American Vernacular English through his authentic and careful use of idioms and dialect.

110. **B.** By deleting "playing the" and adding "lessons" after "piano," the sentence now contains proper parallelism: Tory participates in basketball, softball, and piano lessons.

111. **A.** The second sentence has a problem with the pronoun *he*. It is unclear to the reader whether Jimmy or Austin received recognition from the coach and teammates.

112. **C.** Sociolinguistics is the study of language as it relates to society, including class, race, and gender.

113. **C.** In the publishing stage of the writing process, a writer is LEAST likely to use the Internet to search for writing ideas. This task is more likely to occur during the prewriting stage.

114. **B.** Bartlett's *Familiar Quotations* is the foremost print and online source of famous quotations.

115. **A.** "Dear Sir or Madam:" is an appropriate greeting in a business letter. Please note that a business letter requires the use of a colon, not comma, at the end of the greeting.

116. **A.** Listing writing topics is an excellent prewriting activity.

117. **D.** *Restroom* is a euphemism for the toilet room. A euphemism is a polite way to discuss a topic that may bring about discomfort.

118. **C.** Concrete poetry emphasizes shape and visual effects to create meaning.

119. **D.** A canto is the main section of a long poem, especially found in epics. Dante's *Divine Comedy* is comprised of 100 cantos and Ezra Pound's *The Cantos* has 120 cantos.

120. **B.** The emotional atmosphere created by the author is the mood of a literary work.

121. **B.** Hermia and Robin Goodfellow, a puck who causes much mischief, are characters in *A Midsummer Night's Dream.*

122. **D.** *The Giver, 1984,* and *The Lord of the Rings* are all science fiction/fantasy novels.

123. **C.** *Fahrenheit 451* takes place in the future—in the 24th century.

124. **B.** Lewis Carroll is the author of the poem "Jabberwocky," which is a nonsense poem. The authors in choices A, C, and D also composed nonsense poems.

125. B. "Jabberwocky" was written in the Victorian period of British literature.

126. A. Tituba uses dialect from the area her family comes from. Scholars believe that Tituba, a slave in the Parris household, was most likely from South America, not Africa.

127. B. A compound/complex sentence has two or more independent clauses and one or more dependent clauses.

128. D. The Beat Generation comprised a group of U.S. authors whose literature explored and influenced American culture in the post–World War II literary period. Famous authors include Allen Ginsberg and Jack Kerouac.

129. D. Reliable Internet sources should be checked for authorship, accuracy, purpose, and access (so that others can find the information again).

130. D. Writers should consider the audience for their writing—who the intended reader is, what his or her background knowledge is, and how this piece might be purposeful beyond the classroom.

Chapter 8

English Language Arts: Content and Analysis (5039)

This chapter includes one full-length practice test for the Praxis English Language Arts: Content and Analysis (5039) test. This practice test will give you a sense of the format of the test and help you determine which content areas you need to study. You also may want to practice your pacing while taking this full-length practice test. Remember, you will have a total of 150 minutes to complete the selected response section, plus 30 minutes to write two constructed responses.

After you complete the practice test, score your answers and use the explanations to assess content areas to study in chapters 3–5 of this book. Note that the English Language Arts Instruction content in chapter 6 is not assessed on this test.

It's time to set yourself up in a quiet place with no interruptions, get your pencils ready, take a look at the clock, and begin your practice test.

IMPORTANT NOTE: For ease of studying, all questions in the first section of this practice test are single-selection multiple-choice.

Answer Sheet

1 Ⓐ Ⓑ Ⓒ Ⓓ	46 Ⓐ Ⓑ Ⓒ Ⓓ	91 Ⓐ Ⓑ Ⓒ Ⓓ
2 Ⓐ Ⓑ Ⓒ Ⓓ	47 Ⓐ Ⓑ Ⓒ Ⓓ	92 Ⓐ Ⓑ Ⓒ Ⓓ
3 Ⓐ Ⓑ Ⓒ Ⓓ	48 Ⓐ Ⓑ Ⓒ Ⓓ	93 Ⓐ Ⓑ Ⓒ Ⓓ
4 Ⓐ Ⓑ Ⓒ Ⓓ	49 Ⓐ Ⓑ Ⓒ Ⓓ	94 Ⓐ Ⓑ Ⓒ Ⓓ
5 Ⓐ Ⓑ Ⓒ Ⓓ	50 Ⓐ Ⓑ Ⓒ Ⓓ	95 Ⓐ Ⓑ Ⓒ Ⓓ
6 Ⓐ Ⓑ Ⓒ Ⓓ	51 Ⓐ Ⓑ Ⓒ Ⓓ	96 Ⓐ Ⓑ Ⓒ Ⓓ
7 Ⓐ Ⓑ Ⓒ Ⓓ	52 Ⓐ Ⓑ Ⓒ Ⓓ	97 Ⓐ Ⓑ Ⓒ Ⓓ
8 Ⓐ Ⓑ Ⓒ Ⓓ	53 Ⓐ Ⓑ Ⓒ Ⓓ	98 Ⓐ Ⓑ Ⓒ Ⓓ
9 Ⓐ Ⓑ Ⓒ Ⓓ	54 Ⓐ Ⓑ Ⓒ Ⓓ	99 Ⓐ Ⓑ Ⓒ Ⓓ
10 Ⓐ Ⓑ Ⓒ Ⓓ	55 Ⓐ Ⓑ Ⓒ Ⓓ	100 Ⓐ Ⓑ Ⓒ Ⓓ
11 Ⓐ Ⓑ Ⓒ Ⓓ	56 Ⓐ Ⓑ Ⓒ Ⓓ	101 Ⓐ Ⓑ Ⓒ Ⓓ
12 Ⓐ Ⓑ Ⓒ Ⓓ	57 Ⓐ Ⓑ Ⓒ Ⓓ	102 Ⓐ Ⓑ Ⓒ Ⓓ
13 Ⓐ Ⓑ Ⓒ Ⓓ	58 Ⓐ Ⓑ Ⓒ Ⓓ	103 Ⓐ Ⓑ Ⓒ Ⓓ
14 Ⓐ Ⓑ Ⓒ Ⓓ	59 Ⓐ Ⓑ Ⓒ Ⓓ	104 Ⓐ Ⓑ Ⓒ Ⓓ
15 Ⓐ Ⓑ Ⓒ Ⓓ	60 Ⓐ Ⓑ Ⓒ Ⓓ	105 Ⓐ Ⓑ Ⓒ Ⓓ
16 Ⓐ Ⓑ Ⓒ Ⓓ	61 Ⓐ Ⓑ Ⓒ Ⓓ	106 Ⓐ Ⓑ Ⓒ Ⓓ
17 Ⓐ Ⓑ Ⓒ Ⓓ	62 Ⓐ Ⓑ Ⓒ Ⓓ	107 Ⓐ Ⓑ Ⓒ Ⓓ
18 Ⓐ Ⓑ Ⓒ Ⓓ	63 Ⓐ Ⓑ Ⓒ Ⓓ	108 Ⓐ Ⓑ Ⓒ Ⓓ
19 Ⓐ Ⓑ Ⓒ Ⓓ	64 Ⓐ Ⓑ Ⓒ Ⓓ	109 Ⓐ Ⓑ Ⓒ Ⓓ
20 Ⓐ Ⓑ Ⓒ Ⓓ	65 Ⓐ Ⓑ Ⓒ Ⓓ	110 Ⓐ Ⓑ Ⓒ Ⓓ
21 Ⓐ Ⓑ Ⓒ Ⓓ	66 Ⓐ Ⓑ Ⓒ Ⓓ	111 Ⓐ Ⓑ Ⓒ Ⓓ
22 Ⓐ Ⓑ Ⓒ Ⓓ	67 Ⓐ Ⓑ Ⓒ Ⓓ	112 Ⓐ Ⓑ Ⓒ Ⓓ
23 Ⓐ Ⓑ Ⓒ Ⓓ	68 Ⓐ Ⓑ Ⓒ Ⓓ	113 Ⓐ Ⓑ Ⓒ Ⓓ
24 Ⓐ Ⓑ Ⓒ Ⓓ	69 Ⓐ Ⓑ Ⓒ Ⓓ	114 Ⓐ Ⓑ Ⓒ Ⓓ
25 Ⓐ Ⓑ Ⓒ Ⓓ	70 Ⓐ Ⓑ Ⓒ Ⓓ	115 Ⓐ Ⓑ Ⓒ Ⓓ
26 Ⓐ Ⓑ Ⓒ Ⓓ	71 Ⓐ Ⓑ Ⓒ Ⓓ	116 Ⓐ Ⓑ Ⓒ Ⓓ
27 Ⓐ Ⓑ Ⓒ Ⓓ	72 Ⓐ Ⓑ Ⓒ Ⓓ	117 Ⓐ Ⓑ Ⓒ Ⓓ
28 Ⓐ Ⓑ Ⓒ Ⓓ	73 Ⓐ Ⓑ Ⓒ Ⓓ	118 Ⓐ Ⓑ Ⓒ Ⓓ
29 Ⓐ Ⓑ Ⓒ Ⓓ	74 Ⓐ Ⓑ Ⓒ Ⓓ	119 Ⓐ Ⓑ Ⓒ Ⓓ
30 Ⓐ Ⓑ Ⓒ Ⓓ	75 Ⓐ Ⓑ Ⓒ Ⓓ	120 Ⓐ Ⓑ Ⓒ Ⓓ
31 Ⓐ Ⓑ Ⓒ Ⓓ	76 Ⓐ Ⓑ Ⓒ Ⓓ	121 Ⓐ Ⓑ Ⓒ Ⓓ
32 Ⓐ Ⓑ Ⓒ Ⓓ	77 Ⓐ Ⓑ Ⓒ Ⓓ	122 Ⓐ Ⓑ Ⓒ Ⓓ
33 Ⓐ Ⓑ Ⓒ Ⓓ	78 Ⓐ Ⓑ Ⓒ Ⓓ	123 Ⓐ Ⓑ Ⓒ Ⓓ
34 Ⓐ Ⓑ Ⓒ Ⓓ	79 Ⓐ Ⓑ Ⓒ Ⓓ	124 Ⓐ Ⓑ Ⓒ Ⓓ
35 Ⓐ Ⓑ Ⓒ Ⓓ	80 Ⓐ Ⓑ Ⓒ Ⓓ	125 Ⓐ Ⓑ Ⓒ Ⓓ
36 Ⓐ Ⓑ Ⓒ Ⓓ	81 Ⓐ Ⓑ Ⓒ Ⓓ	126 Ⓐ Ⓑ Ⓒ Ⓓ
37 Ⓐ Ⓑ Ⓒ Ⓓ	82 Ⓐ Ⓑ Ⓒ Ⓓ	127 Ⓐ Ⓑ Ⓒ Ⓓ
38 Ⓐ Ⓑ Ⓒ Ⓓ	83 Ⓐ Ⓑ Ⓒ Ⓓ	128 Ⓐ Ⓑ Ⓒ Ⓓ
39 Ⓐ Ⓑ Ⓒ Ⓓ	84 Ⓐ Ⓑ Ⓒ Ⓓ	129 Ⓐ Ⓑ Ⓒ Ⓓ
40 Ⓐ Ⓑ Ⓒ Ⓓ	85 Ⓐ Ⓑ Ⓒ Ⓓ	130 Ⓐ Ⓑ Ⓒ Ⓓ
41 Ⓐ Ⓑ Ⓒ Ⓓ	86 Ⓐ Ⓑ Ⓒ Ⓓ	
42 Ⓐ Ⓑ Ⓒ Ⓓ	87 Ⓐ Ⓑ Ⓒ Ⓓ	
43 Ⓐ Ⓑ Ⓒ Ⓓ	88 Ⓐ Ⓑ Ⓒ Ⓓ	
44 Ⓐ Ⓑ Ⓒ Ⓓ	89 Ⓐ Ⓑ Ⓒ Ⓓ	
45 Ⓐ Ⓑ Ⓒ Ⓓ	90 Ⓐ Ⓑ Ⓒ Ⓓ	

Practice Test 5039

Selected Response

Time: 150 minutes
130 questions

Directions: Each of the questions or statements below is followed by four suggested answers or completions. In each case, select the answer that is best.

---

1. The following literary works were written during which period in British literature?

Isabella by Keats
Prometheus Unbound by Shelley
Don Juan by Byron

   A. Renaissance
   B. Romantic
   C. Modern
   D. Harlem

Questions 2 and 3 are based on the following excerpt from a Robert Frost poem.

Two roads diverged in a yellow wood,
And sorry I could not travel both
And be one traveler, long I stood
And looked down one as far as I could
To where it bent in the undergrowth;

2. Which of the following is the correct title of the poem from which this excerpt is taken?

   A. "The Long and Winding Road"
   B. "The Road Less Traveled"
   C. "Life Is a Road"
   D. "The Road Not Taken"

3. Which of the following describes the rhyme scheme and meter of this excerpt?

   I.   ABAAB
   II.   Iambic pentameter
   III.   Couplet
   IV.   Trochaic septameter

   A. I
   B. I, II
   C. I, IV
   D. All of the above

GO ON TO THE NEXT PAGE

Questions 4–6 are based on this opening scene from Shakespeare's Macbeth.

FIRST WITCH: When shall we three meet again?
In thunder, lightning, or in rain?

SECOND WITCH: When the hurleyburley's done,
When the battle's lost and won.

THIRD WITCH: That will be ere the set of sun.

FIRST WITCH: Where the place?

SECOND WITCH: Upon the heath.

THIRD WITCH: There to meet with Macbeth.

FIRST WITCH: I come, Graymalkin.

ALL: Paddock calls. Anon!
Fair is foul, and foul is fair.
Hover through the fog and filthy air.

4. Who or what is Graymalkin in this scene?

   A. A sentry
   B. One of the witches
   C. A familiar in the form of a toad
   D. An evil servant in the form of a cat

5. Which of the following is synonymous with the word *heath*?

   A. Moor
   B. Desert
   C. Valley
   D. Mountain

6. What does the term *ere* mean in the line "That will be ere the set of the sun"?

   A. Before
   B. After
   C. During
   D. Until

GO ON TO THE NEXT PAGE

Questions 7 and 8 are based on the following excerpt from Alfred Lord Tennyson's poem "The Lady of Shallot."

On either side the river lie
Long fields of barley and of rye,
That clothe the wold and meet the sky;
And thro' the field the road runs by
To many-tower'd Camelot;
And up and down the people go,
Gazing where the lilies blow
Round an island there below,
The island of Shallot.

7. Which of the following best describes the versification of the lines above?

    A. Iambic pentameter

    B. Iambic tetrameter

    C. Anapestic pentameter

    D. Anapestic tetrameter

8. This poem contains an allusion to Malory's *Le Morte d'Arthur*. Which of the following words in this excerpt alludes to this work from the Middle English period?

    A. Island

    B. Lilies

    C. Wold

    D. Camelot

Questions 9 and 10 are based on the following excerpt from a poem written by Thomas Gray.

Here rests his head upon the lap of Earth
A youth to Fortune and to Fame unknown.
Fair Science frowned not on his humble birth,
And Melancholy marked him for her own.

Large was his bounty, and his soul sincere,
Heaven did a recompense as largely send:
He gave to Misery all he had, a tear,
He gained from Heaven ('twas all he wish'd) a friend.

No farther seek his merits to disclose,
Or draw his frailties from their dread abode
(There they alike in trembling hope repose),
The bosom of his Father and his God.

9. The title of this poem is _____.

    A. "When Lilacs Last in the Dooryard Bloom'd"

    B. "To my Lord"

    C. "O Captain! My Captain!"

    D. "Elegy Written in a Country Churchyard"

10. Thomas Gray's poem is mourning the loss of _____.

    A. the President of the United States

    B. a way of life

    C. a close personal friend

    D. W. B. Yeats

GO ON TO THE NEXT PAGE

11. Which of the following best describes the writing process?

    A. Stagelike

    B. Developmental

    C. Exclusionary

    D. Recursive

Questions 12 and 13 are based on the following poem, "A Birthday," by Christina Rossetti.

My heart is like a singing bird
    Whose nest is in a watered shoot;
My heart is like an apple-tree
    Whose boughs are bent with thick-set fruit;
My heart is like a rainbow shell
    That paddles in a halcyon sea;
My heart is gladder than all these,
    Because my love is come to me.

Raise me a dais of silk and down;
    Hang it with vair and purple dyes;
Carve it in doves and pomegranates,
    And peacocks with a hundred eyes;
Work it in gold and silver grapes,
    In leaves and silver fleurs-de-lys;
Because the birthday of my life
    Is come, my love is come to me.

12. Which of the following best describes the theme of this poem?

    A. Love can be fraught with peril and delight.

    B. Dreams really do come true.

    C. The natural world can enhance self-expression.

    D. Good things come to those who wait.

13. During which literary time period did Rossetti write?

    A. Pre-Raphaelite

    B. Modern

    C. The Beat Generation

    D. Renaissance

14. Which of the following authors is associated with the Victorian period of British literature?

    A. Shakespeare

    B. Whitman

    C. Dickens

    D. Emerson

GO ON TO THE NEXT PAGE

Questions 15–17 are based on the following excerpt from Nathaniel Hawthorne's "Young Goodman Brown."

Young Goodman Brown came forth at sunset into the street at Salem village; but put his head back, after crossing the threshold, to exchange a parting kiss with his young wife. And Faith, as the wife was aptly named, thrust her own pretty head into the street, letting the wind play with the pink ribbons of her cap while she called to Goodman Brown.

"Dearest heart," whispered she, softly and rather sadly, when her lips were close to his ear, "prithee put off your journey until sunrise and sleep in your own bed to-night. A lone woman is troubled with such dreams and such thoughts that she's afeard of herself sometimes. Pray tarry with me this night, dear husband, of all nights in the year."

"My love and my Faith," replied young Goodman Brown, "of all nights in the year, this one night must I tarry away from thee. My journey, as thou callest it, forth and back again, must needs be done 'twixt now and sunrise. What, my sweet, pretty wife, dost thou doubt me already, and we but three months married?"

"Then God bless you!" said Faith, with the pink ribbons; "and may you find all well when you come back."

"Amen!" cried Goodman Brown. "Say thy prayers, dear Faith, and go to bed at dusk, and no harm will come to thee."

So they parted; and the young man pursued his way until, being about to turn the corner by the meeting-house, he looked back and saw the head of Faith still peeping after him with a melancholy air, in spite of her pink ribbons.

"Poor little Faith!" thought he, for his heart smote him. "What a wretch am I to leave her on such an errand! She talks of dreams, too. Methought as she spoke there was trouble in her face, as if a dream had warned her what work is to be done tonight. But no, no; 't would kill her to think it. Well, she's a blessed angel on earth; and after this one night I'll cling to her skirts and follow her to heaven."

15. Based on your reading of the excerpt above, which of the following best describes the role of the character Faith in this short story?

    A. To contrast the role of men and women in society

    B. To represent the stability of home

    C. To acknowledge religion

    D. To suggest the frailty of women

16. In a short story such as "Young Goodman Brown," brief _____ prose is used to give readers a glimpse of an event or life experience.

    A. theatrical

    B. poetic

    C. nonfiction

    D. fictional

17. Nathaniel Hawthorne wrote during which literary period?

    A. Medieval

    B. Transcendental

    C. Romantic

    D. Victorian

18. Which of the following names the "legend" of Washington Irving's "The Legend of Sleepy Hollow"?

    A. Satchmo

    B. Rip van Winkle

    C. Tam O'Shanter

    D. The Headless Horseman

GO ON TO THE NEXT PAGE

19. Each of the following novels is correctly paired with its author EXCEPT

    A. *Peyton Place,* Hawthorne
    B. *Pride and Prejudice,* Austen
    C. *Waiting for Godot,* Beckett
    D. *The Catcher in the Rye,* Salinger

20. Of the following lines, which ones contain alliteration?

    I.   If ever man were loved by wife, then thee;

    II.   Or all the riches that the East doth hold

    III.   Then while we live, in love let's so persevere

    IV.   That when we live no more, we may live ever

    A. I
    B. I, II
    C. I, II, III
    D. All of the above

Questions 21–25 are based on the following excerpt from the final chapter of Charles Dickens' Great Expectations.

Estella was the next to break the silence that ensued between us.

"I have very often hoped and intended to come back, but have been prevented by many circumstances. Poor, poor old place!"

The silvery mist was touched with the first rays of the moonlight, and the same rays touched the tears that dropped from her eyes. Not knowing that I saw them, and setting herself to get the better of them, she said quietly:

"Were you wondering, as you walked along, how it came to be left in this condition?"

"Yes, Estella."

"The ground belongs to me. It is the only possession I have not relinquished. Everything else has gone from me, little by little, but I have kept this. It was the subject of the only determined resistance I made in all the wretched years."

"Is it to be built on?"

"At last it is. I came here to take leave of it before its change. And you," she said, in a voice of touching interest to a wanderer, "you live abroad still?"

"Still."

"And do well, I am sure?"

"I work pretty hard for a sufficient living, and therefore—Yes, I do well."

"I have often thought of you," said Estella.

"Have you?"

"Of late, very often. There was a long hard time when I kept far from me, the remembrance of what I had thrown away when I was quite ignorant of its worth. But, since my duty has not been incompatible with the admission of that remembrance, I have given it a place in my heart."

"You have always held your place in my heart," I answered.

And we were silent again, until she spoke.

"I little thought," said Estella, "that I should take leave of you in taking leave of this spot. I am very glad to do so."

"Glad to part again, Estella? To me, parting is a painful thing. To me, the remembrance of our last parting has been ever mournful and painful."

"But you said to me," returned Estella, very earnestly, "'God bless you, God forgive you!' And if you could say that to me then, you will not hesitate to say that to me now—now, when suffering has been stronger than all other teaching, and has taught me to understand what your heart used to be. I have been bent and broken, but—I hope—into a better shape. Be as considerate and good to me as you were, and tell me we are friends."

"We are friends," said I, rising and bending over her, as she rose from the bench.

"And will continue friends apart," said Estella.

GO ON TO THE NEXT PAGE

I took her hand in mine, and we went out of the ruined place; and, as the morning mists had risen long ago when I first left the forge, so the evening mists were rising now, and in all the broad expanse of tranquil light they showed to me, I saw no shadow of another parting from her.

21. Dickens' concluding line of *Great Expectations* includes imagery of evening mists, tranquil light, and no shadow when Estella parted from Pip. Which of the following best summarizes the author's meaning in the closing of the novel?

   A. Pip will always regret losing Estella.
   B. The dark mists, the evening, and the shadow signify the anger Pip still holds for Estella.
   C. Pip is at peace with his relationship with Estella and can let her go.
   D. Pip had great expectations for his home and Estella that never came to fruition.

22. The house that is referred to in this excerpt is known as _____ House in *Great Expectations*.

   A. Tara
   B. Satis
   C. Havisham
   D. Bleak

23. This final chapter of *Great Expectations* is best known as which of the following?

   A. Denouement
   B. Climax
   C. Suspense
   D. Plot

24. Which of the following is the correct MLA-format citation for the book *Great Expectations*?

   A. Dickens, C. Great expectations. New York: Random House, 1907. Print.
   B. Dickens, C. (1907). <u>Great Expectations.</u> New York: Random House. Print.
   C. Dickens, Charles. *Great Expectations*. New York: Random House, 1907. Print.
   D. Dickens, Charles. *Great expectations.* New York; Random House, 1907. Print.

25. Which of the following is the correct APA-format citation for the book *Great Expectations*?

   A. Charles Dickens, <u>Great Expectations.</u> New York: Random House, 1907.
   B. Dickens, C. (1907). *Great expectations.* New York: Random House.
   C. Dickens, C. (1907). *Great Expectations.* New York: Random House
   D. Dickens, Charles. (1907). *Great expectations.* New York: Random House.

26. Which of the following lines from a Robert Louis Stevenson poem do NOT contain an example of onomatopoeia?

   I. The squalling cat and the squeaking mouse,
   II. The howling dog by the door of the house,
   III. The bat that lies in bed at noon,
   IV. All love to be out by the light of the moon.

   A. II, III, IV
   B. III, IV
   C. I, II
   D. All of the above

GO ON TO THE NEXT PAGE

Questions 27 and 28 are based on the following excerpt from a Shakespearean work, which you will be asked to identify below.

I have heard that guilty creatures sitting at a play
Have, by the very cunning of the scene,
Been struck so to the soul that presently
They have proclaimed their malefactions.

27. Which of the following Shakespearean tragedies, identified by the excerpt above, contains a play within a play in which the villainous king is invited to *The Mousetrap* to see a reenactment of the murder of his brother?

    A. *Hamlet*
    B. *Macbeth*
    C. *Julius Caesar*
    D. *King Richard III*

28. Which villainous character from this work is meant to proclaim his "malefactions"?

    A. Polonius
    B. Macbeth
    C. Claudius
    D. Caesar

Questions 29–31 are based on the following excerpt from the Declaration of Independence.

When in the Course of human events, it becomes necessary for one people to dissolve the political bands which have connected them with another, and to assume among the powers of the earth, the separate and equal situation to which the Laws of Nature and of Nature's God entitle them, a decent respect to the opinions of mankind requires that they should declare the causes which impel them to the separation.

29. Which of the following authors wrote the first draft of the Declaration of Independence?

    A. George Washington
    B. Thomas Jefferson
    C. Patrick Henry
    D. John Hancock

30. Which of the following best describes the meaning of the phrase "to dissolve the political bands which have connected them with another"?

    A. To seek a resolution to the political nature of a conflict
    B. To sever political ties with England
    C. To seek a change in the political structure of the homeland
    D. To seek religious freedom

31. The phrase "a decent respect to the opinions of mankind" works persuasively because it appeals to the reader's sense of _____.

    A. audience
    B. propriety
    C. rationale
    D. manhood

GO ON TO THE NEXT PAGE

Questions 32–34 are based on the following passage from Gulliver's Travels *by Jonathan Swift.*

We arrived at Lisbon, Nov. 5, 1715. At our landing, the captain forced me to cover myself with his cloak, to prevent the rabble from crowding about me. I was conveyed to his own house; and at my earnest request, he led me up to the highest room backwards. I conjured him to "conceal from all persons what I had told him of the Houyhnhnms; because the least hint of such a story would not only draw numbers of people to see me, but probably put me in danger of being imprisoned, or burnt by the Inquisition." The captain persuaded me to accept a suit of clothes newly made; but I would not suffer the tailor to take my measure; however, Don Pedro being almost of my size, they fitted me well enough. He accoutred me with other necessaries, all new, which I aired for twenty-four hours before I would use them.

32. Which of the following best describes this excerpt from *Gulliver's Travels*?

    A. Realistic fiction
    B. Lyrical poetry
    C. Prose in comparison-and-contrast structure
    D. Prose in chronological sequence

33. Which of the following best describes the meaning of the phrase "would not suffer the tailor to take my measure"?

    A. Because of Gulliver's personality, he does not have the patience for the tailor.
    B. Due to Gulliver's size, the tailor would not be equipped to prepare a suit for Gulliver.
    C. Gulliver did not want the tailor to go to the trouble of measuring him.
    D. The tailor would suffer if he took Gulliver's measurement.

34. In which of the following periods was *Gulliver's Travels* written and first published?

    A. Early 1600s
    B. Early 1700s
    C. Early 1800s
    D. Early 1900s

35. If a student makes several errors like those in the following sentence, the teacher should plan for more instruction in _____.

    One sunny morning sixty-seven years ago Southern New England was going well until everything changed.

    A. verb tense
    B. syntax
    C. paraphrasing
    D. comma usage

36. Each of the following pairs are homophones, EXCEPT

    A. sell/cell
    B. read/read
    C. waist/waste
    D. witch/which

37. Which of the following is the best example of a rhetorical question?

    A. Can you help me locate the main office?
    B. Do you need anything else to help make your lesson more effective?
    C. Do we really expect that schools will be funded by property taxes alone?
    D. Do you think you will pass the Praxis English Subject Assessment test?

GO ON TO THE NEXT PAGE

38. One phonological feature of African American Vernacular English (also known as Black English) is
_____.

    A. the use of sporting expressions such as "bowled over" to mean "taken by surprise" and "football" to mean "soccer"

    B. the pronunciation of the final *-ng* in one-syllable words: *sing* becomes *sin* or *ring* becomes *rin*

    C. the pronunciation of the final *-ng* in two-syllable words: *wedding* becomes *weddin* or *nothing* becomes *nuffin*

    D. the use of the word *ja* in place of the word *yes,* as in, "You're alright, ja?"

39. In the quote "To err is human; to forgive divine," which of the following rhetorical devices is used?

    A. Persuasion

    B. Rhetorical question

    C. Parallel structure

    D. Emotive language

40. Abraham Lincoln is credited as having said, "You can fool some of the people all of the time, and all of the people some of the time, but you cannot fool all of the people all of the time." Which of the following rhetorical devices was President Lincoln using?

    A. Simile

    B. Hyperbole

    C. Metaphor

    D. Repetition

Questions 41 and 42 are based on this excerpt from "O Captain! My Captain!" by Walt Whitman.

O Captain! my Captain! our fearful trip is done,
The ship has weather'd every rack, the prize we sought is won,
The port is near, the bells I hear, the people all exulting,
While follow eyes the steady keel, the vessel grim and daring;
But O heart! heart! heart!
O the bleeding drops of red,
Where on the deck my Captain lies,
Fallen cold and dead.

41. In the first line of this stanza, which poetic device is used?

    A. Apostrophe

    B. Rhyme

    C. Hubris

    D. Irony

42. Who is memorialized in this Whitman poem?

    A. Lincoln

    B. Keating

    C. Browning

    D. Washington

GO ON TO THE NEXT PAGE

43. During which period did the British Romantics such as Keats, Shelley, and Byron write?

    A. 1660–1700
    B. 1780–1840
    C. 1880–1930
    D. 1900–2000

Questions 44–46 are based on this excerpt from William Shakespeare's "Sonnet 18."

Shall I compare thee to a summer's day?
Thou art more lovely and more temperate:
Rough winds do shake the darling buds of May,
And summer's lease hath all too short a date:
Sometime too hot the eye of heaven shines,
And often is his gold complexion dimm'd;
And every fair from fair sometime declines,
By chance, or nature's changing course untrimm'd;
But thy eternal summer shall not fade,
Nor lose possession of that fair thou ow'st,
Nor shall death brag thou wander'st in his shade,
When in eternal lines to time thou grow'st;
So long as men can breathe, or eyes can see,
So long lives this, and this gives life to thee.

44. Which of the following is another name for this Shakespearean sonnet?

    A. Ode
    B. Elegy
    C. Epic poem
    D. Lyric poem

45. Which of the following describe the metrics of Shakespeare's "Sonnet 18"?

    I.   14 lines
    II.   Iambic pentameter
    III.   Approximately 10 syllables per line
    IV.   Rhyming couplet

    A. I
    B. II
    C. I, II, III
    D. All of the above

46. Which of the following best describes this sonnet's rhyme scheme?

    A. BABA; DCDC; FEFE; GG
    B. ABAB; CDCD; EFEF; GG
    C. AABB; CCDD; EEFF; GG
    D. Three quatrains and two couplets

GO ON TO THE NEXT PAGE

Questions 47 and 48 are based on the following excerpt from Don Quixote.

So then, his armour being furbished, his morion turned into a helmet, his hack christened, and he himself confirmed, he came to the conclusion that nothing more was needed now but to look out for a lady to be in love with; for a knight-errant without love was like a tree without leaves or fruit, or a body without a soul. As he said to himself, "If, for my sins, or by my good fortune, I come across some giant hereabouts, a common occurrence with knights-errant, and overthrow him in one onslaught, or cleave him asunder to the waist, or, in short, vanquish and subdue him, will it not be well to have some one I may send him to as a present, that he may come in and fall on his knees before my sweet lady, and in a humble, submissive voice say, 'I am the giant Caraculiambro, lord of the island of Malindrania, vanquished in single combat by the never sufficiently extolled knight Don Quixote of La Mancha, who has commanded me to present myself before your Grace, that your Highness dispose of me at your pleasure'?"

47. The phrase "for a knight-errant without love was like a tree without leaves or fruit, or a body without a soul" includes which of the following literary devices?

   A. Rhetorical question
   B. Personification
   C. Paradox
   D. Simile

48. Who is the author of *Don Quixote*?

   A. Escobar
   B. Achebe
   C. Cervantes
   D. More

Question 49 is based on this haiku by Raizan.

You rice-field maidens!
The only things not muddy
Are the songs you sing.

49. Haiku is often written in 17 syllables with three lines divided into _____.

   A. 5, 7, 5 syllables
   B. 3, 7, 7 syllables
   C. 5, 7, 5 words
   D. 5, 7, 7 words

50. Which of the following is best described as a cliché?

   A. You can't teach an old dog new tricks.
   B. My grandmother passed away last April.
   C. The Holocaust victims were executed in a concentration camp.
   D. Agent Orange was a chemical used during the Vietnam War.

GO ON TO THE NEXT PAGE

Questions 51 and 52 are based on the following Thomas Hardy poem, "To a Lady."

Now that my page upcloses, doomed, maybe,
Never to press thy cosy cushions more,
Or wake thy ready Yeas as heretofore,
Or stir thy gentle vows of faith in me:

Knowing thy natural receptivity,
I figure that, as flambeaux banish eve,
My sombre image, warped by insidious heave
Of those less forthright, must lose place in thee.

So be it. I have borne such. Let thy dreams
Of me and mine diminish day by day,
And yield their space to shine of smugger things;
Till I shape to thee but in fitful gleams,
And then in far and feeble visitings,
And then surcease. Truth will be truth alway.

51. The poet's use of the word *upcloses* indicates which of the following meanings?

    A. His feelings have died.
    B. He is up close and personal with this woman.
    C. His book is complete.
    D. His relationship is coming to an end.

52. Which of the following rhetorical devices does Hardy use in the last line of this poem?

    A. Rhetorical question
    B. Repetition
    C. Extended metaphor
    D. Contrast

53. Which of the following lines contains an allusion?

    A. Men are April when they woo, December when they wed.
    B. Knaves and robbers can obtain only what was before possessed by others.
    C. Town Manager Kern is a "man for all seasons."
    D. The couple had a bliss-filled marriage.

GO ON TO THE NEXT PAGE

Questions 54 and 55 are based on the following excerpt from The Scarlet Letter.

The effect of the symbol—or rather, of the position in respect to society that was indicated by it—on the mind of Hester Prynne herself, was powerful and peculiar. All the light and graceful foliage of her character had been withered up by this red-hot brand, and had long ago fallen away, leaving a bare and harsh outline, which might have been repulsive, had she possessed friends or companions to be repelled by it.

54. Which of the following best describes the main conflict in *The Scarlet Letter*?

    A. Person versus nature

    B. Person versus person

    C. Person versus society

    D. Person versus fate

55. Which of the following authors wrote *The Scarlet Letter*?

    A. Edwards

    B. Emerson

    C. Hawthorne

    D. Miller

Questions 56 and 57 are based on this final scene from Henrik Ibsen's play A Doll's House.

NORA: That's right. Now it is all over. I have put the keys here. The maids know all about everything in the house—better than I do. Tomorrow, after I have left her, Christine will come here and pack up my own things that I brought with me from home. I will have them sent after me.

HELMER: All over! All over!—Nora, shall you never think of me again?

NORA: I know I shall often think of you, the children, and this house.

HELMER: May I write to you, Nora?

NORA: No—never. You must not do that.

HELMER: But at least let me send you—

NORA: Nothing—nothing—

HELMER: Let me help you if you are in want.

NORA: No. I can receive nothing from a stranger.

HELMER: Nora—can I never be anything more than a stranger to you?

NORA: *(Taking her bag)* Ah, Torvald, the most wonderful thing of all would have to happen.

HELMER: Tell me what that would be!

NORA: Both you and I would have to be so changed that—. Oh, Torvald, I don't believe any longer in wonderful things happening.

HELMER: But I will believe in it. Tell me! So changed that—?

NORA: That our life together would be a real wedlock. Goodbye. *(She goes out through the hall.)*

GO ON TO THE NEXT PAGE

HELMER: *(Sinks down on a chair at the door and buries his face in his hands)* Nora! Nora! *(Looks around, and rises.)* Empty. She is gone. *(A hope flashes across his mind.)* The most wonderful thing of all—?

(The sound of a door shutting is heard from below.)

56. Ibsen's play *A Doll's House* popularized which of the following types of drama?

   A. Realist
   B. Romantic
   C. Existentialist
   D. Neoclassical

57. The character Nora possesses which of the following character traits at some point in the play?

   I.   Silly
   II. Feminist
   III. Serious
   IV. Open-minded

   A. I, II
   B. I, III
   C. III, IV
   D. All of the above

58. From which of the following works by the playwright Oscar Wilde is the excerpt below?

Morning-room in Algernon's flat in Half-Moon Street. The room is luxuriously and artistically furnished. The sound of a piano is heard in the adjoining room.

(Lane is arranging afternoon tea on the table, and after the music has ceased, Algernon enters.)

ALGERNON: Did you hear what I was playing, Lane?

LANE: I didn't think it polite to listen, sir.

ALGERNON: I'm sorry for that, for your sake. I don't play accurately—anyone can play accurately—but I play with wonderful expression. As far as the piano is concerned, sentiment is my forte. I keep science for Life.

LANE: Yes, sir.

ALGERNON: And, speaking of the science of Life, have you got the cucumber sandwiches cut for Lady Bracknell?

LANE: Yes, sir. *(Hands them on a salver.)*

ALGERNON: *(Inspects them, takes two, and sits down on the sofa.)* Oh! … by the way, Lane, I see from your book that on Thursday night, when Lord Shoreman and Mr. Worthing were dining with me, eight bottles of champagne are entered as having been consumed.

LANE: Yes, sir; eight bottles and a pint.

ALGERNON: Why is it that at a bachelor's establishment the servants invariably drink the champagne? I ask merely for information.

   A. *An Ideal Husband*
   B. *Flowers for Algernon*
   C. *The Importance of Being Earnest*
   D. *Utopia*

GO ON TO THE NEXT PAGE

Questions 59 and 60 are based on this final excerpt from "The Fall of the House of Usher."

From that chamber, and from that mansion, I fled aghast. The storm was still abroad in all its wrath as I found myself crossing the old causeway. Suddenly there shot along the path a wild light, and I turned to see whence a gleam so unusual could have issued; for the vast house and its shadows were alone behind me. The radiance was that of the full, setting, and blood-red moon which now shone vividly through that once barely-discernible fissure of which I have before spoken as extending from the roof of the building, in a zigzag direction, to the base. While I gazed, this fissure rapidly widened—there came a fierce breath of the whirlwind—the entire orb of the satellite burst at once upon my sight—my brain reeled as I saw the mighty walls rushing asunder—there was a long tumultuous shouting sound like the voice of a thousand waters—and the deep and dank tarn at my feet closed sullenly and silently over the fragments of the "House of Usher."

59. Which literary device is used in the excerpt above?

    A. Epitaph

    B. Cliché

    C. Euphemism

    D. Personification

60. Who is the author of "The Fall of the House of Usher"?

    A. Poe

    B. Wilde

    C. Dickens

    D. Hardy

Questions 61 and 62 are based on the following excerpt from the play Pygmalion *by George Bernard Shaw.*

THE FLOWER GIRL: *(To Pickering, as he passes her)* Buy a flower, kind gentleman. I'm short for my lodging.

PICKERING: I really haven't any change. I'm sorry. *(He goes away.)*

HIGGINS: *(Shocked at girl's mendacity)* Liar. You said you could change half-a-crown.

THE FLOWER GIRL: *(Rising in desperation)* You ought to be stuffed with nails, you ought. *(Flinging the basket at his feet)* Take the whole blooming basket for sixpence.

(The church clock strikes the second quarter.)

HIGGINS: *(Hearing in it the voice of God, rebuking him for his Pharisaic want of charity to the poor girl)* A reminder. *(He raises his hat solemnly; then throws a handful of money into the basket and follows Pickering.)*

THE FLOWER GIRL: *(Picking up a half-crown)* Ah—ow—ooh! *(Picking up a couple of florins)* Aaah—ow—ooh! *(Picking up several coins)* Aaaaaah—ow—ooh! *(Picking up a half-sovereign)* Aasaaaaaaaaaah—ow—ooh!!!

FREDDY: *(Springing out of a taxicab)* Got one at last. Hallo! *(To the girl)* Where are the two ladies that were here?

THE FLOWER GIRL: They walked to the bus when the rain stopped.

FREDDY: And left me with a cab on my hands. Damnation!

GO ON TO THE NEXT PAGE

THE FLOWER GIRL: *(With grandeur)* Never you mind, young man. I'm going home in a taxi. *(She sails off to the cab. The driver puts his hand behind him and holds the door firmly shut against her. Quite understanding his mistrust, she shows him her handful of money.)* Eightpence ain't no object to me, Charlie. *(He grins and opens the door.)* Angel Court, Drury Lane, round the corner of Micklejohn's oil shop. Let's see how fast you can make her hop it. *(She gets in and pulls the door to with a slam as the taxicab starts.)*

FREDDY: Well, I'm dashed!

61. Which of the following is the primary setting of *Pygmalion*?

   A. Contemporary France
   B. Modern-day Africa
   C. Puritan times in New England
   D. Great Britain

62. After hearing the church bell, Higgins reflects that he may have expressed a "Pharisaic want of charity" toward the Flower Girl. Which of the following best defines the word Pharisaic in this play?

   A. A member of an ancient Jewish sect
   B. Hypocritically self-righteous
   C. Pragmatic
   D. A kinglike leader of ancient Egypt

Questions 63 and 64 are based on this excerpt from T. S. Eliot's poem "The Waste Land."

April is the cruelest month, breeding
Lilacs out of the dead land, mixing
Memory and desire, stirring
Dull roots with spring rain.
Winter kept us warm, covering
Earth in forgetful snow, feeding
A little life with dried tubers.

63. T. S. Eliot wrote this poem during which of the following periods?

   A. Nationalist period (1828–1836)
   B. Modern period (1900–1945)
   C. Colonial period (1630–1760)
   D. Puritan period (1625–1660)

64. Which of the following literary works does the excerpt above allude to?

   A. *Beowulf*
   B. *The Iliad*
   C. *Canterbury Tales*
   D. *War and Peace*

GO ON TO THE NEXT PAGE

Questions 65–69 are based on the following excerpt from William Shakespeare's Hamlet.

HAMLET: O that this too too sullied flesh would melt,
Thaw, and resolve itself into a dew!
Or that the Everlasting had not fixed
His canon 'gainst self-slaughter! O God, God,
How weary, stale, flat, and unprofitable
Seem to me all the uses of this world!
Fie on't, ah fie! 'tis an unweeded garden
That grows to seed; things rank and gross in nature
Possess it merely. That it should come to this!
But two months dead, nay, not so much, not two.
So excellent a king, that was to this
Hyperion to a satyr; so loving to my mother
That he might not beteem the winds of heaven
Visit her face too roughly. Heaven and earth,
Must I remember? Why, she would hang on him
As if increase of appetite had grown
By what it fed on.

65. Which of the following best describes the phrase "'tis an unweeded garden/That grows to seed"?

   A.   A simile comparing Hamlet to his mother
   B.   A metaphor comparing an unweeded garden to Denmark's ruin after the death of King Hamlet
   C.   A metaphor comparing Hamlet's appetite to a garden
   D.   A simile comparing the king's death to heaven and hell

66. To whom is Hamlet referring in the line "But two months dead, nay, not so much, not two"?

   A.   Fortinbras
   B.   Queen Gertrude
   C.   King Claudius
   D.   King Hamlet

67. Which of the following best describes *Hamlet*?

   A.   Comedy
   B.   Tragedy
   C.   History
   D.   Sonnet

68. This excerpt from *Hamlet* uses which of the following rhetorical devices?

   A.   Sarcasm
   B.   Praise
   C.   Appeal to emotion
   D.   Counterpoints

69. Which of the following is the best interpretation of the lines "...that was to this/Hyperion to a satyr..."?

   A.   It alludes to an entertainment industry giant.
   B.   It alludes to an incomplete poem by Keats.
   C.   It alludes to a star in the universe.
   D.   It alludes to the mythical god of the sun.

GO ON TO THE NEXT PAGE

70. The author of *Beowulf* is _____.

    A. Racine

    B. Socrates

    C. Ulysses

    D. Unknown

Question 71 is based on the following excerpt from Plato's The Republic.

The result, then, is that more plentiful and better-quality goods are more easily produced if each person does one thing for which he is naturally suited, does it at the right time, and is released from having to do any of the others.

71. Which of the following best summarizes Plato's point in this passage?

    A. Each person must do the work that fits his or her own strengths.

    B. Every man for himself.

    C. A philosopher must choose wisely.

    D. A farmer's work is never done.

72. Which of the following terms can be defined as using language persuasively or impressively?

    A. Personification

    B. Rhetoric

    C. Tone

    D. Point of view

73. Which of the following lines contains a simile?

    A. Mine eyes have seen the glory of the coming of the Lord:

    B. Woodman, spare that tree! Touch not a single bough!

    C. Away to the window I flew like a flash.

    D. My candle burns at both ends; it will not last the night;

74. The following poem by Edward Lear is known as a _____.

There was a Young Lady whose eyes,
Were unique as to colour and size;
When she opened them wide,
People all turned aside,
And started away in surprise.

    A. ballad

    B. canto

    C. ode

    D. limerick

75. Which of the following authors wrote *The Catcher in the Rye*?

    A. Alex Haley

    B. John Updike

    C. J. D. Salinger

    D. Sylvia Plath

GO ON TO THE NEXT PAGE

76. In which of the following periods was *The Catcher in the Rye* written?

    A. 20th-century British literature

    B. Contemporary U.S. literature

    C. American Renaissance period

    D. British Victorian period

Questions 77 and 78 are based on the following excerpt from the poem "The Love Song of J. Alfred Prufrock" by T. S. Eliot.

No! I am not Prince Hamlet, nor was meant to be;
Am an attendant lord, one that will do
To swell a progress, start a scene or two,
Advise the prince; no doubt, an easy tool,
Deferential, glad to be of use,
Politic, cautious, and meticulous;
Full of high sentence, but a bit obtuse;
At times, indeed, almost ridiculous—
Almost, at times, the Fool.

I grow old…I grow old…
I shall wear the bottoms of my trousers rolled.

Shall I part my hair behind? Do I dare to eat a peach?
I shall wear white flannel trousers, and walk upon the beach.
I have heard the mermaids singing, each to each.

I do not think that they will sing to me.

77. Which of the following is the best interpretation of the poet's meaning in this excerpt?

    A. Prufrock is paralyzed to act; specifically, to eat a peach.

    B. Prufrock is contemplating murder, like Hamlet.

    C. Prufrock is afraid of growing old.

    D. Prufrock is a man in love with a mermaid.

78. Modernist poets such as T. S. Eliot expressed _____.

    A. the desire to turn to nature for inspiration

    B. the romantic hopes of poets during this time period

    C. the fundamental rights of humanity

    D. the fragile nature of the human psyche in the 20th century

79. A high school English teacher wants to effectively open a lesson on *King Lear*. Which of the following is most likely to motivate adolescent readers?

    A. An analysis of the play by a famous English author

    B. A homework assignment to read Act I

    C. A round-robin read-aloud in which students take turns reading the play without time to practice

    D. A discussion about seeking justice in students' lives, personal experiences, and world events

GO ON TO THE NEXT PAGE

80. Which of the following cognates is most DIFFERENT in meaning and usage from its original Latin root?

    A. Facile

    B. Facilitate

    C. Faction

    D. Facility

81. Which of the following are examples of correlative conjunctions?

    A. and/but

    B. not only/but also

    C. after/before

    D. since/then

82. Which of the following is an appropriate revision-stage activity during the writing process?

    A. Peer conferencing

    B. Peer editing

    C. Teacher editing

    D. Prewriting

83. Which of the following is the best definition of a writing rubric?

    A. A frame story

    B. A writing scoring guide

    C. A description of a writing assignment

    D. A part of a manuscript or book

84. Which of the following correctly cites a source using MLA-format guidelines?

    A. Golding wrote in his opening line of Lord of the Flies, "The boy with fair hair lowered himself down the last few feet of rock and began to pick his way toward the lagoon" (7).

    B. Golding wrote in his opening line of *Lord of the Flies*, "The boy with fair hair lowered himself down the last few feet of rock and began to pick his way toward the lagoon" (7).

    C. Golding wrote in his opening line of <u>Lord of the Flies</u>, "The boy with fair hair lowered himself down the last few feet of rock and began to pick his way toward the lagoon" (Golding, 7).

    D. Golding wrote in his opening line of *Lord of the Flies*, "The boy with fair hair lowered himself down the last few feet of rock and began to pick his way toward the lagoon." (Golding, 7)

85. Which of the following plays by Harold Pinter is seen as an extended metaphor for society in the 1950s, with Stanley representing "angry young men" and his antagonists representing repressive conformists?

    A. *The Birthday Party*

    B. *The Homecoming*

    C. *A Doll's House*

    D. *Waiting for Godot*

GO ON TO THE NEXT PAGE

86. Consider the following sentence:

The Commander's conceited wife rambled on about her upcoming move from one military base to another and was heard to say, "The move is eminent."

The wife's error is known as (a) _____.

- **A.** cliché
- **B.** slang
- **C.** malapropism
- **D.** metaphor

87. Which of the following authors and works represents the Colonial period of literature?

- **A.** Anne Bradstreet's *The Tenth Muse Lately Sprung Up in America*
- **B.** Thomas Hardy's "Winter Words"
- **C.** Washington Irving's "Rip van Winkle"
- **D.** Ben Franklin's "The Contrast"

88. Which of the following characters is the protagonist of the work cited?

- **A.** Claudius in *Hamlet*
- **B.** Nanny in *Their Eyes Were Watching God*
- **C.** Chillingsworth in *The Scarlet Letter*
- **D.** Odysseus in *The Odyssey*

89. Which of the following is the definition of the denouement in a literary work?

- **A.** The conflict or problem
- **B.** The solution or outcome
- **C.** The setting, such as time and place
- **D.** The plot or events in the story

90. Which of the following strategies is used in this excerpt from W. E. B. Du Bois' "Advice to a Black Schoolgirl"?

Ignorance is a cure for nothing. Get the very best training possible and the doors of opportunity will fly open before you as they are flying before thousands of your fellows. On the other hand every time a colored person neglects an opportunity, it makes it more difficult for others of the race to get such an opportunity. Do you want to cut off the chances of the boys and girls of tomorrow?

- **A.** Appeal to emotion
- **B.** Appeal to authority
- **C.** Extended metaphor
- **D.** Counterpoints

GO ON TO THE NEXT PAGE

Questions 91–94 are based on the following excerpt from Theodore Roosevelt's speech "The Strenuous Life," given before the Hamilton Club, Chicago, Illinois, on April 10, 1899.

...I preach to you, then, my countrymen, that our country calls not for the life of ease but for the life of strenuous endeavor. The twentieth century looms before us big with the fate of many nations. If we stand idly by, if we seek merely swollen, slothful ease and ignoble peace, if we shrink from the hard contests where men must win at hazard of their lives and at the risk of all they hold dear, then the bolder and stronger peoples will pass us by, and will win for themselves the domination of the world. Let us therefore boldly face the life of strife, resolute to do our duty well and manfully; resolute to uphold righteousness by deed and by word; resolute to be both honest and brave, to serve high ideals, yet to use practical methods. Above all, let us shrink from no strife, moral or physical, within or without the nation, provided we are certain that the strife is justified, for it is only through strife, through hard and dangerous endeavor, that we shall ultimately win the goal of true national greatness.

91. Roosevelt alludes to what time period in American history in the opening lines of his speech?

    A. Western Expansion and Reform

    B. The Depression and World War II

    C. The Great War and Jazz Age

    D. Civil War

92. Roosevelt uses which of the following rhetorical devices in the following line: "If we stand idly by, if we seek merely swollen, ... if we shrink from the hard contests where men must win at hazard of their lives and at the risk of all they hold dear ..."?

    A. Rhetorical question

    B. Understatement

    C. Oxymoron

    D. Anaphora

93. Which of the following best describes the rhetorical strategy Roosevelt uses in the line "Let us therefore boldly face the life of strife, resolute to do our duty well and manfully; ..."?

    A. Alliteration

    B. Allusion

    C. Prose

    D. Appeal to emotion

94. The sentence "The twentieth century looms before us big with the fate of many nations" can be described as which of the following sentence types?

    A. Single subject, single predicate

    B. Compound subject, single predicate

    C. Independent clause with two or more phrases

    D. Compound subject, compound predicate

95. When a story is written from an omniscient point of view, which of the following statements is true?

    A. The narrator compares two unlike things.

    B. The story is told from the point of view of one of the characters.

    C. The story is told by someone outside of the story.

    D. The narrator is free to tell the story from any and all characters' points of view.

GO ON TO THE NEXT PAGE

96. A poem written in a quintet contains _____.

    A. a five-line stanza

    B. five stanzas

    C. five syllables

    D. parts for five actors

Questions 97–99 are based on a speech given on November 19, 1863, at the dedication of the National Cemetery in Gettysburg, Pennsylvania.

Four score and seven years ago our fathers brought forth on this continent, a new nation, conceived in Liberty, and dedicated to the proposition that all men are created equal.

Now we are engaged in a great civil war, testing whether that nation, or any nation so conceived and so dedicated, can long endure. We are met on a great battlefield of that war. We have come to dedicate a portion of that field, as a final resting place for those who here gave their lives that that nation might live. It is altogether fitting and proper that we should do this.

But, in a larger sense, we cannot dedicate—we cannot consecrate—we cannot hallow—this ground. The brave men, living and dead, who struggled here, have consecrated it, far above our poor power to add or detract. The world will little note, nor long remember what we say here, but it can never forget what they did here. It is for us the living, rather, to be dedicated here to the unfinished work, which they who fought here have thus far so nobly advanced. It is rather for us to be here dedicated to the great task remaining before us—that from these honored dead we take increased devotion to that cause for which they gave the last full measure of devotion—that we here highly resolve that these dead shall not have died in vain—that this nation, under God, shall have a new birth of freedom—and that government of the people, by the people, for the people, shall not perish from the earth.

97. The orator's use of the phrase "four score and seven years ago" exemplifies which of the following rhetorical features?

    A. Tone

    B. Diction

    C. Attitude

    D. Sarcasm

98. The author's description of the National Cemetery as "a final resting place" is known as a(n) _____.

    A. antithesis

    B. epistrophe

    C. euphemism

    D. metaphor

99. Who was the orator of this address?

    A. Lincoln

    B. Kennedy

    C. Roosevelt

    D. Jackson

100. Which of the following best describes the initial setting of *The Grapes of Wrath*?

    A. 1900s Industrial Revolution in the Midwestern United States

    B. 1930s Dust Bowl in the Midwestern United States

    C. 1890s Gold Rush

    D. 1930s pre–World War I England and the United States

GO ON TO THE NEXT PAGE

101. Who is the author of *The Grapes of Wrath*?

    A. Michener
    B. Hemingway
    C. Orwell
    D. Steinbeck

102. In which of the following literary periods was *Le Morte d'Arthur* written?

    A. Middle English period
    B. Elizabethan period
    C. Romantic period
    D. Victorian period

Questions 103 and 104 are based on the following excerpt from Sonnets from the Portuguese.

Beloved, thou hast brought me many flowers
Plucked in the garden, all the summer through,
And winter, and it seemed as if they grew
In this close room, nor missed the sun and showers.
So, in the like name of that love of ours,
Take back these thoughts which here unfolded too,
And which on warm and cold days I withdrew
From my heart's ground. Indeed, those beds and bowers
Be overgrown with bitter weeds and rue,
And wait thy weeding; yet here's eglantine,
Here's ivy!—take them, as I used to do
Thy flowers, and keep them where they shall not pine.
Instruct thine eyes to keep their colours true,
And tell thy soul, their roots are left in mine.

103. Which of the following metric is used in the sonnet above?

    A. Trochaic pentameter
    B. Iambic quintet
    C. Iambic pentameter
    D. Anapestic pentameter

104. Which of the following authors wrote *Sonnets from the Portuguese*?

    A. Emily Dickinson
    B. Elizabeth Barrett Browning
    C. T. S. Eliot
    D. George Eliot

GO ON TO THE NEXT PAGE

Questions 105 and 106 are based on the following excerpt from D. H. Lawrence's essay "Nathaniel Hawthorne and The Scarlet Letter."

Nathaniel Hawthorne writes romance.

And what's romance? Usually, a nice little tale where you have everything *As You Like It,* where rain never wets your jacket and gnats never bite your nose and it's always daisy-time. *As You Like It* and *Forest Lovers,* etc. *Morte d'Arthur.*

Hawthorne obviously isn't this kind of romanticist: though nobody has muddy boots in *The Scarlet Letter,* either.

But there is more to it. *The Scarlet Letter* isn't a pleasant, pretty romance. It is a sort of parable, an earthly story with a hellish meaning.

All the time there is this split in the American art and art-consciousness. On the top it is as nice as pie, goody-goody and lovey-dovey. Like Hawthorne being such a blue-eyed darling, in life, and Longfellow and the rest such sucking-doves. Hawthorne's wife said she 'never saw him in time,' which doesn't mean she saw him too late.

105. Hawthorne's *The Scarlet Letter* is a parable. Which of the following is the best definition of a parable?

    A. A brief story that illustrates a point

    B. A story with a contradictory message or statement

    C. A fictional work meant to tell a story

    D. A story meant to teach a moral lesson

106. Longfellow and Hawthorne were considered _____.

    A. existentialists

    B. transcendentalists

    C. communists

    D. anarchists

107. Which of the following works is from the Middle English period (1066–1550)?

    A. Chaucer's *Canterbury Tales*

    B. Shakespeare's sonnets

    C. Goethe's *Faust*

    D. Homer's *The Iliad*

108. Dorothy Parker's poem "Guinevere at Her Fireside" is from her collection of poems titled _____.

    A. *The Arthurian Legend*

    B. *Enough Rope*

    C. *Death and Taxes*

    D. *The New Yorker Collection*

109. Langston Hughes wrote his poem "Po' Boy Blues" using _____.

    A. iambic pentameter

    B. free verse

    C. authentic setting and meaning

    D. idioms and dialect from African American Vernacular English

GO ON TO THE NEXT PAGE

110. Tory participates in basketball, softball, and playing the piano.

This sentence can be improved by _____.

A. adding "playing" before basketball
B. deleting "playing the" and adding "lessons" after piano
C. deleting "playing"
D. deleting the comma after "softball"

111. Consider the following sentences:

Jimmy and Austin were the highest scorers in the basketball game. He enjoyed the recognition of his accomplishment from the coach and his teammates.

Which of the following grammatical errors is the primary problem in the second sentence above?

A. Pronoun reference
B. Subject-verb agreement
C. Verb tense
D. Coordinating pronoun

112. Sociolinguistics is the study of language as it relates to _____.

A. semantics
B. social skills
C. society
D. psychology

113. Which of the following activities is LEAST likely to occur during the publishing stage of the writing process?

A. Examining a book to learn about the features of the publication
B. Preparing a cover and title page
C. Using the Internet to search for writing ideas
D. Writing an acknowledgment section

114. In which of the following sources is a reader MOST likely to find an aphorism from Benjamin Franklin?

A. Dictionary
B. Bartlett's *Familiar Quotations*
C. Encyclopedia
D. Thesaurus

115. Which of the following is an appropriate greeting in a business letter?

A. Dear Sir or Madam:
B. Dear Sir or Madam,
C. Dear Mary,
D. Hi, Mr. Stevens:

GO ON TO THE NEXT PAGE

116. Which of the following activities is MOST likely to occur in the prewriting stage of the writing process?

  A. Listing topics
  B. Sharing a draft with a peer
  C. Reading the draft to the teacher
  D. Correcting spelling errors

117. The word *restroom* is a(n) _____ for the toilet room.

  A. elegy
  B. anapestic
  C. aphorism
  D. euphemism

118. Concrete poetry is a poetic form in which _____.

  A. formal structure is foremost
  B. stanzas and couplets are used
  C. shape and visual effects are emphasized
  D. onomatopoeia is emphasized

119. *Canto* is best defined as _____.

  A. proficient use of the dictionary
  B. an exact quotation
  C. disregard for meaning with an emphasis on pronunciation
  D. the main section of a long poem

120. The emotional atmosphere created by the author is known as the _____ of a literary work.

  A. setting
  B. mood
  C. plot
  D. denouement

121. Which of the following pairs of characters appears in Shakespeare's *A Midsummer Night's Dream*?

  A. Romeo and Juliet
  B. Hermia and Robin Goodfellow
  C. Caesar and Calpurnia
  D. Gertrude and Claudius

122. *The Giver, 1984,* and *The Lord of the Rings* can all be classified as belonging to which of the following genres?

  A. Realistic fiction
  B. Poetry
  C. Historical fiction
  D. Science fiction/fantasy

123. The setting of *Fahrenheit 451* is_____.

  A. 1984
  B. the 21st century
  C. the 24th century
  D. the 1950s

GO ON TO THE NEXT PAGE

Questions 124 and 125 are based on the poem "Jabberwocky."

'Twas brillig, and the slithy toves
Did gyre and gimble in the wade;
All mimsy were the borogoves,
And the mome raths outgrabe.

"Beware the Jabberwock, my son!
The jaws that bite, the claws that catch!
Beware the Jubjub bird, and shun
The frumious Bandersnatch!"

He took his vorpal sword in hand:
Long time the manxome foe he sought—
So rested he by the Tumtum tree.
And stood awhile in thought.

And as in uffish thought he stood,
The Jabberwock, with eyes of flame,
Came wiffling through the tulgey wood,
And burbled as it came!

One, two! One, two! And through and through
The vorpal blade went snicker-snack!
He left it dead, and with its head
He went galumphing back.

"And hast thou slain the Jabberwock?
Come to my arms, my beamish boy!
O frabjous day! Callooh! Callay!"
He chortled in his joy.

'Twas brillig, and the slithy toves
Did gyre and gimble in the wabe;
All mimsy were the borogoves,
And the mome raths outgrabe.

124. Who is the author of "Jabberwocky"?

  A. e. e. cummings
  B. Lewis Carroll
  C. Edward Lear
  D. Ogden Nash

125. "Jabberwocky" was written during which of the following literary time periods?

  A. Old English
  B. Victorian
  C. Romantic
  D. Contemporary

GO ON TO THE NEXT PAGE

126. Tituba, a character in Arthur Miller's play *The Crucible,* says, "My Betty be hearty soon?" Which of the following best describes Tituba's use of language?

   A. Dialect
   B. Phonology
   C. Pragmatics
   D. Grammatical error

127. The following sentence is a _____ sentence.

   I look forward to teaching, and I plan to teach middle school English because I love literature.

   A. compound
   B. compound/complex
   C. complex
   D. simple

128. Which of the following best describes the beliefs of the Beat Generation in American literature?

   A. Knowledge can be arrived at not only through the senses, but also through intuition and contemplation of the internal spirit.
   B. The literary work's function is to report what happens, without comment or judgment.
   C. Literature helps identify the underlying causes for a person's actions or beliefs.
   D. Unchecked capitalism is destructive to the human spirit and antithetical to social equality.

129. Which of the following criteria should be used when evaluating Internet sources for a research paper?

   I.   Author
   II. Accuracy
   III. Purpose of the site
   IV. Access

   A. I
   B. I, II
   C. I, II, IV
   D. All of the above

130. When a writer considers the _____ for a piece, he or she considers who else will read it and what background knowledge the reader might need to understand the point of the writing.

   A. grade
   B. publisher
   C. location
   D. audience

IF YOU FINISH BEFORE TIME IS CALLED, CHECK YOUR WORK ON THIS SECTION ONLY. DO NOT WORK ON ANY OTHER SECTION IN THE TEST.

Constructed Response

Time: 30 minutes

2 questions

Constructed Response I: Interpreting Literature

Directions: Read the following poem, "To My Dear and Loving Husband" by Anne Bradstreet, carefully. Then discuss how Bradstreet uses metrics, alliteration, and parallelism in the poem. Be sure to cite at least THREE specific examples from the poem to support your points about Bradstreet's use of metrics, alliteration, and parallelism.

To My Dear and Loving Husband

If ever two were one, then surely we.
If ever man were loved by wife, then thee.
If ever wife was happy in a man,
Compare with me, ye women, if you can.
I prize thy love more than whole Mines of gold
Or all the riches that the East doth hold.
My love is such that rivers cannot quench,
Nor ought but love from thee, give recompense.
Thy love is such I can no way repay,
The heavens reward thee manifold, I pray.
Then while we live, in love let's so persevere
That when we live no more, we may live ever.

Constructed Response II: Rhetorical Analysis

Directions: This constructed-response question requires you to discuss the rhetorical elements of a piece of writing. Plan to spend approximately 15 minutes of your testing time on this question. Describe the major organizational and rhetorical features of this opening paragraph from Martin Luther King, Jr.'s March on Washington address. Refer directly to the excerpt to support your description of its organization.

Five score years ago, a great American, in whose symbolic shadow we stand, signed the Emancipation Proclamation. This momentous decree came as a great beacon light of hope to millions of Negro slaves who had been seared in the flames of withering injustice. It came as a joyous daybreak to end the long night of captivity.

But one hundred years later, we face the tragic fact that the Negro is still not free. One hundred years later, the life of the Negro is still sadly crippled by the manacles of segregation and the chains of discrimination. One hundred years later, the Negro lives on a lonely island of poverty in the midst of a vast ocean of material prosperity. One hundred years later, the Negro is still languished in the corners of American society and finds himself an exile in his own land. So we have come here today to dramatize an appalling condition.

IF YOU FINISH BEFORE TIME IS CALLED, CHECK YOUR WORK ON THIS SECTION ONLY. DO NOT WORK ON ANY OTHER SECTION IN THE TEST.

Answer Key for Selected Response

Question	Answer	Content Category	Where to Get More Help
1.	B	Reading and Literature	Chapter 3
2.	D	Reading and Literature	Chapter 3
3.	B	Reading and Literature	Chapter 3
4.	D	Reading and Literature	Chapter 3
5.	A	Reading and Literature	Chapter 3
6.	A	Language Use, Vocabulary, and Linguistics	Chapter 4
7.	B	Language Use, Vocabulary, and Linguistics	Chapter 4
8.	D	Writing, Speaking, and Listening	Chapter 5
9.	D	Writing, Speaking, and Listening	Chapter 5
10.	B	Writing, Speaking, and Listening	Chapter 5
11.	D	Writing, Speaking, and Listening	Chapter 5
12.	C	Writing, Speaking, and Listening	Chapter 5
13.	A	Reading and Literature	Chapter 3
14.	C	Reading and Literature	Chapter 3
15.	B	Reading and Literature	Chapter 3
16.	D	Reading and Literature	Chapter 3
17.	B	Reading and Literature	Chapter 3
18.	D	Reading and Literature	Chapter 3
19.	A	Reading and Literature	Chapter 3
20.	D	Reading and Literature	Chapter 3
21.	C	Language Use, Vocabulary, and Linguistics	Chapter 4
22.	B	Language Use, Vocabulary, and Linguistics	Chapter 4
23.	A	Writing, Speaking, and Listening	Chapter 5
24.	C	Writing, Speaking, and Listening	Chapter 5
25.	B	Writing, Speaking, and Listening	Chapter 5
26.	B	Writing, Speaking, and Listening	Chapter 5
27.	A	Reading and Literature	Chapter 3
28.	C	Reading and Literature	Chapter 3
29.	B	Reading and Literature	Chapter 3
30.	B	Reading and Literature	Chapter 3
31.	B	Reading and Literature	Chapter 3
32.	D	Reading and Literature	Chapter 3
33.	C	Reading and Literature	Chapter 3
34.	B	Reading and Literature	Chapter 3
35.	D	Language Use, Vocabulary, and Linguistics	Chapter 4

Question	Answer	Content Category	Where to Get More Help
36.	B	Language Use, Vocabulary, and Linguistics	Chapter 4
37.	C	Writing, Speaking, and Listening	Chapter 5
38.	C	Writing, Speaking, and Listening	Chapter 5
39.	C	Writing, Speaking, and Listening	Chapter 5
40.	D	Writing, Speaking, and Listening	Chapter 5
41.	A	Writing, Speaking, and Listening	Chapter 5
42.	A	Reading and Literature	Chapter 3
43.	B	Reading and Literature	Chapter 3
44.	D	Reading and Literature	Chapter 3
45.	D	Reading and Literature	Chapter 3
46.	B	Reading and Literature	Chapter 3
47.	D	Reading and Literature	Chapter 3
48.	C	Reading and Literature	Chapter 3
49.	A	Reading and Literature	Chapter 3
50.	A	Language Use, Vocabulary, and Linguistics	Chapter 4
51.	D	Language Use, Vocabulary, and Linguistics	Chapter 4
52.	B	Writing, Speaking, and Listening	Chapter 5
53.	C	Writing, Speaking, and Listening	Chapter 5
54.	C	Reading and Literature	Chapter 3
55.	C	Reading and Literature	Chapter 3
56.	A	Reading and Literature	Chapter 3
57.	D	Reading and Literature	Chapter 3
58.	C	Reading and Literature	Chapter 3
59.	D	Reading and Literature	Chapter 3
60.	A	Reading and Literature	Chapter 3
61.	D	Reading and Literature	Chapter 3
62.	B	Writing, Speaking, and Listening	Chapter 5
63.	B	Writing, Speaking, and Listening	Chapter 5
64.	C	Language Use, Vocabulary, and Linguistics	Chapter 4
65.	B	Language Use, Vocabulary, and Linguistics	Chapter 4
66.	D	Writing, Speaking, and Listening	Chapter 5
67.	B	Writing, Speaking, and Listening	Chapter 5
68.	C	Writing, Speaking, and Listening	Chapter 5
69.	D	Reading and Literature	Chapter 3
70.	D	Reading and Literature	Chapter 3
71.	A	Reading and Literature	Chapter 3

continued

Question	Answer	Content Category	Where to Get More Help
72.	B	Reading and Literature	Chapter 3
73.	C	Reading and Literature	Chapter 3
74.	D	Reading and Literature	Chapter 3
75.	C	Reading and Literature	Chapter 3
76.	B	Reading and Literature	Chapter 3
77.	A	Reading and Literature	Chapter 3
78.	D	Reading and Literature	Chapter 3
79.	D	Language Use, Vocabulary, and Linguistics	Chapter 4
80.	C	Language Use, Vocabulary, and Linguistics	Chapter 4
81.	B	Writing, Speaking, and Listening	Chapter 5
82.	A	Writing, Speaking, and Listening	Chapter 5
83.	B	Writing, Speaking, and Listening	Chapter 5
84.	B	Writing, Speaking, and Listening	Chapter 5
85.	A	Writing, Speaking, and Listening	Chapter 5
86.	C	Reading and Literature	Chapter 3
87.	A	Reading and Literature	Chapter 3
88.	D	Reading and Literature	Chapter 3
89.	B	Reading and Literature	Chapter 3
90.	A	Reading and Literature	Chapter 3
91.	A	Reading and Literature	Chapter 3
92.	D	Writing, Speaking, and Listening	Chapter 5
93.	D	Writing, Speaking, and Listening	Chapter 5
94.	C	Language Use, Vocabulary, and Linguistics	Chapter 4
95.	D	Language Use, Vocabulary, and Linguistics	Chapter 4
96.	A	Writing, Speaking, and Listening	Chapter 5
97.	B	Writing, Speaking, and Listening	Chapter 5
98.	C	Writing, Speaking, and Listening	Chapter 5
99.	A	Reading and Literature	Chapter 3
100.	B	Reading and Literature	Chapter 3
101.	D	Reading and Literature	Chapter 3
102.	A	Reading and Literature	Chapter 3
103.	C	Reading and Literature	Chapter 3
104.	B	Reading and Literature	Chapter 3
105.	D	Reading and Literature	Chapter 3
106.	B	Reading and Literature	Chapter 3
107.	A	Reading and Literature	Chapter 3
108.	C	Reading and Literature	Chapter 3

Question	Answer	Content Category	Where to Get More Help
109.	D	Language Use, Vocabulary, and Linguistics	Chapter 4
110.	B	Language Use, Vocabulary, and Linguistics	Chapter 4
111.	A	Language Use, Vocabulary, and Linguistics	Chapter 4
112.	C	Language Use, Vocabulary, and Linguistics	Chapter 4
113.	C	Writing, Speaking, and Listening	Chapter 5
114.	B	Writing, Speaking, and Listening	Chapter 5
115.	A	Writing, Speaking, and Listening	Chapter 5
116.	A	Writing, Speaking, and Listening	Chapter 5
117.	D	Reading and Literature	Chapter 3
118.	C	Writing, Speaking, and Listening	Chapter 5
119.	D	Writing, Speaking, and Listening	Chapter 5
120.	B	Writing, Speaking, and Listening	Chapter 5
121.	B	Reading and Literature	Chapter 3
122.	D	Reading and Literature	Chapter 3
123.	C	Reading and Literature	Chapter 3
124.	B	Reading and Literature	Chapter 3
125.	B	Reading and Literature	Chapter 3
126.	A	Language Use, Vocabulary, and Linguistics	Chapter 4
127.	B	Language Use, Vocabulary, and Linguistics	Chapter 4
128.	D	Reading and Literature	Chapter 3
129.	D	Writing, Speaking, and Listening	Chapter 5
130.	D	Writing, Speaking, and Listening	Chapter 5

Answer Explanations

Selected Response

1. **B.** Keats, Shelley, and Byron are all Romantic period authors in British literary history.

2. **D.** This excerpt is from the first stanza of Robert Frost's famous poem "The Road Not Taken."

3. **B.** This excerpt is an example of a five-line stanza, so you can rule out choice D immediately because it is not written in couplets (III). The rhyme scheme is ABAAB (I), so choices A, B, and C are viable options. Next, you have to identify the metrical feet of the poem. An iambic metrical foot begins with an unstressed syllable followed by a stressed syllable. A trochaic metrical foot begins with a stressed syllable followed by an unstressed syllable. Each line of this excerpt begins with an unstressed syllable and contains five feet, indicating that choice B (I and II) is the credited response.

4. **D.** Graymalkin is the evil servant of the first witch. In this period, this creature was known as a "familiar," which is synonymous with "evil servant." The toad is the familiar to the second witch, and its name is Paddock.

5. **A.** A heath or moor is a large expanse of land covered with low-growing shrubs such as heather and other varieties of evergreens.

6. **A.** The word *ere* in Elizabethan English means "before."

7. **B.** Iambic tetrameter is the versification of the poem "The Lady of Shallot" by Alfred Lord Tennyson. An iamb is a metrical foot in poetry that has an unstressed first syllable followed by a stressed second syllable. Poetry written in iambic tetrameter will have four of these feet in each line. Whenever you get a question about poetic meter, first count the number of stressed syllables in a few lines, and then eliminate incorrect answers. For example, in this question, two responses (choices A and C) have the word "pentameter," which requires five stressed syllables per line; the poem in question has only four.

8. **D.** Camelot is the setting of *Le Morte d'Arthur* by Malory and cues the reader to the allusion to this famous work from the Middle English period.

9. **D.** "Elegy Written in a Country Churchyard" is a poem written by Thomas Gray (1716–1771).

10. **B.** This elegy is noteworthy in that it mourns the loss of a way of life rather than the loss of a person.

11. **D.** The writing process is a recursive process in which the writer moves through the stages of writing in a unique sequence. The term *recursive* signifies that each writer's process is not linear—going directly from one prescribed stage to another. Rather, the writing process is unique to each writer and is based on that writer's distinct needs.

12. **C.** One theme of Rossetti's poem "The Birthday" is how poetry can provide a natural outlet for one's emotions. The imagery of the "singing bird," which opens the poem, signals the song or poem is as natural as breathing.

13. **A.** Christina Rossetti (1830–1894) lived in England and wrote during the Pre-Raphaelite literary period along with writers and artists Dante Gabriel Rossetti, Thomas Woolner, Aubrey Beardsley, and Algernon Charles Swinburne. Pre-Raphaelites were influenced by the doctrines of the Pre-Raphaelite brotherhood, which called for genuine expression of ideas and the attentive study of nature.

14. **C.** Charles Dickens wrote during the Victorian period of British literary history, approximately 1840–1900. He is the author of many works, including *Great Expectations* and *Oliver Twist*.

15. **B.** The character of Faith, Young Goodman Brown's wife, represents the Puritan view of the importance of domestic life and the stability of home.

16. **D.** A short story is a brief fictional prose that succinctly portrays a life event or experience.

17. **B.** Nathaniel Hawthorne (1804–1864) was an American author who wrote during the Transcendental Movement between 1830 and 1860. Hawthorne also wrote *The Scarlet Letter*.

18. **D.** "The Legend of Sleepy Hollow," a short story whose main character is Ichabod Crane, is about the legend of a headless horseman who lost his head to a cannonball and rides to find his lost head.

19. **A.** *Peyton Place* was written by Grace Metalious in 1957, not by Hawthorne.

20. **D.** Each of the selected lines from Anne Bradstreet's poem "To My Dear and Loving Husband" contains at least one example of alliteration—the repetition of initial consonant sounds (not necessarily the same letter). Below you will see the initial consonant sounds in bold:

    I.   If ever man were loved by wife, **th**en **th**ee;
    II. Or all the riches **th**at **th**e East doth hold
    III. Then **wh**ile **w**e live, in **l**ove **l**et's so persevere
    IV. That **wh**en **w**e **l**ive no more, **w**e may **l**ive ever

21. **C.** The imagery of the tranquility of nightfall and Pip's not envisioning a shadow of another parting with Estella signifies his ability to let his loss of her love go and be at peace with the ending of their relationship.

22. **B.** Satis House is the mansion in which Estella lived her entire childhood with Miss Havisham, who preferred that no light enter the house.

23. **A.** The denouement of a literary work follows the events after the story's climax and serves as the conclusion. The word *denouement* is derived from the Old French term *denoer,* meaning "to untie."

24. **C.** The proper MLA citation of Dickens' *Great Expectations* is:

Dickens, Charles. *Great Expectations.* New York: Random House, 1907. Print.

25. **B.** The proper APA citation of all book titles, such as Dickens' *Great Expectations,* is:

Dickens, C. (1907). *Great expectations.* New York: Random House.

26. **B.** "The bat that lies in bed at noon," and "All love to be out by the light of the moon" are the only lines that do not contain onomatopoeia—the use of sound words to suggest meaning.

27. **A.** *Hamlet* contains at least one play within a play, the primary of which is referred to in this passage. Hamlet invites actors to perform a play he has written, called *The Mousetrap*, which contains parallels to Claudius' marriage to Hamlet's mother and Claudius' murder of his brother, King Hamlet.

28. **C.** Claudius is the villainous man who plays many roles in Hamlet's life—uncle, stepfather, king, traitor, enemy—and is the intended audience of *The Mousetrap*, the play that Hamlet consigns to be performed at the castle in an effort to expose Claudius' evil acts.

29. **B.** The Declaration of Independence was first penned by Thomas Jefferson as a member of a committee with John Adams and Benjamin Franklin.

30. **B.** The meaning of the phrase "to dissolve the political bands which have connected them with another" is best paraphrased in choice B: to sever political ties with England.

31. **B.** The author respectfully sets a purpose for this declaration based on "a decent respect to the opinions of mankind." This rhetorical strategy persuades the reader to read on and respectfully consider this declaration.

32. **D.** This excerpt from *Gulliver's Travels* can best be described as prose in chronological sequence. The narrator first tells the reader about his arrival in Lisbon, then his welcoming at the captain's home, and finally his efforts to be clothed properly and comfortably.

33. **C.** The term *suffer* is used often in *Gulliver's Travels* to express discomfort or trouble.

34. **B.** Jonathan Swift was born in 1667. *Gulliver's Travels* was first published anonymously in 1726.

35. **D.** The student's most important error is in comma usage. This issue should be the teacher's first priority; lessons on word choice and sentence construction could follow.

36. **B.** The words *read* and *read* are not homophones because they are not pronounced the same way. For example, consider the following sentences using *read* and *read:*

I *read* the newspaper yesterday.

I will *read* the newspaper tomorrow.

37. **C.** A rhetorical question is one that the speaker does not truly want answered.

38. **C.** African American Vernacular English (AAVE) has many features, including the pronunciation of two-syllable words that end in *-ng* as *weddin* for *wedding* or *nuffin* for *nothing.*

39. **C.** This quote uses parallel structure as a rhetorical device.

40. **D.** Lincoln, one of the United States' great orators, used repetition in this quote to make his point effectively.

41. **A.** In poetry, apostrophe is a literary device in which some abstraction or personification that is not physically present is addressed, as in the first lines of the poem "O Captain! My Captain!"

42. **A.** Whitman wrote this poem to memorialize President Abraham Lincoln.

43. **B.** The British Romantic period of literature was 1780–1840.

44. **D.** A sonnet is a lyric poem with a formal structure. Lyric poems are usually short and often personal.

45. **D.** This sonnet has 14 lines written in iambic pentameter, which means that each line has 10 syllables, with the stressed syllable or accent on every second syllable in a rhyming couplet.

46. **B.** The Shakespearean sonnet's rhyme scheme is ABAB, CDCD, EFEF, GG: three quatrains followed by one couplet.

47. **D.** This line from *Don Quixote* contains a simile, which is a comparison using *like* or *as*.

48. **C.** Miguel de Cervantes (1547–1616) wrote *Don Quixote*.

49. **A.** Traditional haiku poetry is made up of three lines containing 5, 7, 5 syllables.

50. **A.** Clichés are phrases that are used so often that they lose their expressive power.

51. **D.** Hardy uses the metaphor of a book and its pages to convey the message of this poem, which is that this relationship is coming to an end.

52. **B.** Hardy repeats the word *truth* for emphasis and persuasion.

53. **C.** The allusion "man for all seasons" refers to Thomas More, the author of *Utopia,* who was sent to prison and executed. He was considered a man for all seasons for courageously holding firm to his beliefs. An allusion is a reference to a familiar person, place, thing, or event.

54. **C.** The central conflict in *The Scarlet Letter* is best described as person versus society. Hester Prynne, the main character in the story, has a problem with an element of society; specifically, she has committed adultery and is forced to wear a scarlet letter on her dress at all times.

55. **C.** The author of *The Scarlet Letter* is Nathaniel Hawthorne, who completed this classic novel in 1850.

56. **A.** In the mid-1800s, a time of revolution in Europe, writers like Ibsen began to challenge the romantic traditions that were in vogue at the time. Ibsen, a writer from Norway, is credited with mastering and popularizing realist drama.

57. **D.** Nora is an immature, silly young woman at the opening of the play. By the end, she has grown into a serious, open-minded woman who rejects the traditional roles available to a woman during this time—housewife, mother, dependent.

58. **C.** This opening scene is from *The Importance of Being Earnest* by Oscar Wilde.

59. **D.** Personification is a literary device in which the author describes an inanimate object or abstraction—the storm, in this text—using human qualities or abilities, such as "fierce breath of the whirlwind" and "a long tumultuous shouting sound."

60. **A.** "The Fall of the House of Usher" was written by Edgar Allan Poe (1809–1849). Poe was an American author during the Romantic period, known especially for his stories of the macabre and mysterious.

61. **D.** *Pygmalion* takes place in Great Britain, which is signaled by the mention of Drury Lane, a famous location in Great Britain, and the mention of eightpence, a denomination of British money.

62. **B.** The use of the term *Pharisaic* is best defined as hypocritically self-righteous. Higgins regrets his behavior toward the lower-class Flower Girl and offers her much of the change in his pocket as a sign of his repentance.

63. **B.** T. S. Eliot wrote his most famous poem, "The Waste Land," during the Modern period, 1900–1945.

64. **C.** Eliot's description of the month of April as "cruel" is an ironic allusion to the prologue of Chaucer's *Canterbury Tales,* which describes spring as a time of rebirth and life.

65. **B.** In this scene, Hamlet is despondent over his father's death and his mother's hasty marriage to his uncle. Hamlet uses the metaphor of an unweeded garden to represent that Denmark is in ruin after King Hamlet's death.

66. **D.** Hamlet is referring to his father, King Hamlet.

67. **B.** *Hamlet* is one of Shakespeare's great tragedies.

68. **C.** This excerpt from *Hamlet* uses an appeal to emotion to convey the author's message. We are to feel pity and empathy for Prince Hamlet.

69. D. This allusion to the mythical god of the sun as compared to a cowardly beast contrasts Old King Hamlet and the new King Claudius.

70. D. The author of *Beowulf* is unknown.

71. A. Plato suggests that each person must do the work that fits his or her own strengths.

72. B. Rhetoric can be defined as the use of language in a persuasive or impressive way.

73. C. This line from Clement C. Moore's *A Visit from Saint Nicholas* contains the simile "like a flash."

74. D. This limerick by Edward Lear is a humorous verse form of five anapestic lines with the rhyme scheme AABBA.

75. C. J. D. Salinger is the author of *The Catcher in the Rye*.

76. B. *The Catcher in the Rye* was published in 1951 in the United States. It is considered contemporary U.S. literature.

77. A. Prufrock's name is meant to elicit the image of a prude in a frock who is incapable of action, specifically to eat a peach in the presence of high-society women.

78. D. Modernist poets, such as T. S. Eliot, focused on the inner, artistic, stream of consciousness mind, not the outer concrete world.

79. D. A discussion about seeking justice in students' lives, personal experiences, and world events would activate students' prior knowledge and experiences about a central theme in Shakespeare's *King Lear*.

80. C. *Faction*—a group of persons forming a cohesive, often contentious group—is the word least related to the Latin cognate *facilis,* which means "easy."

81. B. Correlative conjunctions are used only in pairs and include not only/but also, neither/nor, and either/or.

82. A. During a peer conference, students read their writing to hear their ideas aloud and receive feedback from an initial audience. This is an appropriate revision-stage activity in which students re-see their writing to potentially strengthen and change the piece.

83. B. A writing rubric is a scoring guide used to provide feedback to students and help them assess their writing.

84. B. The proper MLA citation is choice B because it contains italics for the book title and only the page number in parentheses since the author's name appears in the sentence.

85. A. *The Birthday Party*, one of Harold Pinter's most famous plays, contains an extended metaphor.

86. C. A malapropism is the unintentional misuse of a word that is confused with one that sounds similar. The correct word here is *imminent* (pending), not *eminent* (distinguished).

87. A. Anne Bradstreet's *The Tenth Muse Lately Sprung Up in America* was written in 1650, during the Colonial period.

88. D. A protagonist is the central character. Odysseus is the central character in the epic *The Odyssey*.

89. B. The denouement is the tying up of loose ends in a story, leading to the outcome or resolution.

90. A. W. E. B. Du Bois effectively uses the rhetorical device of appeal to emotion to persuade the young schoolgirl not to give up and to attend to her studies.

91. A. Theodore Roosevelt alluded to the period in American history called Western Expansion and Reform, which included the life of frontiersmen and women, who placed hard work and the needs of the nation above those of the individual.

92. D. Roosevelt's repetition of "if we stand; if we seek; if we shrink" utilizes the rhetorical strategy anaphora, which builds tension for the listener and a resulting sense of satisfaction due to the parallelism and the resolution at the end of the statement.

93. D. Roosevelt conjures the listeners' sense of pride, masculinity, and duty—all appeals to the listeners' emotions.

94. **C.** This sentence has one independent clause (The twentieth century looms) with three prepositional phrases (before us big; with the fate; of many nations).

95. **D.** In the omniscient point of view, the narrator is free to tell the story from any and all characters' perspectives.

96. **A.** A quintet contains a five-line stanza.

97. **B.** The speaker displays his diction—choice and use of words and phrases—by opening with the phrase "four score and seven years ago" rather than the date of the American Revolution in 1776.

98. **C.** "Final resting place" is a euphemism, a word or phrase that substitutes for a harsher or more blunt term. It is used in the place of the phrase "the battlefield where these men were killed."

99. **A.** President Abraham Lincoln (1809–1865) was the orator of the Gettysburg Address of 1863.

100. **B.** The initial setting of *The Grapes of Wrath* is the 1930s Dust Bowl in the Midwestern United States. The family then heads to California in search of a better life.

101. **D.** John Steinbeck (1902–1968) is the author of *The Grapes of Wrath*.

102. **A.** *Le Morte d'Arthur* was written in the mid-1400s, during the Middle English period (1066–1550).

103. **C.** This is an English sonnet, which is traditionally written in iambic pentameter.

104. **B.** Elizabeth Barrett Browning wrote *Sonnets from the Portuguese,* a collection of 44 love sonnets to her husband, Robert Browning.

105. **D.** A parable is a story meant to teach a moral lesson. Hester Prynne's scarlet letter is meant to symbolize shame, but she integrates it into who she is, empowering her to find her own identity and inner strength.

106. **B.** Transcendentalist authors like Longfellow and Hawthorne were dedicated to the belief that the divine can be found everywhere.

107. **A.** Chaucer's *Canterbury Tales* is from the Middle English period of British literature.

108. **C.** "Guinevere at Her Fireside" is from *Death and Taxes*, which is perhaps the most famous collection of poetry by Dorothy Parker.

109. **D.** Hughes captured the beauty of African American Vernacular English through his authentic and careful use of idioms and dialect.

110. **B.** By deleting "playing the" and adding "lessons" after "piano," the sentence now contains proper parallelism: Tory participates in basketball, softball, and piano lessons.

111. **A.** The second sentence has a problem with the pronoun *he*. It is unclear to the reader whether Jimmy or Austin received recognition from the coach and teammates.

112. **C.** Sociolinguistics is the study of language as it relates to society, including class, race, and gender.

113. **C.** In the publishing stage of the writing process, a writer is LEAST likely to use the Internet to search for writing ideas. This task is more likely to occur during the prewriting stage.

114. **B.** Bartlett's *Familiar Quotations* is the foremost print and online source of famous quotations.

115. **A.** "Dear Sir or Madam:" is an appropriate greeting in a business letter. Please note that a business letter requires the use of a colon, not comma, at the end of the greeting.

116. **A.** Listing writing topics is an excellent prewriting activity.

117. **D.** *Restroom* is a euphemism for the toilet room. A euphemism is a polite way to discuss a topic that may bring about discomfort.

118. **C.** Concrete poetry emphasizes shape and visual effects to create meaning.

119. **D.** A canto is the main section of a long poem, especially found in epics. Dante's *Divine Comedy* is comprised of 100 cantos and Ezra Pound's *The Cantos* has 120 cantos.

120. B. The emotional atmosphere created by the author is the mood of a literary work.

121. B. Hermia and Robin Goodfellow, a puck who causes much mischief, are characters in *A Midsummer Night's Dream.*

122. D. *The Giver, 1984,* and *The Lord of the Rings* are all science fiction/fantasy novels.

123. C. *Fahrenheit 451* takes place in the future—in the 24th century.

124. B. Lewis Carroll is the author of the poem "Jabberwocky," which is a nonsense poem. The authors in choices A, C, and D also composed nonsense poems.

125. B. "Jabberwocky" was written in the Victorian period of British literature.

126. A. Tituba uses dialect from the area her family comes from. Scholars believe that Tituba, a slave in the Parris household, was most likely from South America, not Africa.

127. B. A compound/complex sentence has two or more independent clauses and one or more dependent clauses.

128. D. The Beat Generation comprised a group of U.S. authors whose literature explored and influenced American culture in the post–World War II literary period. Famous authors include Allen Ginsberg and Jack Kerouac.

129. D. Reliable Internet sources should be checked for authorship, accuracy, purpose, and access (so that others can find the information again).

130. D. Writers should consider the audience for their writing—who the intended reader is, what his or her background knowledge is, and how this piece might be purposeful beyond the classroom.

Constructed Response

Constructed Response I: Interpreting Literature

Here is an example of a constructed response that would be scored as a 3.

Anne Bradstreet, an American Puritan period poet, effectively uses alliteration, parallelism, and metrics in her poem "To My Dear and Loving Husband" to convey her message of love for her husband. In this poem, Bradstreet writes about the depth of her love for her husband in a time in which women were required not to show their emotions outwardly, to dress conservatively, and to repress urges of pleasure and passion. It is within this context that Bradstreet's poem is analyzed.

Throughout the poem, Bradstreet uses alliteration to develop an upbeat sense of musical rhythm. Examples of alliteration include then/thee, while/we, and live/love/let's. Each of these alliterative pairs invites the reader into the poet's heart as she writes about her life and her love, and implores her husband to "let us" continue to love for the remainder of their lives. Bradstreet uses parallelism in the opening of the poem to entice and to challenge the reader to compare the depth of her love for her husband with the love in "ye women['s]" life. The first three lines of the poem begin with "if ever" and build to a challenge for other women to compare their love with the poet's:

> *If ever* two were one, then surely we.
> *If ever* man were loved by wife, then thee.
> *If ever* wife was happy in a man,
> Compare with me, ye women, if you can.

The love that Bradstreet holds for her husband is more prized "than whole Mines of gold" and "all the riches that the East doth hold." In this heroic couplet, the poet posits that her love is more valuable than gold or all of the riches of the Far East. She also uses parallelism in the final couplet of the poem in which she repeats the words "we live." She closes with a challenge to her husband—to live and love so deeply that when they die their love will live on forever. The heroic couplets, which contain end rhyme and are written in iambic pentameter, provide a sense of rhythmic joy and celebration of this great love. In summary, Anne Bradstreet is defiantly disobeying the norms of her Puritan time and sharing her heartfelt passion and love for her "dear and loving husband."

Score Explanation

Constructed response questions that earn full credit demonstrate a thorough understanding of the content. This response includes analysis of specific literary elements—alliteration, parallelism, and metrics—with some depth. Sound understanding of Anne Bradstreet's poem "To My Dear and Loving Husband" is evident, and the test-taker supports points with appropriate quotes from the text. Finally, this response demonstrates coherent control of language and facility with conventions of Standard Written English.

Constructed Response II: Rhetorical Analysis

Here is an example of a constructed response that would be scored as a 3.

> Dr. Martin Luther King, Jr., spoke persuasively and effectively as he addressed his large audience in Washington, D.C., in 1963. He used repetition, allusion, and metaphor to capture his listeners' attention and move all who heard him to action.
>
> The orator began with an allusion to Abraham Lincoln's Gettysburg Address by stating, "Five score years ago." Lincoln opened the Gettysburg Address with "Four score and seven years ago." This time reference and the historical context of Lincoln's important speech that addressed the freeing of slaves in the United States provided the context for King's address.
>
> King used repetition with the phrase "one hundred years later" to make the point that the time had come for change and to accentuate the dire circumstance of the African-American people of his day. This phrase is built on the historical context of Lincoln's signing of the Emancipation Proclamation in the late 1800s. King described his people as experiencing segregation, poverty, discrimination, and marginalization.
>
> Dr. King startled the listener when he stated in his second paragraph that "we face the tragic fact that the Negro is still not free." He then used metaphor to make his point. Employing phrases such as "crippled by the manacles of segregation and the chains of discrimination," King evoked images of African Americans as modern-day slaves. He stated that the "the Negro is still languished in the corners of American society" in a similar way that slaves of yesterday were marginalized.
>
> These first two paragraphs of Dr. King's "I have a dream" speech provided the historical context and rhetorical devices for his central message—that African Americans in the 1960s were enslaved by segregation and discrimination.

Score Explanation

This constructed response would earn full credit because it demonstrates a thorough understanding of the content and includes analysis of specific rhetorical devices—allusion and repetition—with some depth. Sound understanding of Dr. Martin Luther King, Jr.'s speech is evident, and the test-taker supports points with appropriate text citations and examples. Finally, this response demonstrates coherent control of language and facility with conventions of Standard Written English.

Chapter 9

Middle School English Language Arts (5047)

This chapter includes one full-length practice test for the Praxis Middle School English Language Arts (5047) test. This practice test will give you a sense of the format of the test and help you determine which content areas you need to study. You may also want to practice your pacing while taking this full-length practice test. Remember, you will have 130 minutes to complete the 110 selected-response questions, plus an additional 30 minutes to write two constructed responses.

After you complete the practice test, score your answers and use the explanations to assess content areas to study in chapters 3–6 of this book.

It's time to set yourself up in a quiet place with no interruptions, get your pencils ready, take a look at the clock, and begin your practice test.

IMPORTANT NOTE: For ease of studying, all questions in the first section of this practice test are single-selection multiple-choice.

Answer Sheet

1 Ⓐ Ⓑ Ⓒ Ⓓ	41 Ⓐ Ⓑ Ⓒ Ⓓ	81 Ⓐ Ⓑ Ⓒ Ⓓ
2 Ⓐ Ⓑ Ⓒ Ⓓ	42 Ⓐ Ⓑ Ⓒ Ⓓ	82 Ⓐ Ⓑ Ⓒ Ⓓ
3 Ⓐ Ⓑ Ⓒ Ⓓ	43 Ⓐ Ⓑ Ⓒ Ⓓ	83 Ⓐ Ⓑ Ⓒ Ⓓ
4 Ⓐ Ⓑ Ⓒ Ⓓ	44 Ⓐ Ⓑ Ⓒ Ⓓ	84 Ⓐ Ⓑ Ⓒ Ⓓ
5 Ⓐ Ⓑ Ⓒ Ⓓ	45 Ⓐ Ⓑ Ⓒ Ⓓ	85 Ⓐ Ⓑ Ⓒ Ⓓ
6 Ⓐ Ⓑ Ⓒ Ⓓ	46 Ⓐ Ⓑ Ⓒ Ⓓ	86 Ⓐ Ⓑ Ⓒ Ⓓ
7 Ⓐ Ⓑ Ⓒ Ⓓ	47 Ⓐ Ⓑ Ⓒ Ⓓ	87 Ⓐ Ⓑ Ⓒ Ⓓ
8 Ⓐ Ⓑ Ⓒ Ⓓ	48 Ⓐ Ⓑ Ⓒ Ⓓ	88 Ⓐ Ⓑ Ⓒ Ⓓ
9 Ⓐ Ⓑ Ⓒ Ⓓ	49 Ⓐ Ⓑ Ⓒ Ⓓ	89 Ⓐ Ⓑ Ⓒ Ⓓ
10 Ⓐ Ⓑ Ⓒ Ⓓ	50 Ⓐ Ⓑ Ⓒ Ⓓ	90 Ⓐ Ⓑ Ⓒ Ⓓ
11 Ⓐ Ⓑ Ⓒ Ⓓ	51 Ⓐ Ⓑ Ⓒ Ⓓ	91 Ⓐ Ⓑ Ⓒ Ⓓ
12 Ⓐ Ⓑ Ⓒ Ⓓ	52 Ⓐ Ⓑ Ⓒ Ⓓ	92 Ⓐ Ⓑ Ⓒ Ⓓ
13 Ⓐ Ⓑ Ⓒ Ⓓ	53 Ⓐ Ⓑ Ⓒ Ⓓ	93 Ⓐ Ⓑ Ⓒ Ⓓ
14 Ⓐ Ⓑ Ⓒ Ⓓ	54 Ⓐ Ⓑ Ⓒ Ⓓ	94 Ⓐ Ⓑ Ⓒ Ⓓ
15 Ⓐ Ⓑ Ⓒ Ⓓ	55 Ⓐ Ⓑ Ⓒ Ⓓ	95 Ⓐ Ⓑ Ⓒ Ⓓ
16 Ⓐ Ⓑ Ⓒ Ⓓ	56 Ⓐ Ⓑ Ⓒ Ⓓ	96 Ⓐ Ⓑ Ⓒ Ⓓ
17 Ⓐ Ⓑ Ⓒ Ⓓ	57 Ⓐ Ⓑ Ⓒ Ⓓ	97 Ⓐ Ⓑ Ⓒ Ⓓ
18 Ⓐ Ⓑ Ⓒ Ⓓ	58 Ⓐ Ⓑ Ⓒ Ⓓ	98 Ⓐ Ⓑ Ⓒ Ⓓ
19 Ⓐ Ⓑ Ⓒ Ⓓ	59 Ⓐ Ⓑ Ⓒ Ⓓ	99 Ⓐ Ⓑ Ⓒ Ⓓ
20 Ⓐ Ⓑ Ⓒ Ⓓ	60 Ⓐ Ⓑ Ⓒ Ⓓ	100 Ⓐ Ⓑ Ⓒ Ⓓ
21 Ⓐ Ⓑ Ⓒ Ⓓ	61 Ⓐ Ⓑ Ⓒ Ⓓ	101 Ⓐ Ⓑ Ⓒ Ⓓ
22 Ⓐ Ⓑ Ⓒ Ⓓ	62 Ⓐ Ⓑ Ⓒ Ⓓ	102 Ⓐ Ⓑ Ⓒ Ⓓ
23 Ⓐ Ⓑ Ⓒ Ⓓ	63 Ⓐ Ⓑ Ⓒ Ⓓ	103 Ⓐ Ⓑ Ⓒ Ⓓ
24 Ⓐ Ⓑ Ⓒ Ⓓ	64 Ⓐ Ⓑ Ⓒ Ⓓ	104 Ⓐ Ⓑ Ⓒ Ⓓ
25 Ⓐ Ⓑ Ⓒ Ⓓ	65 Ⓐ Ⓑ Ⓒ Ⓓ	105 Ⓐ Ⓑ Ⓒ Ⓓ
26 Ⓐ Ⓑ Ⓒ Ⓓ	66 Ⓐ Ⓑ Ⓒ Ⓓ	106 Ⓐ Ⓑ Ⓒ Ⓓ
27 Ⓐ Ⓑ Ⓒ Ⓓ	67 Ⓐ Ⓑ Ⓒ Ⓓ	107 Ⓐ Ⓑ Ⓒ Ⓓ
28 Ⓐ Ⓑ Ⓒ Ⓓ	68 Ⓐ Ⓑ Ⓒ Ⓓ	108 Ⓐ Ⓑ Ⓒ Ⓓ
29 Ⓐ Ⓑ Ⓒ Ⓓ	69 Ⓐ Ⓑ Ⓒ Ⓓ	109 Ⓐ Ⓑ Ⓒ Ⓓ
30 Ⓐ Ⓑ Ⓒ Ⓓ	70 Ⓐ Ⓑ Ⓒ Ⓓ	110 Ⓐ Ⓑ Ⓒ Ⓓ
31 Ⓐ Ⓑ Ⓒ Ⓓ	71 Ⓐ Ⓑ Ⓒ Ⓓ	
32 Ⓐ Ⓑ Ⓒ Ⓓ	72 Ⓐ Ⓑ Ⓒ Ⓓ	
33 Ⓐ Ⓑ Ⓒ Ⓓ	73 Ⓐ Ⓑ Ⓒ Ⓓ	
34 Ⓐ Ⓑ Ⓒ Ⓓ	74 Ⓐ Ⓑ Ⓒ Ⓓ	
35 Ⓐ Ⓑ Ⓒ Ⓓ	75 Ⓐ Ⓑ Ⓒ Ⓓ	
36 Ⓐ Ⓑ Ⓒ Ⓓ	76 Ⓐ Ⓑ Ⓒ Ⓓ	
37 Ⓐ Ⓑ Ⓒ Ⓓ	77 Ⓐ Ⓑ Ⓒ Ⓓ	
38 Ⓐ Ⓑ Ⓒ Ⓓ	78 Ⓐ Ⓑ Ⓒ Ⓓ	
39 Ⓐ Ⓑ Ⓒ Ⓓ	79 Ⓐ Ⓑ Ⓒ Ⓓ	
40 Ⓐ Ⓑ Ⓒ Ⓓ	80 Ⓐ Ⓑ Ⓒ Ⓓ	

Practice Test 5047

Selected Response

Time: 130 minutes
110 questions

Directions: Each of the questions or statements below is followed by four possible answers or completions. Select the one that is best in each case.

1. Which of the following pairs of characters appears in Shakespeare's *A Midsummer Night's Dream*?

   A. Romeo and Juliet
   B. Hermia and Robin Goodfellow
   C. Caesar and Calpurnia
   D. Gertrude and Claudius

2. *The Giver, 1984*, and *The Lord of the Rings* can all be classified as belonging to which of the following genres?

   A. Realistic fiction
   B. Poetry
   C. Historical fiction
   D. Science fiction/fantasy

3. The setting of *Fahrenheit 451* is _____.

   A. 1984
   B. the 21st century
   C. the 24th century
   D. the 1950s

Questions 4 and 5 are based on the following excerpt from the Declaration of Independence.

When in the Course of human events, it becomes necessary for one people to dissolve the political bands which have connected them with another, and to assume among the powers of the earth, the separate and equal situation to which the Laws of Nature and of Nature's God entitle them, a decent respect to the opinions of mankind requires that they should declare the causes which impel them to the separation.

4. Which of the following best describes the meaning of the phrase "to dissolve the political bands which have connected them with another"?

   A. To seek a resolution to the political nature of a conflict
   B. To sever political ties with England
   C. To seek a change in the political structure of the homeland
   D. To seek religious freedom

5. The phrase "a decent respect to the opinions of mankind" works persuasively because it appeals to the reader's sense of _____.

   A. audience
   B. propriety
   C. rationale
   D. manhood

GO ON TO THE NEXT PAGE

6. Tituba, a character in Arthur Miller's play *The Crucible*, says, "My Betty be hearty soon?" Which of the following best describes Tituba's use of language?

   A. Dialect
   B. Phonology
   C. Pragmatics
   D. Grammatical error

7. The following sentence is a _____ sentence.

   I look forward to teaching, and I plan to teach middle school English because I love literature.

   A. compound
   B. compound/complex
   C. complex
   D. simple

8. Which of the following terms can be defined as using language persuasively or impressively?

   A. Personification
   B. Point of view
   C. Tone
   D. Rhetoric

9. Which of the following criteria should be used when evaluating Internet sources for a research paper?

   I. Author
   II. Accuracy
   III. Purpose of the site
   IV. Access

   A. I
   B. I, II
   C. I, II, IV
   D. All of the above

10. Which of the following correctly cites a source using MLA-format guidelines?

    A. Golding wrote in his opening line of Lord of the Flies, "The boy with fair hair lowered himself down the last few feet of rock and began to pick his way toward the lagoon" (7).
    B. Golding wrote in his opening line of *Lord of the Flies*, "The boy with fair hair lowered himself down the last few feet of rock and began to pick his way toward the lagoon" (7).
    C. Golding wrote in his opening line of <u>Lord of the Flies</u>, "The boy with fair hair lowered himself down the last few feet of rock and began to pick his way toward the lagoon" (Golding, 7).
    D. Golding wrote in his opening line of *Lord of the Flies*, "The boy with fair hair lowered himself down the last few feet of rock and began to pick his way toward the lagoon." (Golding, 7)

11. When a writer considers the _____ for a piece, he or she considers who else will read it and what background knowledge the reader might need to understand the point of the writing.

    A. grade
    B. publisher
    C. location
    D. audience

GO ON TO THE NEXT PAGE

Questions 12 and 13 are based on Shakespeare's "Sonnet 18."

Shall I compare thee to a summer's day?
Thou art more lovely and more temperate:
Rough winds do shake the darling buds of May,
And summer's lease hath all too short a date:
Sometime too hot the eye of heaven shines,
And often is his gold complexion dimmed,
And every fair from fair sometime declines,
By chance, or nature's changing course untrimmed:
But thy eternal summer shall not fade,
Nor lose possession of that fair thou ow'st,
Nor shall death brag thou wander'st in his shade,
When in eternal lines to time thou grow'st,
So long as men can breathe, or eyes can see,
So long lives this, and this gives life to thee.

12. "Sonnet 18" is organized as a _____.

    A. sequence
    B. hierarchy
    C. comparison
    D. cause and effect

13. Prior to teaching Shakespeare's "Sonnet 18" to her eighth graders, Miss Judge asks her students open-ended questions about feelings evoked by summer and people they love. This pre-reading activity is called a(n) _____.

    A. anticipation guide
    B. pretest
    C. brainstorm
    D. graphic organizer

14. Prior to reading a news article to her students about the 9/11 terrorist attacks, Miss Bell shows them a replica of the World Trade Center that she saved as a memento from a trip to New York City. Miss Bell is using which of the following methods to activate prior knowledge?

    A. Concept mapping
    B. Replication
    C. Concrete experiences
    D. Semantic feature analysis

15. Mr. Audette makes a point to model the reading strategy to be learned in a lesson, offer guided practice by using the reading strategy in class, and allow his students time to work independently while practicing the new reading strategy. Which of the following best describes the theory behind Mr. Audette's practice?

    A. Chalk and talk
    B. Scaffolding instruction
    C. Lecture
    D. Cooperative learning

GO ON TO THE NEXT PAGE

16. Which of the following authors wrote *The Swiss Family Robinson*?

    A. Geoffrey Chaucer
    B. William Hill Brown
    C. Herman Hesse
    D. Johann Wyss

17. Mrs. Friedman has organized her students into literature circles, with each student taking a role in the group. Which of the following roles is most likely found in a literature circle?

    A. Key grip
    B. Summarizer
    C. Leader
    D. Dictionary worker

18. Tory and Kelly are trying to compare and contrast the film of *The Wizard of Oz* and the book. Which of the following graphic organizers will best support their note-taking?

    A. Culture cluster
    B. Story map
    C. Hierarchical array
    D. Venn diagram

Questions 19 and 20 are based on the following passage from Gulliver's Travels by Jonathan Swift.

We arrived at Lisbon, Nov. 5, 1715. At our landing, the captain forced me to cover myself with his cloak, to prevent the rabble from crowding about me. I was conveyed to his own house, and at my earnest request, he led me up to the highest room backwards. I conjured him to "conceal from all persons what I had told him of the Houyhnhnms, because the least hint of such a story would not only draw numbers of people to see me, but probably put me in danger of being imprisoned, or burnt by the Inquisition." The captain persuaded me to accept a suit of clothes newly made; but I would not suffer the tailor to take my measure; however, Don Pedro being almost of my size, they fitted me well enough. He accoutred me with other necessaries, all new, which I aired for twenty-four hours before I would use them.

19. Which of the following best describes this excerpt from *Gulliver's Travels*?

    A. Prose in chronological sequence
    B. Lyrical poetry
    C. Prose in compare-and-contrast structure
    D. Realistic fiction

20. In which of the following periods was *Gulliver's Travels* written and first published?

    A. Early 1600s
    B. Early 1700s
    C. Early 1800s
    D. Early 1900s

21. Which of the following pairs are collective nouns?

    A. people and schools
    B. Mary's and John's
    C. gaggle and cache
    D. his and her

GO ON TO THE NEXT PAGE

22. Which of the following is the verb tense in the sentence below?

Tory has attended Curtis Corner Middle School for sixth and seventh grades.

   A. Future
   B. Present perfect
   C. Present
   D. Past perfect

23. When a story is written from an omniscient point of view, which of the following is true?

   A. The narrator is free to tell the story from any and all characters' points of view.
   B. The story is told from the point of view of one character.
   C. The story is told by someone outside the story.
   D. The narrator compares two unlike things.

24. Which of the following word pairs demonstrates an analogous relationship to score : concert?

   A. game : inning
   B. record : sound
   C. screenplay : movie
   D. music : video

25. Which of the following best describes the organization of a news article?

   A. Cause and effect
   B. Inverted pyramid
   C. Hierarchical array
   D. Problem/solution

26. Which of the following best defines an editorial?

   A. A fact-and-opinion essay
   B. A news article that covers an important current event
   C. A letter that discusses opinions held by the author
   D. A brief persuasive essay that expresses a viewpoint on a timely or important topic

27. Which of the following best summarizes the plot of *Julie of the Wolves* by Jean Craighead George?

   A. A young Eskimo girl experiences the changes forced upon her culture.
   B. A young girl lives outdoors for a year and removes herself from society's forces.
   C. A young girl is forced to survive alone after a storm kills all the other inhabitants of her island.
   D. A baby girl is abandoned and cared for by a pack of wolves.

28. Which of the following authors wrote *The Outsiders*?

   A. Katherine Paterson
   B. Harper Lee
   C. S. E. Hinton
   D. Walter Dean Myers

GO ON TO THE NEXT PAGE

29. Which of the following pairs are main characters in *The Outsiders*?

    A. Johnny and Maria

    B. Ponyboy and Dallas

    C. Tex and Sherri

    D. Jess and Leslie

30. Which of the following lines contains a metaphor?

    A. "And when I am king, as king I will be—"

    B. "All the world's a stage"

    C. "Neither a borrower nor a lender be"

    D. "How like a winter hath my absence been"

31. Which of the following best defines the literary term *mood*?

    A. A frequently occurring custom or behavior

    B. The emotional state of mind or atmosphere created by an author in a literary work

    C. The special characteristics an author uses in his or her writing

    D. The patterns of ideas organized in a literary work

32. Langston Hughes wrote his poem "Po' Boy Blues" using _____.

    A. iambic pentameter

    B. free verse

    C. authentic setting and meaning

    D. idioms and dialect from African American Vernacular English

33. Which of the following activities is LEAST likely to occur during the publishing stage of the writing process?

    A. Examining a book to learn about the features of the publication

    B. Preparing a cover and title page

    C. Using the Internet to search for writing ideas

    D. Writing an acknowledgment section

34. Which of the following BEST describes the writing process?

    A. Recursive

    B. Developmental

    C. Exclusionary

    D. Step-by-step

35. Which of the following cueing strategies do readers use when they try to figure out an unknown word by thinking about what they know and what might make sense in the sentence?

    A. Vocabulary

    B. Graphophonics

    C. Structure

    D. Semantics

36. The root word in *exceed* and *succeed* is _____.

    A. ed

    B. ceed

    C. cce

    D. eed

GO ON TO THE NEXT PAGE

37. The purpose of a response journal is for students to _____.

    A. write a journal entry to the author

    B. write about the author's message based on a lecture

    C. construct meaning from their experiences and their reading of a text

    D. write an entry that will be graded by the teacher

38. During a writing workshop, which of the following is the best role for the teacher?

    A. Check student work for spelling errors.

    B. Correct quizzes.

    C. Lead writing conferences.

    D. Prepare for the close of the lesson.

39. Which of the following is the correct MLA-format citation for the book *Great Expectations*?

    A. Dickens, C. Great expectations. New York: Random House, 1907. Print.

    B. Dickens, C. (1907). Great Expectations. New York: Random House. Print.

    C. Dickens, Charles. *Great Expectations*. New York: Random House, 1907. Print.

    D. Dickens, Charles. *Great expectations.* New York; Random House, 1907. Print.

40. In which of the following sources is a reader MOST likely to find an aphorism from Benjamin Franklin?

    A. Dictionary

    B. Thesaurus

    C. Encyclopedia

    D. Bartlett's *Familiar Quotations*

41. In an advertisement for legal services, a famous television attorney attests to the merits of the law firm being advertised. Which of the following persuasive techniques is being used in this advertisement?

    A. Appeal to authority

    B. Appeal to tradition

    C. Propaganda

    D. Appeal to excellence

42. Which of the following pairs of words contains a vowel digraph?

    A. freight-believe

    B. right-ring

    C. organize-prioritize

    D. same-tame

43. Mrs. Josephson is an eighth-grade English teacher who is teaching her nonfluent students of English to understand a short story. Which of the following approaches is LEAST effective for Mrs. Josephson's students?

    A. Have students take turns repeat-reading in pairs.

    B. Have students take turns reading aloud passages from the short story to the whole class.

    C. Have students ask preview-and-predict questions prior to reading silently.

    D. Have students work in cooperative learning groups to read the short story.

GO ON TO THE NEXT PAGE

44. What is the main problem or conflict in *Bridge to Terabithia* by Katherine Paterson?

    A. Person versus school
    B. Person versus person
    C. Person versus society
    D. Person versus self

45. What is unique about the main character's name in the novel *Holes*?

    A. His name is a palindrome.
    B. His name is an acrostic.
    C. Her name is a palindrome.
    D. Her name is an acronym.

46. Which of the following topics are present in the novel *Holes*?

    A. Cheating, crocodiles, and the Everglades
    B. Bullying, lizards, and Camp Green Lake
    C. Dribbling, basketball, and the NBA
    D. Hiding, German soldiers, and World War II

47. Which of the following authors wrote *Holes*?

    A. William Golding
    B. Walter Dean Myers
    C. Paul Fleischman
    D. Louis Sachar

48. The main character in Caroline B. Cooney's *The Voice on the Radio* is _____.

    A. Finny, a boy who attends a prep school
    B. Gene, a radio announcer
    C. Janie, a girl who was kidnapped as a child
    D. Caroline, the popular girl in school

49. Which of the following characters appears in *The Adventures of Huckleberry Finn*?

    A. Jim, a runaway slave
    B. Tim Sawyer, a mischievous friend
    C. Sam Clemens, a doctor
    D. Mrs. McGillicutty, a motherly neighbor

50. Which of the following sentences contains a dangling modifier?

    A. After earning a passing score on the Praxis English Subject Assessment test, the teacher certification office awarded her with a teaching license.
    B. The teacher certification office mailed the teaching license.
    C. The Praxis English Subject Assessment test is a teaching licensure test used in Rhode Island and is also required in Florida.
    D. In order to earn a teaching license, she had to complete an accredited program, file an application, and mail it to the teacher certification office.

GO ON TO THE NEXT PAGE

51. Which of the following pairs is made up of compound words?

A. read-read
B. emigrate-immigrate
C. firing-fired
D. bumblebee-rosebush

52. Which of the following is an appropriate revision-stage activity during the writing process?

A. Peer conferencing
B. Peer editing
C. Teacher editing
D. Prewriting

53. When an advertisement includes testimony from a representative of the store who says, "For over 100 years, we have given customers the quality and service they deserve," which of the following persuasive strategies is being used?

A. Appeal to authority
B. Sex appeal
C. Appeal to tradition
D. Appeal to plain folks

54. Which of the following best describes the genre of *The Witch of Blackbird Pond*?

A. Science fiction
B. Realistic fiction
C. Historical fiction
D. Mystery

55. *The Glory Field,* a book about an African American family's present and past, was written by _____.

A. Zora Neale Hurston
B. Langston Hughes
C. Walter Dean Myers
D. Nikki Giovanni

56. The narrator of *The Giver* is _____.

A. Jonas
B. Joseph
C. Noah
D. Nancy

57. Which of the following is a definition for *primary sources*?

A. Commentaries
B. Original documents
C. News articles
D. The first documents one uses in a research paper

GO ON TO THE NEXT PAGE

58. Which of the following is a definition for *secondary sources*?

    A. The second documents one uses in a research paper
    B. Authentic diary entries
    C. Commentaries on primary sources
    D. Information overheard by another

59. In which novel do John and Lorraine tell the story of their lonely neighbor?

    A. *A Separate Peace* by John Knowles
    B. *The Chocolate War* by Robert Cormier
    C. *Holes* by Louis Sachar
    D. *The Pigman* by Paul Zindel

60. Which of the following is the best definition of a *novel*?

    A. An extended, fictional prose narrative
    B. A short, fictional prose narrative
    C. A narrative comprising idealized events far removed from everyday life
    D. An expository text that describes one's life story

61. Which of the following characters is the protagonist in the work cited?

    A. Lord Capulet in *Romeo and Juliet*
    B. Tom Sawyer in *The Adventures of Huckleberry Finn*
    C. Mr. Pendanski in *Holes*
    D. Ponyboy in *The Outsiders*

62. Which of the following text structures shows the relationship between events and their results?

    A. Chronological order
    B. Cause and effect
    C. Comparison
    D. Location

63. Which of the following literary terms can be defined as the turning point in a story?

    A. Falling action
    B. Climax
    C. Denouement
    D. Exposition

64. Which of the following words correctly uses a hyphen with a prefix?

    A. a-gain
    B. cross-stitch
    C. self-help
    D. selectman-elect

65. Which of the following is defined as informal speech made up of new words or expressions?

    A. Rap
    B. Cliché
    C. Slang
    D. Press conference

GO ON TO THE NEXT PAGE

66. In this opening line of *Bridge to Terabithia*, the author uses which of the following literary devices?

"Ba-room, ba-room, ba-room, baripity, baripity, baripity, baripity—Good."

    A. Illusion

    B. Allusion

    C. Personification

    D. Onomatopoeia

67. Which of the following types of writing tries to prove that something is true or convince the reader to see the writer's viewpoint?

    A. Sonnet

    B. Argument

    C. Analysis

    D. Technical

68. Which of the following is a propaganda technique?

    A. News articles

    B. Poster

    C. Bandwagon

    D. Mass marketing

69. In a story told from the first-person point of view, the story is told _____.

    A. by the main antagonist

    B. by someone outside the story

    C. from the perspective of an outside member of society

    D. from the perspective of one of the characters

70. Which of the following lines contains a simile?

    A. Mine eyes have seen the glory of the coming of the Lord:

    B. Woodman, spare that tree! Touch not a single bough!

    C. My candle burns at both ends; it will not last the night;

    D. Away to the window I flew like a flash.

71. Which of the following is LEAST likely to foster reading appreciation in adolescents?

    A. Round-robin reading aloud in class

    B. Helping students find "just right"–level books

    C. Conducting literature circles

    D. Finding an author or series to read

72. Which of the following lines from Shakespeare does NOT contain an insult?

    A. "Tis brief, my lord." "As woman's love."

    B. "Shall I compare thee to a summer's day?"

    C. "Tempt not too much the hatred of my spirit, for I am sick when I do look on thee."

    D. "She speaks yet she says nothing."

GO ON TO THE NEXT PAGE

73. Which of the following techniques should students use to avoid plagiarism?

    I.   Paraphrase the author's words without giving credit to the author

   II.   Summarize in one's own words

  III.   Cite quotations

  IV.   Enclose quoted words in quotation marks

    A. I

    B. I, II

    C. II, III, IV

    D. All of the above

74. The word *restroom* is a(n) _____ for the toilet room.

    A. elegy

    B. anapestic

    C. aphorism

    D. euphemism

75. Which of the following sentences contains a verb in the future tense?

    A. Matthew has attended Dean College.

    B. Matthew enrolled in Dean College for fall 2007.

    C. Matthew will attend Dean College in the fall.

    D. Matthew and Jimmy attend Dean College.

76. Which of the following types of writing captures the meaning of the person, place, or thing being written about?

    A. Scholarly writing

    B. Subject writing

    C. Workplace writing

    D. Persuasive writing

77. Abraham Lincoln is attributed with saying, "You can fool some of the people all of the time, and all of the people some of the time, but you cannot fool all of the people all of the time." Which of the following rhetorical devices was President Lincoln using?

    A. Repetition

    B. Hyperbole

    C. Metaphor

    D. Simile

78. Which of the following activities is MOST likely to appear in an argument written for a composition class?

    A. Run-on sentence

    B. Quarrel

    C. Insertion

    D. Assertion

GO ON TO THE NEXT PAGE

79. Which of the following is an appropriate greeting in a business letter?

    A. Hi, Mr. Stevens:
    B. Dear Sir or Madam,
    C. Dear Mary,
    D. Dear Sir or Madam:

80. Which of the following pairs of words contains at least one open syllable?

    A. careful-carefree
    B. cast-mast
    C. belong-believe
    D. carpet-rug

81. Which of the following BEST defines diction in a composition?

    A. The pronunciation of words
    B. The use and choice of words
    C. The meanings of particular words
    D. The number of syllables in a word

82. Which of the following best describes the theme of Langston Hughes' poem "Harlem"?

    A. Postponing one's deepest-held desires may lead to destruction.
    B. Dreams really do come true.
    C. Life in the city can be fraught with peril and delight.
    D. Good things come to those who wait.

Questions 83–86 are based on the following excerpt from an inaugural address.

I am certain that my fellow Americans expect that on my induction into the presidency I will address them with a candor and a decision, which the present situation of our Nation impels. This is preeminently the time to speak the truth, the whole truth, frankly and boldly. Nor need we shrink from honestly facing conditions in our country today. This great nation will endure as it has endured, will revive and will prosper. So, first of all, let me assert my firm belief that the only thing we have to fear is fear itself—nameless, unreasoning, unjustified terror, which paralyzes needed efforts to convert retreat into advance.

83. Which of the following summarizes the topic sentence of this address?

    A. We have nothing to fear except fear itself.
    B. The president will speak candidly and decisively, as the people expect.
    C. The people should not shrink from fear or problems.
    D. The president will speak the whole truth.

84. Which of the following is a supporting detail in the passage above?

    A. The only thing we have to fear is fear itself.
    B. The president will speak candidly and decisively, as the people expect.
    C. The people will attend the inauguration.
    D. The people have elected this president and, therefore, support him.

GO ON TO THE NEXT PAGE

85. Which of the following best defines the word *preeminently* as used in the address above?

    A. Most important
    B. Right
    C. Formal
    D. Religious

86. Which of the following presidents delivered this inaugural address?

    A. Richard Nixon
    B. Jimmy Carter
    C. Franklin Delano Roosevelt
    D. John F. Kennedy

Questions 87–90 are based on the following poem in Sonnets from the Portuguese.

Beloved, thou hast brought me many flowers
Plucked in the garden, all the summer through,
And winter, and it seemed as if they grew
In this close room, nor missed the sun and showers.
So, in the like name of that love of ours,
Take back these thoughts which here unfolded too,
And which on warm and cold days I withdrew
From my heart's ground. Indeed, those beds and bowers
Be overgrown with bitter weeds and rue,
And wait thy weeding; yet here's eglantine,
Here's ivy!—take them, as I used to do
Thy flowers, and keep them where they shall not pine.
Instruct thine eyes to keep their colours true,
And tell thy soul, their roots are left in mine.

87. Which of the following metrics is used in the English sonnet above?

    A. Iambic pentameter
    B. Iambic quintet
    C. Trochaic pentameter
    D. Anapestic pentameter

88. Which of the following authors wrote *Sonnets from the Portuguese*?

    A. Emily Dickinson
    B. George Eliot
    C. T. S. Eliot
    D. Elizabeth Barrett Browning

89. The phrase "From my heart's ground" uses which of the following literary devices?

    A. Alliteration
    B. Metaphor
    C. Allusion
    D. Phoneme

GO ON TO THE NEXT PAGE

90. Which of the following offers the most likely interpretation of the final line of the sonnet?

  A. The poet is asking her love to remain true to her.
  B. The poet has lost her love.
  C. The poet's husband has cut off the roots of a bouquet.
  D. The poet prefers wildflowers to store-bought flowers.

91. Prior to assigning a short-story writing project, an English teacher can do which of the following to prepare the students for success?

  A. Proofread
  B. Revise
  C. Watch a film
  D. Prewrite

Questions 92 and 93 are based on the following excerpt from Jesse Jackson's speech to the Democratic National Convention on July 20, 1988.

… We meet tonight at the crossroads, a point of decision.

Shall we expand, be inclusive, find unity and power; or suffer division and impotence?

We come to Atlanta, the cradle of the old South, the crucible of the new South. Tonight, there is a sense of celebration, because we are moved, fundamentally moved from racial battlegrounds by law, to economic common ground. Tomorrow we will challenge to move to higher ground.

Common ground! Think of Jerusalem—the intersection where many trails met. A small village that became the birthplace of three great religions—Judaism, Christianity, and Islam.

92. Which of the following best describes the rhetorical strategy Jackson uses in the line "Jerusalem—the intersection where many trails met"?

  A. Alliteration
  B. Allusion
  C. Prosody
  D. Appeal to emotion

93. Jackson's line "Shall we expand, be inclusive, find unity and power; or suffer division and impotence?" is called which of the following?

  A. Allusion
  B. Personification
  C. Extended metaphor
  D. Rhetorical question

94. Which of the following is a type of story that includes characters and events that represent an idea or generalization about life?

  A. Allegory
  B. Biography
  C. Ballad
  D. Analogy

GO ON TO THE NEXT PAGE

95. Mrs. Wildes opens her lesson on *The Giver* with a series of questions that have no right or wrong answer. The questions are meant to inspire discussion and debate on issues related to themes in the novel. Which of the following is the name of this instructional technique?

   A. Anticipation guide
   B. Post-test
   C. Story map
   D. Concrete experience

96. Structure cues, also known as graphophonic cues, are being used in which of the following situations?

   A. Jimmy skips a difficult word in *The Adventures of Huckleberry Finn* to try to figure out its meaning.
   B. Matt reads a chapter of *The Iliad* and then summarizes what he's read.
   C. Tory sounds out the word *yisgadal* in *Night*.
   D. Jim comes upon a passage in the newspaper that is about basketball, a topic he knows a lot about.

97. Which of the following types of assessment helps inform an English teacher's day-to-day instruction?

   A. Summative assessment
   B. Formative assessment
   C. Norm-referenced assessment
   D. Achievement assessment

98. Maria is participating in a class taught entirely in English even though she has just moved to the United States from Central America. Her lessons are offered in simplified English so that she can learn both English and the academic content. Which of the following best describes the type of instruction Maria is receiving?

   A. Primary language instruction
   B. English immersion instruction
   C. Bilingual instruction
   D. Ebonics

99. Mrs. McGuire assigns her students different portions of a chapter to read and respond to for homework. When the students return to class, they work in small groups with students who have read differing portions of the chapter. The students discuss and make sense of their reading together. Which of the following is the name for this instructional strategy?

   A. Think-Pair-Share
   B. Student Teams Achievement Division
   C. Advance organizer
   D. Jigsaw

100. If a teacher wants to ask lower-level questions, which of the following types of questions from Bloom's taxonomy would she use?

   A. Comprehension and discussion
   B. Analysis and synthesis
   C. Knowledge and literal
   D. Open-ended and reflective

GO ON TO THE NEXT PAGE

Questions 101 and 102 are based on the following passage.

Dee is a new student in Mrs. Meyer's ninth-grade English class. Mrs. Meyer learns from Dee's school records that she has recently moved to the United States from Cambodia and that her family speaks Vietnamese at home. Dee has been nearly silent in the classroom during the first month of school, and Mrs. Meyer would like to get to know Dee's literacy and educational needs better. Mrs. Meyer has three other students who speak both Vietnamese and English in her class this year and hopes that the students can help her teach Dee.

101. Which of the following best describes Dee's current language/literacy status?

    A. Primary language not English

    B. Illiterate

    C. Mentally handicapped

    D. Developmentally delayed

102. Which of the following strategies will best help Dee as she learns English in Mrs. Meyer's classroom?

    A. Conduct whole-group discussions and hope that Dee learns English.

    B. Provide Dee with a hall pass to meet with the librarian to find books she can read.

    C. Give Dee the opportunity to talk with peers in small groups.

    D. Send home notes to Dee's parents to help them understand how important it is for Dee to learn English.

103. Mrs. Josephson is a ninth-grade English teacher who is teaching her nonfluent students of English to understand a short story. Which of the following approaches would be LEAST effective for Mrs. Josephson's students?

    A. Have students take turns repeat-reading in pairs.

    B. Have students take turns reading aloud passages from the short story to the whole class.

    C. Have students ask preview-and-predict questions prior to reading silently.

    D. Have students work in cooperative learning groups to read the short story.

104. Mrs. Dougherty has several students in her class who are English language learners. She strives to teach English at an appropriate level for her students, and she teaches in English between 70 and 90 percent of the time. Which of the following describes the program Mrs. Dougherty uses?

    A. Ebonics

    B. Structured English immersion

    C. Phonics approach

    D. Total physical approach

105. Which of the following instructional strategies is most likely to benefit an English language learner?

    I. Pre-teach vocabulary

    II. Provide an overview of the lesson prior to instruction

    III. Assign silent reading followed by a chapter test

    IV. Allow time for small-group discussion

    A. I, II, III

    B. I, II, IV

    C. I

    D. I, III

GO ON TO THE NEXT PAGE

106. Miss Ellsworth is teaching *A Separate Peace* to her tenth-grade students in a diverse urban high school. Several of her students are recent immigrants to the United States and speak more than one language. *A Separate Peace* is set in New England during World War II, and Miss Ellsworth is concerned that all of her students may not be familiar with the cultural context of the work. Which of the following openings to the lesson would be most effective for all of Miss Ellsworth's students?

    A. Who can tell us about World War II?

    B. How many of you have read *A Separate Peace* before?

    C. The next book we'll read is about Phineas and Gene, who are attending a boys' boarding school in New England. Have any of you been to New England or to a boarding school? What do you think it is like?

    D. The next book we'll read is about conflict. We all experience conflict in our lives—such as arguments with siblings and friends or larger conflicts such as war. Think about a small or large conflict you have experienced and then turn to your partner and discuss your conflict.

107. Nishita is a gifted twelfth grader who accurately and thoroughly completes her assignments 30 minutes earlier than her peers. Recently, Nishita appears bored with her schoolwork and is spending time visiting with classmates while they are trying to complete their work. Nishita also has started to forget to hand in her classwork. Which of the following instructional strategies may be most helpful to Nishita?

    A. Cooperative learning

    B. Jigsaw

    C. Curriculum compacting

    D. Curriculum chunking

108. Mrs. Horton is teaching a reading lesson to her tenth-grade students. She has already discussed the story's structure. Next, she would like her students to identify the story's main characters, setting, and basic plot elements. Which of the following graphic organizers would be most helpful in Mrs. Horton's lesson?

    A. Story map

    B. Sequence chart

    C. Hierarchical array

    D. Venn diagram

109. Which of the following is an important comprehension strategy that involves teaching students to use a double-entry notebook or SQ3R to comprehend written materials that can be incorporated into lessons?

    A. Reinforcing and providing recognition

    B. Identifying similarities and differences

    C. Creating nonlinguistic representations

    D. Summarizing and note-taking

110. Which of the following words is known as a portmanteau word?

    A. Fedora

    B. Gardening

    C. Basketball

    D. Ebonics

IF YOU FINISH BEFORE TIME IS CALLED, CHECK YOUR WORK ON THIS SECTION ONLY. DO NOT WORK ON ANY OTHER SECTION IN THE TEST.

Constructed Response

Time: 30 minutes

2 questions

Constructed Response I: Textual Interpretation

Directions: This constructed-response question requires you to interpret a piece of literary or nonfiction text. Plan to spend approximately 15 minutes of your testing time on this question. The excerpt below is from Emily Dickinson's poem "Success." Discuss the theme of the poem and explain how Dickinson uses poetic form to convey meaning in her poem.

Success is counted sweetest
By those who ne'er succeed.
To comprehend a nectar
Requires sorest need.

Not one of all the purple host
Who took the flag to-day
Can tell the definition,
So clear, of victory,

As he, defeated, dying,
On whose forbidden ear
The distant strains of triumph
Break, agonized and clear!

GO ON TO THE NEXT PAGE

Constructed Response II: Teaching Writing

Directions: Students in a sixth-grade class were asked to write a descriptive essay for an audience of their peers from the perspective of a woman in their lives. What follows is the final draft of one student's response to this assignment. Read the student's response carefully, paying special attention to the features of writing listed below, and then compose one constructed response that addresses the three tasks that follow the student's essay. Plan to spend approximately 15 minutes of your testing time on this question.

Features of Writing

- Content/Supporting Ideas
- Organization
- Vocabulary
- Sentence Structure
- Mechanics

Student Essay

The Battle for Life

After the longest car-ride home from the hospital that I ever had, I stepped into my house, walked down the hallway, went through the living room, and kitchen, then, as I approached the back room my heart started pounding. "Girls, I think you should sit down, (I was talking to my two high school-aged daughters) I am very sorry that I have to tell you this but … I have breast cancer." Once I told Sarah (my older daughter) and Melissa, they scurried up to their rooms and were sobbing non-stop. It took them quite a while to realize that overcoming something like breast cancer is possible, but once they did, we were all striving for survival.

First, I had my surgery. After that, I went through chemotherepy and lost all of my hair. It was so devestating having to loose parts of me along the journey, but I knew that it would all be worth it in the end. Along with chemotherepy, there were other obstacles getting in the way like not being able to get enough sleep. So I did a lot of yoga and was fortunate to have people in my family like my brother Jim always being there for me and knowing that I could call him any time if I needed him.

Today, I have survived, and I am very healthy. I also have a wonderful family and great brothers, neices, nefews, and a wonderful father to look forward to seeing.

Tasks

1. Identify ONE feature of the student's writing you view as a strength for a sixth-grade writer. Be sure to support your response with examples from the student's essay. Do NOT discuss facility in the use of standard written English (grammar, punctuation, spelling) in this part of your response.

2. Identify ONE feature of the student's writing you view as a weakness for a sixth-grade writer. Be sure to support your response with examples from the student's essay. Do NOT discuss facility in the use of standard written English (grammar, punctuation, spelling) in this part of your response.

3. Describe one follow-up assignment you would give this student that would build on the strength you described in Task 1 OR address the weakness you identified in Task 2. Explain how the assignment would help this sixth-grade student writer.

IF YOU FINISH BEFORE TIME IS CALLED, CHECK YOUR WORK ON THIS SECTION ONLY. DO NOT WORK ON ANY OTHER SECTION IN THE TEST.

Answer Key for Selected Response

Question	Answer	Content Category	Where to Get More Help
1.	B	Reading and Literature	Chapter 3
2.	D	Reading and Literature	Chapter 3
3.	C	Reading and Literature	Chapter 3
4.	B	Reading and Literature	Chapter 3
5.	B	Writing, Speaking, and Listening	Chapter 5
6.	A	Language Use, Vocabulary, and Linguistics	Chapter 4
7.	B	Language Use, Vocabulary, and Linguistics	Chapter 4
8.	D	Writing, Speaking, and Listening	Chapter 5
9.	D	Writing, Speaking, and Listening	Chapter 5
10.	B	Writing, Speaking, and Listening	Chapter 5
11.	D	Writing, Speaking, and Listening	Chapter 5
12.	C	Writing, Speaking, and Listening	Chapter 5
13.	A	Reading and Literature Study	Chapter 3
14.	C	Reading and Literature Study	Chapter 3
15.	B	Reading and Literature Study	Chapter 3
16.	D	Reading and Literature Study	Chapter 3
17.	B	Reading and Literature Study	Chapter 3
18.	D	Reading and Literature Study	Chapter 3
19.	A	Writing, Speaking, and Listening	Chapter 5
20.	B	Writing, Speaking, and Listening	Chapter 5
21.	C	Language Use, Vocabulary, and Linguistics	Chapter 4
22.	B	Language Use, Vocabulary, and Linguistics	Chapter 4
23.	A	Writing, Speaking, and Listening	Chapter 5
24.	C	Writing, Speaking, and Listening	Chapter 5
25.	B	Writing, Speaking, and Listening	Chapter 5
26.	D	Writing, Speaking, and Listening	Chapter 5
27.	A	Reading and Literature Study	Chapter 3
28.	C	Reading and Literature	Chapter 3
29.	B	Reading and Literature	Chapter 3
30.	B	Reading and Literature	Chapter 3
31.	B	Reading and Literature	Chapter 3
32.	D	Reading and Literature	Chapter 3
33.	C	Writing, Speaking, and Listening	Chapter 5
34.	A	Writing, Speaking, and Listening	Chapter 5
35.	D	Language Use, Vocabulary, and Linguistics	Chapter 4
36.	B	Language Use, Vocabulary, and Linguistics	Chapter 4
37.	C	Writing, Speaking, and Listening	Chapter 5
38.	C	Writing, Speaking, and Listening	Chapter 5
39.	C	Writing, Speaking, and Listening	Chapter 5
40.	D	Writing, Speaking, and Listening	Chapter 5

continued

Question	Answer	Content Category	Where to Get More Help
41.	A	Writing, Speaking, and Listening	Chapter 5
42.	A	Language Use, Vocabulary, and Linguistics	Chapter 4
43.	B	Language Use, Vocabulary, and Linguistics	Chapter 4
44.	D	Reading and Literature	Chapter 3
45.	A	Reading and Literature	Chapter 3
46.	B	Reading and Literature	Chapter 3
47.	D	Reading and Literature	Chapter 3
48.	C	Reading and Literature	Chapter 3
49.	A	Reading and Literature	Chapter 3
50.	A	Language and Linguistics	Chapter 4
51.	D	Language and Linguistics	Chapter 4
52.	A	Writing, Speaking, and Listening	Chapter 5
53.	C	Writing, Speaking, and Listening	Chapter 5
54.	C	Reading and Literature	Chapter 3
55.	C	Reading and Literature	Chapter 3
56.	A	Reading and Literature	Chapter 3
57.	B	Writing, Speaking, and Listening	Chapter 5
58.	C	Writing, Speaking, and Listening	Chapter 5
59.	D	Reading and Literature Study	Chapter 3
60.	A	Writing, Speaking, and Listening	Chapter 5
61.	D	Writing, Speaking, and Listening	Chapter 5
62.	B	Writing, Speaking, and Listening	Chapter 5
63.	B	Writing, Speaking, and Listening	Chapter 5
64.	C	Language Use, Vocabulary, and Linguistics	Chapter 4
65.	C	Language Use, Vocabulary, and Linguistics	Chapter 4
66.	D	Writing, Speaking, and Listening	Chapter 5
67.	B	Writing, Speaking, and Listening	Chapter 5
68.	C	Writing, Speaking, and Listening	Chapter 5
69.	D	Reading and Literature Study	Chapter 3
70.	D	Reading and Literature Study	Chapter 3
71.	A	Reading and Literature Study	Chapter 3
72.	B	Reading and Literature Study	Chapter 3
73.	C	Reading and Literature Study	Chapter 3
74.	D	Language Use, Vocabulary, and Linguistics	Chapter 4
75.	C	Language Use, Vocabulary, and Linguistics	Chapter 4
76.	B	Writing, Speaking, and Listening	Chapter 5
77.	A	Writing, Speaking, and Listening	Chapter 5
78.	D	Writing, Speaking, and Listening	Chapter 5
79.	D	Language and Linguistics	Chapter 4
80.	C	Language and Linguistics	Chapter 4
81.	B	Writing, Speaking, and Listening	Chapter 5
82.	A	Writing, Speaking, and Listening	Chapter 5

Question	Answer	Content Category	Where to Get More Help
83.	A	Writing, Speaking, and Listening	Chapter 5
84.	B	Writing, Speaking, and Listening	Chapter 5
85.	A	Writing, Speaking, and Listening	Chapter 5
86.	C	Reading and Literature	Chapter 3
87.	A	Reading and Literature	Chapter 3
88.	D	Reading and Literature	Chapter 3
89.	B	Reading and Literature	Chapter 3
90.	A	Reading and Literature	Chapter 3
91.	D	Writing, Speaking, and Listening	Chapter 5
92.	B	Writing, Speaking, and Listening	Chapter 5
93.	D	Writing, Speaking, and Listening	Chapter 5
94.	A	Reading and Literature	Chapter 3
95.	A	Reading and Literature	Chapter 3
96.	C	Reading and Literature	Chapter 3
97.	B	Reading and Literature	Chapter 3
98.	B	English Language Arts Instruction	Chapter 6
99.	D	English Language Arts Instruction	Chapter 6
100.	C	English Language Arts Instruction	Chapter 6
101.	A	Language Use, Vocabulary, and Linguistics	Chapter 4
102.	C	Language Use, Vocabulary, and Linguistics	Chapter 4
103.	B	Language Use, Vocabulary, and Linguistics	Chapter 4
104.	B	Language Use, Vocabulary, and Linguistics	Chapter 4
105.	B	Language Use, Vocabulary, and Linguistics	Chapter 4
106.	D	Language Use, Vocabulary, and Linguistics	Chapter 4
107.	C	Reading and Literature	Chapter 3
108.	A	Reading and Literature	Chapter 3
109.	D	Reading and Literature	Chapter 3
110.	D	Reading and Literature	Chapter 3

Answer Explanations

Selected Response

1. **B.** Hermia and Robin Goodfellow, a puck who causes much mischief, are characters in *A Midsummer Night's Dream.*

2. **D.** *The Giver, 1984,* and *The Lord of the Rings* are all science fiction/fantasy novels.

3. **C.** *Fahrenheit 451* takes place in the future—in the 24th century.

4. **B.** The meaning of the phrase "to dissolve the political bands which have connected them with another" is best paraphrased in choice B: to sever political ties with England.

5. **B.** The author respectfully sets a purpose for this declaration based on "a decent respect to the opinions of mankind." This rhetorical strategy persuades the reader to read on and respectfully consider this declaration.

6. **A.** Tituba uses dialect from the area her family comes from. Scholars believe that Tituba, a slave in the Parris household, was most likely a slave from South America, not Africa.

7. **B.** A compound/complex sentence has two or more independent clauses and one or more dependent clauses.

8. **D.** Rhetoric can be defined as the use of language in a persuasive or impressive way.

9. **D.** Reliable Internet sources should be checked for authorship, accuracy, purpose, and access (so that others can find the information again).

10. **B.** The proper MLA citation is choice B because it contains italics for the book title and only the page number in parentheses, since the author's name appears in the sentence.

11. **D.** Writers should consider the audience for their writing—who the intended reader is, what his or her background knowledge is, and how this piece might be purposeful beyond the classroom.

12. **C.** Shakespeare's "Sonnet 18" is organized as a comparison. It compares a loved one to summer.

13. **A.** An anticipation guide is a series of open-ended questions intended to prepare students for the major themes or concepts in an upcoming reading assignment.

14. **C.** Miss Bell uses a replica of the Twin Towers as a concrete experience to start a discussion about 9/11 and activate students' prior knowledge before reading.

15. **B.** Mr. Audette is scaffolding instruction—offering students a model, guided practice, and independent practice with the support of a capable adult.

16. **D.** Johann Wyss wrote *The Swiss Family Robinson* in 1813.

17. **B.** In literature circles, students play key roles such as summarizer, word finder, passage master, and illustrator to make sense of their reading collaboratively.

18. **D.** A Venn diagram is a graphic organizer made up of overlapping circles and is best used to compare and contrast information.

19. **A.** This excerpt from *Gulliver's Travels* can best be described as prose in chronological sequence. The narrator first tells the reader about his arrival in Lisbon, then his welcome at the captain's home, and finally his efforts to be clothed properly and comfortably.

20. **B.** Jonathan Swift was born in 1667. *Gulliver's Travels* was first published anonymously in 1726.

21. **C.** A collective noun names a group or unit, such as gaggle of geese or cache of jewels.

22. **B.** The verb tense in this sentence is present perfect because the action (*attending*) began in the past but continues into the present.

23. **A.** In the omniscient point of view, the narrator is free to tell the story from any and all characters' perspectives.

24. **C.** Choice C, screenplay : movie, has an analogous relationship to score : concert because a score is the text of a concert and a screenplay is the text of a movie.

25. **B.** A news article typically follows an inverted pyramid structure with the lead first, followed by details presented in the order of importance.

26. **D.** An editorial is a brief persuasive essay that expresses a viewpoint on a timely or important topic.

27. **A.** *Julie of the Wolves* is the story of a young Eskimo girl who experiences the changes inflicted upon her culture by outside forces.

28. **C.** S. E. Hinton wrote *The Outsiders* when she was 16 years old.

29. **B.** Ponyboy and Dallas are two of the main characters in the novel *The Outsiders*.

30. **B.** "All the world's a stage" is a metaphor comparing life to a play.

31. **B.** The mood of a literary work is the emotional state of mind or atmosphere created by the author.

32. **D.** Hughes captured the beauty of African American Vernacular English through his authentic and careful use of idioms and dialect.

33. **C.** In the publishing stage of the writing process, a writer is least likely to use the Internet to search for writing ideas. This task is more likely to occur in the prewriting stage.

34. **A.** The writing process is a recursive process in which the writer moves through the stages of writing in a unique sequence. The term *recursive* signifies that each writer's process is not linear—going directly from one prescribed stage to another. Rather, the writing process is unique to each writer based on that writer's distinct needs.

35. **D.** Readers use three cueing systems: semantics, syntax, and structure. When a reader draws upon what he or she knows, the reader is using the semantic, or meaning, cueing system.

36. **B.** The root word *ceed* or *cede* means "to go" or "to yield."

37. **C.** Response journals are intended to enable students to construct meaning from their experiences and their reading of a text.

38. **C.** Writing teachers can best use writing workshop time to lead writing conferences with students.

39. **C.** The proper MLA citation of Dickens' *Great Expectations* is:

Dickens, Charles. *Great Expectations*. New York: Random House, 1907. Print.

40. **D.** Bartlett's *Familiar Quotations* is the foremost print and online source of famous quotations.

41. **A.** In an appeal to authority, advertisers hire sports, television, film, and other celebrities to attest to the value of a product.

42. **A.** *Freight* and *believe* contain the vowel digraphs *ei* and *ie*. A vowel digraph is a pair of vowel letters used to create one sound.

43. **B.** Students who are nonfluent in English can read silently and comprehend with some proficiency before they can read aloud well; therefore, choice B is the least likely to be supportive for nonfluent English readers.

44. **D.** In *Bridge to Terabithia,* Jess has to overcome the loss of a friend. Of the choices available, the main conflict is person versus self.

45. **A.** The main character in *Holes* is Stanley Yelnats, whose name is a palindrome—a word that is the same when spelled backward and forward.

46. **B.** *Holes* is a story about bullying, lizards, and Camp Green Lake. The main character, Stanley Yelnats, is sent to Camp Green Lake as punishment for allegedly stealing a pair of sneakers. He is forced to dig a hole every day in the former location of Green Lake, and in those holes he finds yellow-spotted lizards.

47. **D.** *Holes* was written by Louis Sachar, the author of several young-adolescent books, including the *Wayside School* series and the *Marvin Redpost* series.

48. **C.** Janie, a girl who was kidnapped as a child, is the main character in *The Voice on the Radio,* a companion novel to *The Face on the Milk Carton* and *Whatever Happened to Janie?*.

49. **A.** Jim, a runaway slave, joins Huck Finn on his adventure down the Mississippi River. Note that choice B is meant to trick you. Tom Sawyer, not Tim Sawyer, is the mischievous friend in *The Adventures of Huckleberry Finn*.

50. **A.** The sentence in choice A contains a dangling modifier—a modifier that fails to refer logically to the word it modifies. In this case, the teacher certification office did not take the Praxis English Subject Assessment test.

51. **D.** Compound words are made up of two smaller words that together create new meaning.

52. **A.** During a peer conference, students read their writing to hear their ideas out loud and receive feedback from an initial audience. This is an appropriate revision-stage activity in which students re-see their writing in an effort to strengthen and change the piece.

53. C. In this advertisement, an appeal to tradition is being used.

54. C. *The Witch of Blackbird Pond* is a historical fiction novel that takes place in Connecticut in the late 1600s.

55. C. *The Glory Field* was written by Walter Dean Myers.

56. A. The narrator of *The Giver* is Jonas, a young boy chosen to keep all the memories of a society.

57. B. Primary sources are original documents, such as journals, diaries, laws, and maps.

58. C. Secondary sources are commentaries on primary sources.

59. D. *The Pigman* by Paul Zindel is the story of two high school sophomores who befriend Mr. Angelo Pignati, the Pigman.

60. A. A novel is best defined as an extended, fictional prose narrative.

61. D. Ponyboy in *The Outsiders* is the protagonist, or the central character in a narrative or drama.

62. B. Cause-and-effect texts are organized to show the relationship between events and their results.

63. B. The climax is the turning point in a story, when the problem is at its worst.

64. C. The prefix *self* is correctly followed by a hyphen.

65. C. Slang is informal speech made up of newly coined expressions or common words used in a new way.

66. D. Paterson opens *Bridge to Terabithia* with onomatopoeia, a literary device in which sound words are used.

67. B. Argument is a type of writing that tries to prove that something is true or convince the reader to see the writer's viewpoint.

68. C. One propaganda technique is to suggest that everyone is doing or believing something, so you should jump on the bandwagon, too.

69. D. In the first-person point of view, the story is told from the perspective of one of the characters.

70. D. This line from Clement C. Moore's *A Visit from Saint Nicholas* contains the simile "like a flash."

71. A. Round-robin reading aloud in class is a practice that often demotivates students for several reasons, including tuning out between reading turns, listening to less proficient readers, and fearing embarrassment while reading to the whole class.

72. B. "Shall I compare thee to a summer's day?" is the first line of a love sonnet; it is not an insult.

73. C. To avoid plagiarism, students should summarize in their own words, cite quotations, and enclose quoted words in quotation marks.

74. D. *Restroom* is a euphemism for the toilet room. A euphemism is a polite way to discuss a topic that may bring about discomfort.

75. C. The verb *will attend* is in the future tense.

76. B. Subject writing includes writing interviews, accounts, or biographies to capture the meaning of the subject being written about.

77. A. Lincoln, one of the United States' great orators, used repetition in this quote to make his point effectively.

78. D. A well-written argument contains an assertion, a premise, and a conclusion.

79. D. "Dear Sir or Madam:" is an appropriate greeting in a business letter. Please note that a business letter requires the use of a colon, not a comma, at the end of the greeting.

80. C. The words *belong* and *believe* contain one open syllable, *be-*.

81. B. When an author uses good diction, he or she chooses words that accurately convey the intended meaning and suit the occasion of the piece.

82. **A.** Hughes' poem "Harlem" is commonly referred to as "Dream Deferred." In this poem, the dream that is deferred, or put off, could be lost or destroyed. Lines such as "fester in the sun" and "stink like rotten meat" support this interpretation of the theme.

83. **A.** The topic sentence of this paragraph appears in the last line. The speaker's point in this paragraph is that the people have nothing to fear except fear itself, which results in inaction. Choice B is a supporting detail sentence and a distractor because topic sentences are typically the first sentence of paragraphs in academic writing.

84. **B.** A supporting detail in this paragraph is, "The president will speak candidly and decisively, as the people expect," which is found in the first sentence of the paragraph. As noted in the explanation for item 83 above, while the first sentence of a paragraph is often topic sentence, this is not always the case.

85. **A.** *Preeminently* means "most important" in the context of this speech.

86. **C.** Franklin Delano Roosevelt delivered this, his first inaugural address, in 1933.

87. **A.** This is an English sonnet, which is traditionally written in iambic pentameter.

88. **D.** Elizabeth Barrett Browning wrote *Sonnets from the Portuguese,* a collection of 44 love sonnets to her husband, Robert Browning.

89. **B.** The poet uses an extended metaphor comparing her love to a garden.

90. **A.** The poet is asking her love to remain true to her.

91. **D.** The prewriting stage of the writing process gives students an opportunity to brainstorm ideas for the short-story assignment with the teacher's guidance.

92. **B.** Jackson's reference to Jerusalem in the speech is meant to allude to the Bible and appeal emotionally to the listener.

93. **D.** Jackson uses a rhetorical question, one that he does not actually want answered, to motivate his listeners and persuade them of the importance of his message.

94. **A.** An allegory is a story in which the events and characters symbolize ideas about human life or for a historical or political event.

95. **A.** Mrs. Wildes uses an anticipation guide to open the lesson on *The Giver.* This short questionnaire prompts the students to debate and discuss issues related to the book prior to reading.

96. **C.** Structure cues are used when a student sounds out a word and uses visual and phonics cues to determine how to pronounce or read a word.

97. **B.** Formative assessment is used before or during instruction to inform instructional planning and enhance student achievement.

98. **B.** English immersion instruction consists of classroom discourse conducted in English only, even if students speak other languages. The teacher offers simplified English so that Maria can learn both English and the academic content.

99. **D.** Jigsaw is a cooperative learning structure in which students are responsible for only a portion of a task and then work together with the students who have the remainder of the information; collectively, they assemble complete understanding. In this way, the task is "jigsawed."

100. **C.** Lower-level questions in Bloom's taxonomy include knowledge and literal questions.

101. **A.** Based on the passage, Dee's language/literacy status is best described as primary language not English (PLNE). Mrs. Meyer can support Dee by building on her culture, supporting Dee's language/literacy proficiency in her primary language (Vietnamese), and offering opportunities for Dee to work in small groups. It is common for PLNE students to remain nearly silent in the classroom for several months until they gain proficiency in English.

102. **C.** Students who are learning a new language benefit from opportunities to speak in small groups with peers. Small groups give students more opportunities to interact and take risks with language when the whole class is not listening.

103. **B.** Students who are nonfluent in English can read silently and comprehend with some proficiency before they can read aloud proficiently; therefore, choice B is the least likely to be supportive for nonfluent English readers.

104. **B.** Structured English immersion programs emphasize instruction in English between 70 and 90 percent of the school day and prioritize teaching at the students' language level proficiency.

105. **B.** English language learners will benefit from all of the instructional strategies except silent reading followed by a chapter test. While silent reading is expected at some point, the reading should be accompanied by pre-teaching of vocabulary and key concepts.

106. **D.** Teachers of English language learners should be aware that many texts contain cultural, contextual information that may need to be taught to students. Teachers can start with broad, universal concepts, such as conflict in this example, and then build on students' background knowledge to teach them the necessary background information.

107. **C.** Of the choices offered, Nishita would benefit most from curriculum compacting, or determining the key components of the curriculum that must be met and offering a compacted version of the work. Students like Nishita may become bored or even develop discipline problems when the work is not challenging.

108. **A.** A story map is the best graphic organizer to present information such as characters, plot, and setting, which are also known as story elements or story grammar. A sequence chart (choice B) is best used to support instruction about the beginning, middle, and ending events in a story. A hierarchical array (choice C) shows the relationship between a concept/term and its related elements, which are presented below the concept or term. A Venn diagram (choice D) is best used to show the similarities and differences among elements in a story.

109. **D.** Summarizing and note-taking are essential instructional strategies that teach students to better comprehend materials.

110. **D.** A portmanteau word is a word that has been melded together, such as Ebonics, which is a combination of *ebony* and *phonics*.

Constructed Response

Constructed Response I: Textual Interpretation

Here is an example of a constructed response that would be scored as a 3:

> In this constructed response, I will analyze the poetic form used in Emily Dickinson's "Success" and then discuss the poem's theme. "Success" is written in three stanzas of four lines each, which is known as a quatrain. Dickinson uses iambic trimeter (each line has three iambic feet) and iambic tetrameter (each line has four iambic feet). An iambic foot is made up of one unstressed syllable followed by one stressed syllable. For example, the first line "Success is counted sweetest" is written in iambic tetrameter, with the last foot incomplete. The second line, "By those who ne'er succeed," is written in iambic trimeter. The poem's rhyme scheme uses an ABCB pattern; in other words, the second and fourth lines in each stanza are the only ones that rhyme.
>
> The theme is paradoxical in nature and is established in the first quatrain. The first two lines may be interpreted as: success is most understood by those who have not succeeded. The next lines, "To comprehend a nectar/Requires sorest need," further develop the theme with a specific example: the one who most appreciates and understands the special nature of nectar (a delicious drink or in mythology, the drink of the gods) is the one who most desperately needs it. In the remaining two quatrains, Dickinson conjures military imagery, such as the purple host (bloodied soldiers) "defeated, dying" on the battlefield, who "can tell the definition,/So clear, of victory." Finally, the poet closes with a dying soldier who hears his triumphant enemy celebrating success.

Score Explanation

Constructed response questions that earn full credit demonstrate a thorough understanding of the content. This response includes analysis of specific poetic features—form, rhyme, meter, and theme—with some depth. Sound understanding of Emily Dickinson's poem "Success" is evident, and the test-taker supports points with appropriate quotes from the poem. For example, the test-taker provides accurate analysis of the lines, "To comprehend a nectar/Requires sorest need." Finally, this response demonstrates coherent control of language and facility with conventions of Standard Written English.

Constructed Response II: Teaching Writing

Here is an example of a constructed response that would be scored as a 3:

One strength of this descriptive essay is its attention to the task of writing from the perspective of an important woman in the writer's life. The lead sentence engages the reader and creates a sense of mystery, "After the longest car-ride home from the hospital that I ever had, … my heart started pounding." The writer appropriately and sensitively takes the perspective of her family member who is battling breast cancer. The essay remains on task as the author develops details such as the teenage daughters' distress, the trials of treatment ("It was so devestating having to loose parts of me along the journey."), and the journey's end ("Today, I have survived …"). This essay, based on a realistic personal experience, is likely to appeal to a sixth-grade peer audience.

One area of weakness this writer demonstrates is the limited use of illustrative examples. For example, in the second paragraph about obstacles, such as not getting enough sleep, the writer does not describe what it's like to experience sleepless nights, the causes, the thoughts and feelings the narrator is experiencing. The closing sentences are particularly lacking in detail, and the sentences are quite simple—"Today, I have survived, and I am very healthy. I also have a wonderful family …"

One suggestion for revision is to address the lack of illustrative details by first highlighting the strength of the student's lead sentence, which is filled with detail and pulls the reader into the day this woman had to tell her daughters about her breast cancer diagnosis. Then the teacher and student could brainstorm ways to build rich detail into the second and third paragraphs. For example, the student states, "So I did a lot of yoga …" and could develop more vivid images in the reader's mind about the ways yoga made the woman feel— more powerful, healthy, alive. The lead sentence of the second paragraph might be revised to signal the reader about the main idea of this paragraph and offer an allusion to the long battle ahead.

The purpose of this follow-up assignment would be to encourage the student to develop stamina as a writer by including rich, illustrative details, not only in the lead sentence of the essay, but throughout the piece. The essay surely remains focused on the important person in the writer's life and is clearly organized, but lacks descriptive details after the first paragraph. To extend the assignment above, the student and teacher could also look for examples of rich detail in the works of favorite young-adult authors.

Score Explanation

This is a full-credit response because it addresses all three prompts with strong evidence of how to support a student in strengthening an essay and understanding features of writing. The response to Prompt 1 correctly identifies one strength as the development of writing from another's perspective in an essay assignment. The response to Prompt 2, identifying one weakness of the essay, discusses the need for illustrative details. Analysis of specific instances where the writer loses reader interest follows with specific text cites. The response to Prompt 3 offers specific follow-up assignments to support the student writer's efforts to maintain reader interest through mini lessons using author study of texts with vivid detail. These suggestions for revision are very strong, including what should be done and why these revisions would improve the essay. The response shows a clear understanding of how a writing teacher's actions highlight a student's strengths and support the development of a student's skills and development as a writer.

Chapter 10

Middle School: Content Knowledge—Literature and Language Studies Subtest (5146)

This chapter includes one full-length practice test for the Literature and Language Studies section of the Praxis Middle School: Content Knowledge (5146) test. This practice subtest will give you a sense of the format of the test and help you determine which content areas you need to study. You may also want to practice your pacing while taking this full-length practice test. There are 30 selected-response questions for the Literature and Language Studies subtest, so you will want to plan for approximately 30 minutes of testing time. Remember, you will have a total of 2 hours to complete all four content areas on the test, which is made up of a total of 120 selected-response questions. The other subtests have 30 selected-response questions each in the following content areas: mathematics, history/social studies, and science.

After you complete the practice test, score your answers and use the explanations to assess content areas to study in chapters 3–5 of this book. For additional preparation for this actual test, you may want to complete, or at least review, the other full-length practice tests in chapters 7–9 to determine further content areas to study. Even though these additional practice tests are written for other English Subject Assessment tests, the broad content categories of the questions—Reading and Literature; Language Use, Vocabulary, and Linguistics; and Writing, Speaking, and Listening—remain virtually the same. Note that the English Language Arts Instruction content is not assessed on test 5146.

It's time to set yourself up in a quiet place with no interruptions, get your pencils ready, take a look at the clock, and begin your practice test.

IMPORTANT NOTE: For ease of studying, all questions in this practice test are single-selection multiple-choice.

Answer Sheet

1	Ⓐ	Ⓑ	Ⓒ	Ⓓ
2	Ⓐ	Ⓑ	Ⓒ	Ⓓ
3	Ⓐ	Ⓑ	Ⓒ	Ⓓ
4	Ⓐ	Ⓑ	Ⓒ	Ⓓ
5	Ⓐ	Ⓑ	Ⓒ	Ⓓ
6	Ⓐ	Ⓑ	Ⓒ	Ⓓ
7	Ⓐ	Ⓑ	Ⓒ	Ⓓ
8	Ⓐ	Ⓑ	Ⓒ	Ⓓ
9	Ⓐ	Ⓑ	Ⓒ	Ⓓ
10	Ⓐ	Ⓑ	Ⓒ	Ⓓ
11	Ⓐ	Ⓑ	Ⓒ	Ⓓ
12	Ⓐ	Ⓑ	Ⓒ	Ⓓ
13	Ⓐ	Ⓑ	Ⓒ	Ⓓ
14	Ⓐ	Ⓑ	Ⓒ	Ⓓ
15	Ⓐ	Ⓑ	Ⓒ	Ⓓ
16	Ⓐ	Ⓑ	Ⓒ	Ⓓ
17	Ⓐ	Ⓑ	Ⓒ	Ⓓ
18	Ⓐ	Ⓑ	Ⓒ	Ⓓ
19	Ⓐ	Ⓑ	Ⓒ	Ⓓ
20	Ⓐ	Ⓑ	Ⓒ	Ⓓ
21	Ⓐ	Ⓑ	Ⓒ	Ⓓ
22	Ⓐ	Ⓑ	Ⓒ	Ⓓ
23	Ⓐ	Ⓑ	Ⓒ	Ⓓ
24	Ⓐ	Ⓑ	Ⓒ	Ⓓ
25	Ⓐ	Ⓑ	Ⓒ	Ⓓ
26	Ⓐ	Ⓑ	Ⓒ	Ⓓ
27	Ⓐ	Ⓑ	Ⓒ	Ⓓ
28	Ⓐ	Ⓑ	Ⓒ	Ⓓ
29	Ⓐ	Ⓑ	Ⓒ	Ⓓ
30	Ⓐ	Ⓑ	Ⓒ	Ⓓ

Literature and Language Subtest

Time: 30 minutes

30 questions

Directions: Each of the questions or statements below is followed by four possible answers or completions. Select the one that is best in each case.

1. Which of the following pairs of characters appears in Shakespeare's *A Midsummer Night's Dream*?

   A. Romeo and Juliet
   B. Hermia and Robin Goodfellow
   C. Caesar and Calpurnia
   D. Gertrude and Claudius

2. *The Giver, 1984*, and *The Lord of the Rings* can all be classified as belonging to which of the following genres?

   A. Realistic fiction
   B. Poetry
   C. Historical fiction
   D. Science fiction/fantasy

3. The setting of *Fahrenheit 451* is _____.

   A. 1984
   B. the 21st century
   C. the 24th century
   D. the 1950s

Questions 4 and 5 are based on the following excerpt from the Declaration of Independence.

When in the Course of human events, it becomes necessary for one people to dissolve the political bands which have connected them with another, and to assume among the powers of the earth, the separate and equal situation to which the Laws of Nature and of Nature's God entitle them, a decent respect to the opinions of mankind requires that they should declare the causes which impel them to the separation.

4. Which of the following best describes the meaning of the phrase "to dissolve the political bands which have connected them with another"?

   A. To seek a resolution to the political nature of a conflict
   B. To sever political ties with England
   C. To seek a change in the political structure of the homeland
   D. To seek religious freedom

5. The phrase "a decent respect to the opinions of mankind" works persuasively because it appeals to the reader's sense of _____.

   A. audience
   B. propriety
   C. rationale
   D. manhood

GO ON TO THE NEXT PAGE

6. Tituba, a character in Arthur Miller's play *The Crucible*, says, "My Betty be hearty soon?" Which of the following best describes Tituba's use of language?

    A. Dialect

    B. Phonology

    C. Pragmatics

    D. Grammatical error

7. The following sentence is a _____ sentence.

I look forward to teaching, and I plan to teach middle school English because I love literature.

    A. compound

    B. compound/complex

    C. complex

    D. simple

8. Which of the following terms can be defined as using language persuasively or impressively?

    A. Personification

    B. Point of view

    C. Tone

    D. Rhetoric

9. Which of the following criteria should be used when evaluating Internet sources for a research paper?

    I. Author

    II. Accuracy

    III. Purpose of the site

    IV. Access

    A. I

    B. I, II

    C. I, II, IV

    D. All of the above

10. Which of the following correctly cites a source using MLA-format guidelines?

    A. Golding wrote in his opening line of Lord of the Flies, "The boy with fair hair lowered himself down the last few feet of rock and began to pick his way toward the lagoon" (7).

    B. Golding wrote in his opening line of *Lord of the Flies*, "The boy with fair hair lowered himself down the last few feet of rock and began to pick his way toward the lagoon" (7).

    C. Golding wrote in his opening line of Lord of the Flies, "The boy with fair hair lowered himself down the last few feet of rock and began to pick his way toward the lagoon" (Golding, 7).

    D. Golding wrote in his opening line of *Lord of the Flies*, "The boy with fair hair lowered himself down the last few feet of rock and began to pick his way toward the lagoon." (Golding, 7)

11. When a writer considers the _____ for a piece, he or she considers who else will read it and what background knowledge the reader might need to understand the point of the writing.

    A. grade

    B. publisher

    C. location

    D. audience

GO ON TO THE NEXT PAGE

Questions 12 and 13 are based on Shakespeare's "Sonnet 18."

Shall I compare thee to a summer's day?
Thou art more lovely and more temperate:
Rough winds do shake the darling buds of May,
And summer's lease hath all too short a date:
Sometime too hot the eye of heaven shines,
And often is his gold complexion dimmed,
And every fair from fair sometime declines,
By chance, or nature's changing course untrimmed:
But thy eternal summer shall not fade,
Nor lose possession of that fair thou ow'st,
Nor shall death brag thou wander'st in his shade,
When in eternal lines to time thou grow'st,
So long as men can breathe, or eyes can see,
So long lives this, and this gives life to thee.

12. "Sonnet 18" is organized as a _____.

    A. sequence
    B. hierarchy
    C. comparison
    D. cause and effect

13. Prior to teaching Shakespeare's "Sonnet 18" to her eighth graders, Miss Judge asks her students open-ended questions about feelings evoked by summer and people they love. This pre-reading activity is called a(n) _____.

    A. anticipation guide
    B. pretest
    C. brainstorm
    D. graphic organizer

14. Prior to reading a news article to her students about the 9/11 terrorist attacks, Miss Bell shows them a replica of the World Trade Center that she saved as a memento from a trip to New York City. Miss Bell is using which of the following methods to activate prior knowledge?

    A. Concept mapping
    B. Replication
    C. Concrete experiences
    D. Semantic feature analysis

15. Mr. Audette makes a point to model the reading strategy to be learned in a lesson, offer guided practice by using the reading strategy in class, and allow his students time to work independently while practicing the new reading strategy. Which of the following best describes the theory behind Mr. Audette's practice?

    A. Chalk and talk
    B. Scaffolding instruction
    C. Lecture
    D. Cooperative learning

GO ON TO THE NEXT PAGE

16. Which of the following authors wrote *The Swiss Family Robinson*?

    A. Geoffrey Chaucer
    B. William Hill Brown
    C. Herman Hesse
    D. Johann Wyss

17. Mrs. Friedman has organized her students into literature circles, with each student taking a role in the group. Which of the following roles is most likely found in a literature circle?

    A. Key grip
    B. Summarizer
    C. Leader
    D. Dictionary worker

18. Tory and Kelly are trying to compare and contrast the film of *The Wizard of Oz* and the book. Which of the following graphic organizers will best support their note-taking?

    A. Culture cluster
    B. Story map
    C. Hierarchical array
    D. Venn diagram

Questions 19 and 20 are based on the following passage from Gulliver's Travels *by Jonathan Swift.*

We arrived at Lisbon, Nov. 5, 1715. At our landing, the captain forced me to cover myself with his cloak, to prevent the rabble from crowding about me. I was conveyed to his own house, and at my earnest request, he led me up to the highest room backwards. I conjured him to "conceal from all persons what I had told him of the Houyhnhnms, because the least hint of such a story would not only draw numbers of people to see me, but probably put me in danger of being imprisoned, or burnt by the Inquisition." The captain persuaded me to accept a suit of clothes newly made; but I would not suffer the tailor to take my measure; however, Don Pedro being almost of my size, they fitted me well enough. He accoutred me with other necessaries, all new, which I aired for twenty-four hours before I would use them.

19. Which of the following best describes this excerpt from *Gulliver's Travels*?

    A. Prose in chronological sequence
    B. Lyrical poetry
    C. Prose in compare-and-contrast structure
    D. Realistic fiction

20. In which of the following periods was *Gulliver's Travels* written and first published?

    A. Early 1600s
    B. Early 1700s
    C. Early 1800s
    D. Early 1900s

21. Which of the following pairs are collective nouns?

    A. people and schools
    B. Mary's and John's
    C. gaggle and cache
    D. his and her

GO ON TO THE NEXT PAGE

22. Which of the following is the verb tense in the sentence below?

Tory has attended Curtis Corner Middle School for sixth and seventh grades.

A. Future
B. Present perfect
C. Present
D. Past perfect

23. When a story is written from an omniscient point of view, which of the following is true?

A. The narrator is free to tell the story from any and all characters' points of view.
B. The story is told from the point of view of one character.
C. The story is told by someone outside the story.
D. The narrator compares two unlike things.

24. Which of the following word pairs demonstrates an analogous relationship to score : concert?

A. game : inning
B. record : sound
C. screenplay : movie
D. music : video

25. Which of the following best describes the organization of a news article?

A. Cause and effect
B. Inverted pyramid
C. Hierarchical array
D. Problem/solution

26. Which of the following best defines an editorial?

A. A fact-and-opinion essay
B. A news article that covers an important current event
C. A letter that discusses opinions held by the author
D. A brief persuasive essay that expresses a viewpoint on a timely or important topic

27. Which of the following best summarizes the plot of *Julie of the Wolves* by Jean Craighead George?

A. A young Eskimo girl experiences the changes forced upon her culture.
B. A young girl lives outdoors for a year and removes herself from society's forces.
C. A young girl is forced to survive alone after a storm kills all the other inhabitants of her island.
D. A baby girl is abandoned and cared for by a pack of wolves.

28. Which of the following authors wrote *The Outsiders*?

A. Katherine Paterson
B. Harper Lee
C. S. E. Hinton
D. Walter Dean Myers

GO ON TO THE NEXT PAGE

29. Which of the following pairs are main characters in *The Outsiders*?

A. Johnny and Maria

B. Ponyboy and Dallas

C. Tex and Sherri

D. Jess and Leslie

30. Which of the following lines contain a metaphor?

A. "And when I am king, as king I will be—"

B. "All the world's a stage"

C. "Neither a borrower nor a lender be"

D. "How like a winter hath my absence been"

Answer Key

Question	Answer	Content Category	Where to Get More Help
1.	B	Reading and Literature	Chapter 3
2.	D	Reading and Literature	Chapter 3
3.	C	Reading and Literature	Chapter 3
4.	B	Reading and Literature	Chapter 3
5.	B	Writing, Speaking, and Listening	Chapter 5
6.	A	Language Use, Vocabulary, and Linguistics	Chapter 4
7.	B	Language Use, Vocabulary, and Linguistics	Chapter 4
8.	D	Writing, Speaking, and Listening	Chapter 5
9.	D	Writing, Speaking, and Listening	Chapter 5
10.	B	Writing, Speaking, and Listening	Chapter 5
11.	D	Writing, Speaking, and Listening	Chapter 5
12.	C	Writing, Speaking, and Listening	Chapter 5
13.	A	Reading and Literature Study	Chapter 3
14.	C	Reading and Literature Study	Chapter 3
15.	B	Reading and Literature Study	Chapter 3
16.	D	Reading and Literature Study	Chapter 3
17.	B	Reading and Literature Study	Chapter 3
18.	D	Reading and Literature Study	Chapter 3
19.	A	Writing, Speaking, and Listening	Chapter 5
20.	B	Writing, Speaking, and Listening	Chapter 5
21.	C	Language Use, Vocabulary, and Linguistics	Chapter 4
22.	B	Language Use, Vocabulary, and Linguistics	Chapter 4
23.	A	Writing, Speaking, and Listening	Chapter 5
24.	C	Writing, Speaking, and Listening	Chapter 5
25.	B	Writing, Speaking, and Listening	Chapter 5
26.	D	Writing, Speaking, and Listening	Chapter 5
27.	A	Reading and Literature Study	Chapter 3
28.	C	Reading and Literature	Chapter 3
29.	B	Reading and Literature	Chapter 3
30.	B	Reading and Literature	Chapter 3

Answer Explanations

1. **B.** Hermia and Robin Goodfellow, a puck who causes much mischief, are characters in *A Midsummer Night's Dream.*

2. **D.** *The Giver, 1984,* and *The Lord of the Rings* are all science fiction/fantasy novels.

3. **C.** *Fahrenheit 451* takes place in the future—in the 24th century.

4. **B.** The meaning of the phrase "to dissolve the political bands which have connected them with another" is best paraphrased in choice B: to sever political ties with England.

5. **B.** The author respectfully sets a purpose for this declaration based on "a decent respect to the opinions of mankind." This rhetorical strategy persuades the reader to read on and respectfully consider this declaration.

6. **A.** Tituba uses dialect from the area her family comes from. Scholars believe that Tituba, a slave in the Parris household, was most likely a slave from South America, not Africa.

7. **B.** A compound/complex sentence has two or more independent clauses and one or more dependent clauses.

8. **D.** Rhetoric can be defined as the use of language in a persuasive or impressive way.

9. **D.** Reliable Internet sources should be checked for authorship, accuracy, purpose, and access (so that others can find the information again).

10. **B.** The proper MLA citation is choice B because it contains italics for the book title and only the page number in parentheses, since the author's name appears in the sentence.

11. **D.** Writers should consider the audience for their writing—who the intended reader is, what his or her background knowledge is, and how this piece might be purposeful beyond the classroom.

12. **C.** Shakespeare's "Sonnet 18" is organized as a comparison. It compares a loved one to summer.

13. **A.** An anticipation guide is a series of open-ended questions intended to prepare students for the major themes or concepts in an upcoming reading assignment.

14. **C.** Miss Bell uses a replica of the Twin Towers as a concrete experience to start a discussion about 9/11 and activate students' prior knowledge before reading.

15. **B.** Mr. Audette is scaffolding instruction—offering students a model, guided practice, and independent practice with the support of a capable adult.

16. **D.** Johann Wyss wrote *The Swiss Family Robinson* in 1813.

17. **B.** In literature circles, students play key roles such as summarizer, word finder, passage master, and illustrator to make sense of their reading collaboratively.

18. **D.** A Venn diagram is a graphic organizer made up of overlapping circles and is best used to compare and contrast information.

19. **A.** This excerpt from *Gulliver's Travels* can best be described as prose in chronological sequence. The narrator first tells the reader about his arrival in Lisbon, then his welcome at the captain's home, and finally his efforts to be clothed properly and comfortably.

20. **B.** Jonathan Swift was born in 1667. *Gulliver's Travels* was first published anonymously in 1726.

21. **C.** A collective noun names a group or unit, such as gaggle of geese or cache of jewels.

22. **B.** The verb tense in this sentence is present perfect because the action (*attending*) began in the past but continues into the present.

23. **A.** In the omniscient point of view, the narrator is free to tell the story from any and all characters' perspectives.

24. **C.** Choice C, screenplay : movie, has an analogous relationship to score : concert because a score is the text of a concert and a screenplay is the text of a movie.

25. **B.** A news article typically follows an inverted pyramid structure with the lead first, followed by details presented in the order of importance.

26. **D.** An editorial is a brief persuasive essay that expresses a viewpoint on a timely or important topic.

27. **A.** *Julie of the Wolves* is the story of a young Eskimo girl who experiences the changes inflicted upon her culture by outside forces.

28. **C.** S. E. Hinton wrote *The Outsiders* when she was 16 years old.

29. **B.** Ponyboy and Dallas are two of the main characters in the novel *The Outsiders*.

30. **B.** "All the world's a stage" is a metaphor comparing life to a play.

Appendix

Resources

This appendix provides a list of resources that you may find helpful as you prepare for the content of your Praxis English Subject Assessment test.

Suggested References

The suggested print references in this section may help prepare you for the content of your Praxis English Subject Assessment test; many will also prove helpful in your English classroom one day soon.

Abrams, M. H., and Greenblatt, S. (Eds.) (2006). *The Norton Anthology of English Literature* (8th ed.). New York: Norton.

American Psychological Association (2009). *Publication Manual of the American Psychological Association* (6th ed.). Washington, D.C.: Author.

Baym, N. (Ed.) (2007). *The Norton Anthology of American Literature* (7th ed.). New York: Norton.

Calkins, L. M. (1994). *The Art of Teaching Writing.* Portsmouth, NH: Heinemann.

Dornan, E. A., and Dawe, C. W. (2003). *The Brief English Handbook: A Guide to Writing, Thinking, Grammar, and Research* (7th ed.). Boston: Longman.

Ferguson, M., Salter, M. J., and Stallworthy, J. (Eds.) (2004). *The Norton Anthology of Poetry.* New York: Norton.

Gates, H. L., and McKay, N. Y. (Eds.) (2003). *The Norton Anthology of African American Literature* (2nd ed.). New York: Norton.

Gibaldi, J. (2003). *MLA Handbook for Writers of Research Papers* (6th ed.). New York: Modern Language Association.

Hacker, D. (2009). *A Writer's Reference* (6th ed.). Boston: Bedford/St. Martin's.

Harris, T. L., and Hodges, R. E. (Eds.) (1995). *The Literacy Dictionary: The Vocabulary of Reading and Writing.* Newark, DE: International Reading Association.

Raffel, B. (1994). *How to Read a Poem.* New York: Penguin Group.

Robb, L., Klemp, R., and Schwartz, W. (2002). *The Reader's Handbook: A Student Guide for Reading and Learning.* Wilmington, MA: Great Source.

Internet Resources

The following online resources are comprehensive and free!

American Passages: A Literary Survey (Annenberg Foundation): www.learner.org/resources/series164.html

Bartleby.com: Great Books Online: www.bartleby.com

Developing Writers: A Workshop for High School Teachers (Annenberg Foundation): www.learner.org/resources/series194.html

Diana Hacker's Rules for Writers, 6th edition: bcs.bedfordstmartins.com/rules7e/#t_669460____

Electronic Texts for the Study of American Culture at the University of Virginia: http://xroads.virginia.edu/~HYPER/hypertex.html

GoodReads: Best Young Adult Books: www.goodreads.com/list/show/43.Best_Young_Adult_Books

Luminarium: Anthology of English Literature: www.luminarium.org

The Norton Anthology of American Literature: www.wwnorton.com/college/english/naal8/

The Norton Anthology of English Literature: www.wwnorton.com/college/english/nael

The Norton Anthology of Poetry: http://books.wwnorton.com/books/webad.aspx?id=10360

The Norton Anthology of World Literature: www.wwnorton.com/college/english/nawol3/

OWL at Purdue Online Writing Lab (for MLA and APA citations): http://owl.english.purdue.edu/owl/resource/560/9/

Project Gutenberg: Online Book Catalog: www.gutenberg.org/catalog

Major Works and Authors

In this section, you will find a list of authors, their nationalities, their years of birth and death, and the genres the authors are best known for, as well as their major works. While not exhaustive, this section is meant to help you create a reading list in preparation for your exam and for your work as an English teacher. Of course, you most likely have not read *all* of these works and will not need to do so to be successful on your Praxis English Subject Assessment test. While the majority of literary works tested will be works of fiction and usually from the Western literary canon, you can also expect to be asked to compare, paraphrase, and interpret a variety of other types of works, such as poetry, young adult literature, world literature, essays, autobiographies, dramas, and graphic representations. The list is organized by the birth year of the author to also help you place the author's work in its historical context.

Major Works and Authors

Author	Nationality	Birth	Death	Genre(s)	Major Works
Homer	Greek	850 B.C.	800 B.C.	Epic poetry	*The Iliad; The Odyssey*
Sophocles	Greek	c. 497–496 B.C.	c. 406–405 B.C.	Tragedy	*Oedipus the King; Antigone*
Euripides	Greek	c. 480 B.C.	c. 406 B.C.	Plays	*Medea; Cyclops*
Virgil	Roman	70 B.C.	20 B.C.	Epic poetry, pastoral poetry, didactic poetry	*Eclogues (or Bucolics); Georgics; The Aeneid*
Horace	Roman	65 B.C.	9 B.C.	Lyric poetry	*Odes; Satires; Ars Poetica*
Ovid	Roman	43 B.C.	A.D. 17 or 18	Elegies, plays, epic poetry	*Metamorphoses*
Anonymous	Old English	8th to 11th centuries A.D.	8th to 11th centuries A.D.	Narrative heroic poetry	*Beowulf*
Murasaki Shibiku	Japanese	c. 973	c. 1014–1025	Novels, poetry	*Tale of Genji*
Rumi	Persian	1207	1273	Poetry	*Spiritual Couplets*

Author	Nationality	Birth	Death	Genre(s)	Major Works
Dante Alighieri	Italian	1265	1321	Poetry, language theory	*The Divine Comedy; Inferno*
Boccaccio	Italian	1313	1375	Poetry, dialogue	*The Decameron; On Famous Women*
Geoffrey Chaucer	English	1343	1400	Poetry, philosophy, Middle English vernacular	*The Canterbury Tales*
Sir Thomas Malory	English	1405	1471	Medieval prose romance	*Le Morte d'Arthur*
François Rabelais	French	1494	1553	Fantasy, satire, the grotesque, bawdy songs and jokes	*Gargantua and Pantagruel*
Miguel de Cervantes	Spanish	1547	1616	Plays, poetry, novels	*Don Quixote*
Edmund Spenser	English	c. 1552	1599	Epic poetry	*The Faerie Queene*
Christopher Marlowe	English	1564	1593	Plays, poetry, blank verse	*Dr. Faustus; Tamburlaine the Great;* "The Passionate Shepherd to His Love"
William Shakespeare	English	c. 1564	1616	Sonnets, plays	*Hamlet; Much Ado About Nothing; Othello; The Taming of the Shrew; A Midsummer Night's Dream; Macbeth; Julius Caesar; King Lear; Shakespeare's Sonnets*
Ben Jonson	English	1572	1637	Plays, poetry	*Volpone; The Alchemist; Bartholomew Fair*
John Donne	English	1572	1631	Satire, love poetry, elegies, sermons	"A Valediction: Forbidding Mourning"; "Elegy XIX: To His Mistress Going to Bed"; "A Fever"; "Death Be Not Proud"
Robert Herrick	English	1591	1674	Poetry	"To the Virgins, to Make Much of Time"
John Milton	English	1608	1674	Epic poetry	*Paradise Lost; Areopagitica*
Anne Bradstreet	American	1612	1672	Poetry	"Here Follows Some Verses upon the Burning of Our House, July 10, 1666"; "To My Dear and Loving Husband"
Andrew Marvell	English	1621	1678	Poetry	"To His Coy Mistress"; "The Garden"; "An Horatian Ode"

continued

Author	Nationality	Birth	Death	Genre(s)	Major Works
Henry Vaughn	Welsh	1621	1695	Poetry	"The World"; "Peace"; "Silex Scintillans"
Molière	French	1622	1673	Plays (comedies)	*Tartuffe; The Misanthrope; The School for Wives*
John Bunyan	English	1628	1688	Allegories, sermons	*The Pilgrim's Progress*
Isaac Newton	English	1642	1727	Monographs	*Principia Mathematica*
Jonathan Swift	English/Irish	1667	1745	Satire, essays, poetry	"A Modest Proposal"; *Gulliver's Travels*
Alexander Pope	English	1688	1744	Poetry	*Pastorals; The Rape of the Lock;* "Elegy to the Memory of an Unfortunate Lady"; "Ode on Solitude"
Voltaire	French	1694	1778	Plays, essays, histories, philosophy, poetry	*Candide; The Age of Louis XIV; Essay on the Customs and the Spirit of the Nations*
Jonathan Edwards	American	1703	1758	Sermons	"Sinners in the Hands of an Angry God"
Benjamin Franklin	American	1706	1790	Satire, proverbs, autobiography	*Poor Richard's Almanack; The Autobiography*
Samuel Johnson	English	1709	1784	Poetry, essays, literary criticism, biography, lexicography	*The Life of Richard Savage;* "London"; "The Vanity of Human Wishes"; *Irene; The Oxford English Dictionary*
Denis Diderot	French	1713	1784	Philosophy, reference	*Encyclopédie*
Thomas Gray	English	1716	1771	Poetry	"Elegy Written in a Country Churchyard"
Horatio Walpole	English	1717	1797	Gothic period novels and letters	*A Gothic Story; Letters*
Patrick Henry	American	1736	1799	Oration	Speech to the Virginia Convention
Thomas Paine	English/ American	1737	1809	Prose	*Common Sense; The Age of Reason;* "The Crisis, No. 1"
Thomas Jefferson	American	1743	1826	Essays, tracts	The Declaration of Independence
Olaudah Equiano	Nigerian	1745	1797	Autobiography	*The Interesting Narrative of the Life of Olaudah Equiano*
Phyllis Wheatley	American	1753	1784	Poetry	*Poems on Various Subjects;* "To the Right Honorable William, Earl of Dartmouth"

Author	Nationality	Birth	Death	Genre(s)	Major Works
William Blake	English	1757	1827	Poetry, epic poetry	*Songs of Innocence; Songs of Experience; Milton: A Poem;* "The Tyger"
Mary Wollstonecraft	English	1759	1797	Novels, historical essays	*A Vindication of the Rights of Woman*
William Wordsworth	English	1770	1850	Poetry	*Lyrical Ballads;* "Lines Composed a Few Miles Above Tintern Abbey," "I Wandered Lonely as a Cloud," "Composed Upon Westminster Bridge," "The World is Too Much with Us"
Samuel Taylor Coleridge	English	1772	1834	Poetry, lyrical ballads	*The Rime of the Ancient Mariner;* "Kubla Khan"; "Christabel"
Jane Austen	English	1775	1817	Romance novels	*Sense and Sensibility; Emma; Pride and Prejudice*
Washington Irving	American	1783	1859	Short stories	"The Legend of Sleepy Hollow"; "Rip van Winkle"; "The Devil and Tom Walker"
Lord Byron	English	1788	1824	Poetry, narrative poetry	"She Walks in Beauty"; "When We Two Parted"; *Don Juan*
James Fenimore Cooper	American	1789	1851	Historical romances, novels	*Leatherstocking Tales; The Last of the Mohicans*
Percy Bysshe Shelley	English	1792	1822	Lyric poetry, drama, essays	"To a Skylark"; "Ozymandias"; "Ode to the West Wind"; "Music"; *Queen Mab*
John Keats	English	1795	1821	Poetry, odes	"Ode to a Grecian Urn"; "When I Have Fears That I May Cease to Be"; "Ode to a Nightingale"; "To Autumn"; "On First Looking into Chapman's Homer"
Mary Shelley	English	1797	1851	Gothic novels, essays, biography	*Frankenstein*
Ralph Waldo Emerson	American	1803	1882	Essays, poetry	"Nature"; "Self-Reliance"; "Brahma"; "Concord Hymn"
Nathaniel Hawthorne	American	1804	1864	Short stories, novels	"The Minister's Black Veil"; "Dr. Heidegger's Experiment"; *The Scarlet Letter; The House of the Seven Gables*

continued

Author	Nationality	Birth	Death	Genre(s)	Major Works
Elizabeth Barrett Browning	English	1806	1861	Poetry	"Sonnet 43: How do I love thee," "Sonnet 14: If thou must love me, let it be for nought" (both from *Sonnets from the Portuguese*); "The Cry of the Children"; "Grief"
Henry Wadsworth Longfellow	American	1807	1882	Poetry, lyric poetry	"The Tide Rises, the Tide Falls"; "Paul Revere's Ride"; "The Cross of Snow"; *The Song of Hiawatha; Evangeline*
Nikolai Gogol	Ukrainian/ Russian	1809	1852	Plays, short stories, novels	"The Overcoat"; "Diary of a Madman"; *The Inspector General*
Oliver Wendell Holmes	American	1809	1894	Poetry, prose	"Old Ironsides"; "The Last Leaf"; *The Autocrat of the Breakfast-Table*
Alfred, Lord Tennyson	English	1809	1892	Poetry	"In Memorium A.H.H."; "The Charge of the Light Brigade"; "Idylls of the King"; "Ulysses"; "Break, Break, Break"; "The Lady of Shalott"
Edgar Allan Poe	American	1809	1849	Poetry, gothic tales	"The Raven"; "The Pit and the Pendulum"; "The Tell-Tale Heart"; "The Fall of the House of Usher"; "Eldorado"; "To Helen"
Abraham Lincoln	American	1809	1865	Speeches, letters, essays	The Gettysburg Address
Harriet Beecher Stowe	American	1811	1896	Novels	*Uncle Tom's Cabin; Little Foxes* (under the pen name Christopher Crowfield)
William Makepeace Thackeray	English	1811	1863	Satire	*Vanity Fair*
Robert Browning	English	1812	1889	Poetry, dramatic monologue	"My Last Duchess"; *The Pied Piper of Hamelin;* "Porphyria's Lover"; "The Ring and the Book"; "Men and Women"
Charles Dickens	English	1812	1870	Novels	*Great Expectations; David Copperfield; Oliver Twist; Bleak House*
Harriet Ann Jacobs	American	1813	1897	Autobiographical narratives	*Incidents in the Life of a Slave Girl*
Charlotte Brontë	English	1816	1855	Romance novels	*Jane Eyre; Villette*

Author	Nationality	Birth	Death	Genre(s)	Major Works
Henry David Thoreau	American	1817	1862	Autobiography, essays	*Walden;* "Civil Disobedience"; "Resistance to Civil Government"
Emily Brontë	English	1818	1848	Romance novels	*Wuthering Heights*
Frederick Douglass	American	1818	1895	Autobiography	*A Narrative of the Life of Frederick Douglass, an American Slave*
George Eliot	English	1819	1880	Novels	*The Mill on the Floss; Silas Marner; Middlemarch*
Herman Melville	American	1819	1891	Novels, short stories	*Moby-Dick; Billy Budd;* "Bartleby, the Scrivener"
Walt Whitman	American	1819	1892	Poetry (considered the father of free verse), elegies, essays	*Leaves of Grass*
Fyodor Dostoyevsky	Russian	1821	1881	Novels, short stories, essays	*Notes from Underground; Crime and Punishment; The Idiot*
John Rollin Ridge	American	1827	1867	Novels	*The Life and Adventures of Joaquin Murieta*
Henrik Ibsen	Norwegian	1828	1906	Plays	*A Doll's House; Hedda Gabler; Ghosts; An Enemy of the People*
Dante Gabriel Rossetti	English	1828	1882	Poetry	"Silent Noon"; "Broken Music"; "Insomnia"
Leo Tolstoy	Russian	1828	1910	Novels, plays, philosophy	*The Power of Darkness; War and Peace; Anna Karenina; A Confession;* "How Much Land Does a Man Need?"
Emily Dickinson	American	1830	1886	Poetry	"I'm Nobody, Who Are You?"; "A Bird Came Down a Walk"; "If Those I Loved Were Lost"; "Because I could not stop for Death"; "Heart, We Will Not Forget Him!"; "Success is counted sweetest"; "The Soul selects her own Society"; "If you were coming in the Fall"
Christina Rossetti	English	1830	1894	Poetry	"Goblin Market"; "Remember"
Louisa May Alcott	American	1832	1888	Novels	*Little Women*

continued

Author	Nationality	Birth	Death	Genre(s)	Major Works
Charles Lutwidge Dodgson (Lewis Carroll)	English	1832	1898	Fantasy, poetry	*Alice's Adventures in Wonderland;* "Jabberwocky"; "The Hunting of the Snark"
Samuel Langhorne Clemens (Mark Twain)	American	1835	1910	Fiction, historical fiction, essays, nonfiction	*The Adventures of Tom Sawyer; The Adventures of Huckleberry Finn;* "The Celebrated Jumping Frog of Calaveras County"; *A Connecticut Yankee in King Arthur's Court*
Algernon Charles Swinburne	English	1837	1909	Poetry (created the roundel form)	"The Roundel"; "A Ballad of Dreamland"; "A Baby's Death"
Thomas Hardy	English	1840	1928	Poetry, novels	"The Man He Killed"; "The Ruined Maid"; "The Convergence of the Twain"; "Drummer Hodge"; *Jude the Obscure; Tess of the d'Ubervilles*
Ambrose Bierce	American	1842	1913	Satire, short stories	"The Damned Thing"; "An Occurrence at Owl Creek Bridge"; "The Devil's Dictionary"
Henry James	American/ English	1843	1916	Novels, short stories (known for literary realism)	*The American; Daisy Miller; The Portrait of a Lady; The Turn of the Screw*
Bram Stoker	Irish/English	1847	1912	Novels, short stories	*Dracula*
August Strindberg	Swedish	1849	1912	Plays, novels, essays	*The Father; Miss Julie; The Red Room*
Kate Chopin	American	1850	1904	Short stories, novels	"Desiree's Baby"; "The Story of an Hour"; "The Storm"; *The Awakening;* "A Pair of Silk Stockings"
Guy de Maupassant	French	1850	1893	Short stories, poetry	"The Jewelry," "The Necklace," "Useless Beauty"
Robert Louis Stevenson	Scottish/English	1850	1894	Novels	*The Strange Case of Dr. Jekyll and Mr. Hyde; Treasure Island; Kidnapped*
Oscar Wilde	Irish	1854	1900	Plays, poetry	"To My Wife - With a Copy of My Poems"; "Sonnet to Liberty"; *The Picture of Dorian Gray; The Importance of Being Earnest*

Author	Nationality	Birth	Death	Genre(s)	Major Works
George Bernard Shaw	Irish/English	1856	1950	Plays	*Pygmalion; Mrs. Warren's Profession; Candida*
Joseph Conrad	Polish/English	1857	1924	Novels	*Heart of Darkness; Lord Jim*
Sir Arthur Conan Doyle	English	1859	1930	Detective fiction	*Sherlock Holmes* novels
Kenneth Grahame	Scottish	1859	1932	Fantasy	*The Wind in the Willows; The Reluctant Dragon*
A. E. Housman	English	1859	1936	Poetry	"To an Athlete Dying Young"; "Loveliest of Trees"; "When I was One-and-Twenty"
J. M. Barrie	Scottish/English	1860	1937	Novels, plays	*Peter Pan; The Little White Bird*
Anton Chekov	Russian	1860	1904	Plays, short stories	"The Bet"; "The Steppe"; "Misery"; *The Cherry Orchard; Three Sisters*
Edith Wharton	American	1862	1937	Novels, short stories	*The Age of Innocence; The House of Mirth; Ethan Frome;* "The Reckoning"
W. W. Jacobs	English	1863	1943	Short stories, novels	"The Monkey's Paw"
Rudyard Kipling	English	1865	1936	Short stories, novels, poetry	*The Jungle Book; Just So Stories;* "The Man Who Would Be King"; *Gunga Din*
William Butler Yeats	Irish	1865	1939	Poetry	"Sailing to Byzantium"; "The Second Coming"; "The Wild Swans at Coole"; *The Tower; The Winding Stair and Other Poems*
W. E. B. Du Bois	American/Ghanaian	1868	1963	Essays	"The Souls of Black Folk"; "Black Reconstruction in America"; "The Crisis"
Mahatma Gandhi	Indian	1869	1948	Speeches, essays	"On Nonviolent Resistance"
Stephen Crane	American	1871	1900	Novels, short stories	*Maggie, A Girl of the Streets; The Red Badge of Courage;* "The Open Boat"; "The Bride Comes to Yellow Sky"; "A Mystery of Heroism"; "War Is Kind"
Theodore Dreiser	American	1871	1945	Novels	*Sister Carrie; An American Tragedy*

continued

Author	Nationality	Birth	Death	Genre(s)	Major Works
James Weldon Johnson	American	1871	1938	Autobiography, poetry	*Autobiography of an Ex-Colored Man;* "Lift Evry' Voice and Sing"
Willa Cather	American	1873	1947	Novels	*My Antonia; One of Ours; O Pioneers!;* "A Wagner Matinée"
Robert Frost	American	1874	1963	Poetry	"Stopping by Woods on a Snowy Evening"; "The Road Not Taken"; "Nothing Gold Can Stay"; "Fire and Ice"; "Birches"; "The Lockless Door"; "Design"; "Mending Wall"; "The Death of the Hired Man"
Winston Churchill	English	1874	1965	Historical and biographical nonfiction	*The Second World War; A History of the English-Speaking Peoples;* "Blood, Sweat and Tears"
Amy Lowell	American	1874	1925	Poetry	"Petals"; "A Fairy Tale"; "Sea Shell"
Jack London	American/ English	1876	1916	Novels, short stories	"To Build a Fire"; *The Call of the Wild; White Fang; The Iron Heel*
Hermann Hesse	German/Swiss	1877	1962	Novels	*Siddhartha; Steppenwolf; The Glass Bead Game*
Upton Sinclair	American	1878	1968	Novels	*The Jungle*
Wallace Stevens	American	1879	1955	Poetry	"The Snowman"; "Valley Candle"; "Anecdote of the Jar"; "The Idea of Order at Key West"; "Sunday Morning"
Juan Ramón Jiménez	Spanish	1881	1958	Poetry	*Spiritual Sonnets; Stones and Sky; Poetry in Prose and Verse; Voices of My Song*
James Joyce	Irish	1882	1941	Novels, poetry (stream of consciousness)	*Ulysses;* "Araby" and "Eveline" (from *Dubliners*); *A Portrait of the Artist as a Young Man; Finnegan's Wake*
Virginia Woolf	English	1882	1941	Novels, essays	*A Room of One's Own; Mrs. Dalloway; To the Lighthouse; Orlando*
Franz Kafka	Czechoslovakian/ Austrian-Hungarian	1883	1924	Novels, short stories	*The Metamorphosis*

Author	Nationality	Birth	Death	Genre(s)	Major Works
William Carlos Williams	American	1883	1963	Poetry	"This is Just to Say"; "The Red Wheelbarrow"; "The Great Figure"; *Spring and All*
D. H. Lawrence	English	1885	1930	Novels, short stories	*Sons and Lovers; Lady Chatterley's Lover;* "Odour of Chrysanthemums"; "The Rocking-Horse Winner"
Ezra Pound	American/Italian	1885	1972	Poetry	*Ripostes; Hugh Selwyn Mauberley; The Cantos;* "A Girl"; "The River Merchant's Wife: A Letter"; "The Garden"
T. S. Eliot	American/ English	1888	1965	Poetry (stream of consciousness)	"The Waste Land; "The Love Song of J. Alfred Prufrock"; *Four Quartets*
Eugene O'Neill	American	1888	1953	Plays	*Long Day's Journey into Night; The Iceman Cometh; Ah, Wilderness; Anna Christie*
Anna Gorenko (Anna Akhmatova)	Russian	1889	1966	Poetry	"Lot's Wife"; "All the unburied ones"
Zora Neale Hurston	American	1891	1960	Novels, short stories, plays, essays, autobiography	*Their Eyes Were Watching God; Mule Bone: A Comedy of Negro Life; Dust Tracks on a Road;* "Sweat"
Pearl S. Buck	American	1892	1973	Novels	*The Good Earth*
Edna St. Vincent Millay	American	1892	1950	Lyrical poetry	"Renascence"; "The Ballad of the Harp-Weaver"; "First Fig"; "I, Being a Born a Woman and Distressed"; "Love is not all"
J. R. R. Tolkien	English	1892	1973	Fantasy	*The Hobbit; The Lord of the Rings*
Dorothy Parker	American	1893	1967	Poetry, short stories, satire	*Enough Rope; A Star Is Born; Sunset Gun*
e. e. cummings	American	1894	1962	Poetry	"i carry your heart with me"; "somewhere i have never travelled, somewhere beyond"; "anyone lived in a pretty how town"; "what if a much of a which of a wind"
James Thurber	American	1894	1961	Short stories, cartoons, essays	*My Life and Hard Times;* "The Secret Life of Walter Mitty"

continued

Author	Nationality	Birth	Death	Genre(s)	Major Works
F. Scott Fitzgerald	American	1896	1940	Novels, short stories, letters	*The Great Gatsby; This Side of Paradise; Tender Is the Night;* "Bernice Bobs Her Hair"; "The Curious Case of Benjamin Button"; "Winter Dreams"; "A Letter to His Daughter"
William Faulkner	American	1897	1962	Novels, short stories	*The Sound and the Fury; As I Lay Dying; Light in August;* "The Bear"; "A Rose for Emily"; "Barn Burning"
Thornton Wilder	American	1897	1975	Plays, novels	*Our Town; The Bridge of San Luis Rey; The Skin of Our Teeth; The Eighth Day*
Ernest Hemingway	American	1899	1961	Novels, short stories	*The Sun Also Rises; A Farewell to Arms; For Whom the Bell Tolls; The Old Man and the Sea; A Moveable Feast;* "Indian Camp"; "The Snows of Kilimanjaro"; "Soldier's Home"; "Speech, 1954"
Yasunari Kawabata	Japanese	1899	1972	Short stories, novels	"The Silver Fifty-Sen Pieces"
Langston Hughes	American	1902	1967	Poetry, plays	"The Negro Speaks of Rivers"; "The Dream Keeper"; "Mother to Son"; "Dream Deferred"; "The Weary Blues"; "Let America Be America Again"; "I, Too, Sing America"; "My People"; *Mule Bone: A Comedy of Negro Life*
Ogden Nash	American	1902	1971	Poetry	"What I Know About Life"; "Carnival of Animals"
John Steinbeck	American	1902	1968	Novels, novellas, short stories	*The Grapes of Wrath; Of Mice and Men; The Red Pony; East of Eden; Travels with Charley: In Search of America; Tortilla Flat; Cannery Row;* "The Leader of the People"
Countee Cullen	American	1903	1946	Poetry	"Tableau"; "Incident"
Eric Arthur Blair (George Orwell)	English	1903	1950	Dystopian novels, satire, essays	*1984; Animal Farm;* "Shooting an Elephant"

Author	Nationality	Birth	Death	Genre(s)	Major Works
Pablo Neruda	Chilean	1904	1973	Poetry	"Plenos poderes" ("Full Powers"); *Twenty Love Poems and a Song of Despair;* "Sonnet 79"
Jean-Paul Sartre	French	1905	1980	Plays	*No Exit; Nausea; The Roads to Freedom* trilogy: *The Age of Reason; The Reprieve; Troubled Sleep*
Samuel Beckett	Irish	1906	1989	Plays (theater of the absurd)	*Waiting for Godot; Endgame*
W. H. Auden	English/ American	1907	1973	Poetry	"In Memory of W. B. Yeats"; "The Unknown Citizen"; "Funeral Blues"; "September 1, 1939"; "Musée des Beaux Arts"
Theodore Roethke	American	1908	1963	Poetry	"In a Dark Time"; "Night Journey"; "The Waking"; "Words for the Wind"; "The Far Field"
Richard Wright	American	1908	1960	Plays, fiction, nonfiction	*Native Son; Uncle Tom's Children; Black Boy; The Outsider*
Eudora Welty	American	1909	2001	Southern literature, memoirs, novels, short stories	*The Optimist's Daughter;* "A Worn Path"
Elizabeth Bishop	American	1911	1979	Poetry, short stories, villanelles	"The Fish"; "One Art"
William Golding	English	1911	1993	Novels	*The Lord of the Flies; Rites of Passage*
Tennessee Williams	American	1911	1983	Plays, short stories	*The Glass Menagerie; A Streetcar Named Desire; The Rose Tattoo; Cat on a Hot Tin Roof;* "The Field of Blue Children"
Albert Camus	French	1913	1960	Novels (absurdist)	*The Stranger*
Robert Hayden	American	1913	1980	Poetry	"El-Hajj Malik El-Shabazz (Malcolm X)"; "Frederick Douglass"; "Those Winter Sundays"; "The Whipping"
John Berryman	American	1914	1972	Poetry	*The Dream Songs*
Ralph Ellison	American	1914	1994	Novels, essays	*Invisible Man; Shadow and Act; Going to the Territory*
Randall Jarrell	American	1914	1965	Poetry, essays, novels	"The Death of the Ball Turret Gunner"; *The Woman at the Washington Zoo; The Lost World*

continued

Author	Nationality	Birth	Death	Genre(s)	Major Works
Dylan Thomas	Welsh	1914	1953	Poetry	"Do Not Go Gentle into that Good Night"; *Under Milk Wood;* "In my Craft or Sullen Art"; "Fern Hill"; "And Death Shall Have no Dominion"
Arthur Miller	American	1915	2005	Plays	*Death of a Salesman; The Crucible; A View from the Bridge*
Robert Lowell	American	1917	1977	Poetry, confessional poetry	"For the Union Dead"; "The Quaker Graveyard in Nantucket"; *Lord Weary's Castle*
Lawrence Ferlinghetti	American	1919		Poetry (Beat poet)	*A Coney Island of the Mind;* "I Am Waiting"; "Junkman's Obbligato"
Doris Lessing	English	1919	2013	Short stories, poetry, biography, novels	"No Witchcraft for Sale"; *The Grass is Singing*
J. D. Salinger	American	1919	2010	Novels, short stories	*The Catcher in the Rye;* "A Perfect Day for Bananafish"; *Franny and Zooey*
Ray Bradbury	American	1920	2012	Dystopian novels, science fiction, horror	*Fahrenheit 451; The Martian Chronicles; The Illustrated Man*
Jack Kerouac	American	1922	1969	Novels, poetry (Beat poet)	*On the Road; Big Sur; Mexico City Blues*
Joseph Heller	American	1923	1999	Satirical novels, short stories	*Catch-22; Something Happened*
Wisława Szymborska	Polish	1923	2012	Poetry	"Discovery"; "The End and the Beginning"
Robert Cormier	American	1925	2000	Young adult novels	*The Chocolate War; I Am the Cheese; After the First Death*
Allen Ginsberg	American	1926	1997	Poetry (Beat poet)	"Howl"; "America"; "Homework"
John Knowles	American	1926	2001	Novels	*A Separate Peace*
Harper Lee	American	1926	2016	Novels	*To Kill a Mockingbird*
Rudolfo Anaya	American	1937		Novels	*Bless Me, Ultima*
Gabriel García Márquez	Colombian	1927	2014	Novels, short stories	*One Hundred Years of Solitude; Love in the Time of Cholera; Autumn of the Patriarch;* "The Handsomest Drowned Man in the World"

Author	Nationality	Birth	Death	Genre(s)	Major Works
Maya Angelou	American	1928	2014	Poetry, autobiography	"Still I Rise"; "Phenomenal Woman"; *I Know Why the Caged Bird Sings*
Anne Sexton	American	1928	1974	Poetry, confessional poetry	"All My Pretty Ones"; "Crossing the Atlantic"; "The Moss of His Skin"; "The Bells"; "Young"
Elie Wiesel	Romanian/ American	1928		Memoirs	*Night*; "Never Shall I Forget"
Anne Frank	German	1929	1945	Diary, young adult literature	*Anne Frank: The Diary of a Young Girl*
Martin Luther King, Jr.	American	1929	1968	Letters, sermons, essays, speeches	Letter from Birmingham Jail; "I Have a Dream"
Adrienne Rich	American	1929	2012	Poetry, essays	"Dreamwood"; *A Change of World*; "Compulsory Heterosexuality and Lesbian Existence"
Chinua Achebe	Nigerian	1930	2013	Novels, poetry	*Things Fall Apart; No Longer at Ease; Arrow of God; A Man of the People*; "Marriage is a Private Affair"
Lorraine Hansberry	American	1930	1965	Plays	*A Raisin in the Sun; The Drinking Gourd*
Shel Silverstein	American	1930	1999	Poetry	*The Giving Tree; Falling Up; A Light in the Attic*; "Messy Room"; "Whatif"; "Bear in There"; "Boa Constrictor"
Toni Morrison	American	1931		Novels	*Beloved; The Bluest Eye; Song of Solomon; Sula*
Sylvia Plath	American	1932	1963	Novels, poetry	"Daddy"; "Ariel"; "Metaphors"; "Lady Lazarus"; "A Life"; "Mushrooms"; "Mirror"; *The Bell Jar*
John Updike	American	1932	2009	Novels, short stories	*Rabbit Angstrom* novels (including *Rabbit Is Rich, Rabbit at Rest*); *The Witches of Eastwick*
Amiri Baraka	American	1934	2014	Poetry, essays	"Somebody Blew Up America"; *Tales of the Out and the Gone*
N. Scott Momaday	American	1934		Novels, memoirs	*House Made of Dawn; The Way to Rainy Mountain*

continued

Author	Nationality	Birth	Death	Genre(s)	Major Works
Paul Zindel	American	1936	2003	Plays, young adult novels	*The Effect of Gamma Rays on Man-in-the-Moon Marigolds; My Darling, My Hamburger; The Pigman*
Lois Lowry	American	1937		Young adult novels	*The Giver; Number the Stars*
Seamus Heaney	Irish	1939	2013	Poetry, plays	"Digging"; *Opened Ground: Poems 1966–1996*
Maxine Hong Kingston	American	1940		Memoirs, novels	*The Woman Warrior; Tripmaster Monkey; China Men*
Robert Pinsky	American	1940		Poetry	"A Classic Moment"; "Catatonic"
Jack Prelutsky	American	1940		Young adult poetry	*The New Kid on the Block; A Pizza the Size of the Sun; Be Glad Your Nose Is on Your Face;* "As Soon as Fred Gets Out of Bed"; "Bleezer's Ice Cream"
Billy Collins	American	1941		Poetry	"Man Listening to Disc"; "The Names"; *Poetry 180: A Turning Back to Poetry*
Pat Mora	American	1942		Poetry	"Now and Then, America"; *My Own True Name: New and Selected Poems for Young Adults*
Francisco Jiménez	Mexican	1943		Memoirs, young adult novels	*The Circuit: Stories of the Life of a Migrant Child*
Mildred D. Taylor	American	1943		Young adult novels	*Roll of Thunder, Hear My Cry*
Alice Walker	American	1944		Novels, short stories	*The Color Purple; You Can't Keep a Good Woman Down: Stories;* "In Search of Our Mother's Gardens"
Tim O'Brien	American	1946		Memoirs, short stories	*The Things They Carried;* "Speaking of Courage"
S. E. Hinton	American	1950		Young adult novels	*The Outsiders; That Was Then, This Is Now; Rumble Fish; Tex*
Naomi Shihab Nye	American	1952		Poetry	"Trying to Name What Doesn't Change"; "Alaska"; "Burning the Old Year"; "Jerusalem"
Amy Tan	American	1952		Novels	*The Joy Luck Club; The Bonesetter's Daughter*

Author	Nationality	Birth	Death	Genre(s)	Major Works
Mark Doty	American	1953		Poetry	*My Alexandria; Firebird;* "Coastal"
Sandra Cisneros	American	1954		Novels, short stories, essays	*The House on Mango Street; Woman Hollering Creek and Other Stories;* "Straw into Gold"
Ben Okri	Nigerian	1959		Novels , essays, poetry	*The Famished Road; Starbook;* "In the Shadow of War"
J. K. Rowling	English	1965		Fantasy, young adult novels	*Harry Potter* series
Jhumpa Lahiri	American	1967		Short stories, novels	"When Mr. Prizada Came to Dine"; "Mrs. Sen's" (from *Interpreter of Maladies*); *The Namesake; Unaccustomed Earth*